History of
Participatory Media

Routledge Studies in Cultural History

1. The Politics of Information in Early Modern Europe
Edited by Brendan Dooley and Sabrina Baron

2. The Insanity of Place/The Place of Insanity
Essays on the History of Psychiatry
Andrew Scull

3. Film, History, and Cultural Citizenship
Sites of Production
Edited by Tina Mai Chen and David S. Churchill

4. Genre and Cinema
Ireland and Transnationalism
Edited by Brian McIlroy

5. Histories of Postmodernism
Edited by Mark Bevir, Jill Hargis, and Sara Rushing

6. Africa after Modernism
Transitions in Literature, Media, and Philosophy
Michael Janis

7. Rethinking Race, Politics, and Poetics
C.L.R. James' Critique of Modernity
Brett St Louis

8. Making British Culture
English Readers and the Scottish Enlightenment, 1740–1830
David Allan

9. Empires and Boundaries
Rethinking Race, Class, and Gender in Colonial Settings
Edited by Harald Fischer-Tiné and Susanne Gehrmann

10. Tabacco in Russian History and Culture
From the Seventeenth Century to the Present
Edited by Matthew P. Romaniello and Tricia Starks

11. History of Islam in German Thought
From Leibniz to Nietzsche
Ian Almond

12. Israeli-Palestinian Conflict in the Francophone World
Edited by Nathalie Debrauwere-Miller

13. History of Participatory Media
Politics and Publics, 1750–2000
Edited by Anders Ekström, Solveig Jülich, Frans Lundgren and Per Wisselgren

History of Participatory Media

Politics and Publics, 1750–2000

Edited by Anders Ekström,
Solveig Jülich, Frans Lundgren,
and Per Wisselgren

First published 2011
by Routledge
270 Madison Avenue, New York, NY 10016

Simultaneously published in the UK
by Routledge
2 Park Square, Milton Park, Abingdon, Oxon OX14 4RN

Routledge is an imprint of the Taylor & Francis Group, an informa business

© 2011 Taylor & Francis

The right of Anders Ekström, Solveig Jülich, Frans Lundgren, and Per Wisselgren to be identified as the authors of the editorial material, and of the authors for their individual chapters, has been asserted by them in accordance with sections 77 and 78 of the Copyright, Designs and Patents Act 1988.

Typeset in Sabon by IBT Global.

All rights reserved. No part of this book may be reprinted or reproduced or utilised in any form or by any electronic, mechanical, or other means, now known or hereafter invented, including photocopying and recording, or in any information storage or retrieval system, without permission in writing from the publishers.

Trademark Notice: Product or corporate names may be trademarks or registered trademarks, and are used only for identification and explanation without intent to infringe.

Library of Congress Cataloging-in-Publication Data
  History of participatory media : politics and publics, 1750–2000 / edited by Anders Ekstrom . . . [et al.].
    p. cm. — (Routledge studies in cultural history)
  Includes bibliographical references and index.
  1. Mass media—Audiences. 2. Mass media—Social aspects. 3. Mass media and culture. 4. Mass media—Influence. I. Ekström, Anders, 1965–
  P96.A83H57 2010
  302.23—dc22
                          2010021427

ISBN13: 978-0-415-88068-8 (hbk)
ISBN13: 978-0-203-83932-4 (ebk)

Contents

List of Figures		vii
Acknowledgements		xi
1	Participatory Media in Historical Perspective: An Introduction ANDERS EKSTRÖM, SOLVEIG JÜLICH, FRANS LUNDGREN, AND PER WISSELGREN	1
2	From Enlightened Participation to Liberal Professionalism: On the Historiography of the Press as a Resource for Legitimacy PATRIK LUNDELL	10
3	Knowing Audiences, Knowing Media: Performing Publics at the Early Twentieth-Century Fun Fair ANDERS EKSTRÖM	20
4	Civic Media: City Exhibitions and the Visual Culture of Community, c. 1900 FRANS LUNDGREN	32
5	Creating Audiences, Making Participants: The Cylinder Phonograph in Ethnographic Fieldwork MATHIAS BOSTRÖM	49
6	The Interactivity of the Model Home MARK B. SANDBERG	63
7	Touring the Congo: Mobility and Materiality in Missionary Media LOTTEN GUSTAFSSON REINIUS	81

vi *Contents*

8   Say Milk, Say Cheese! Inscribing Public Participation in the
    Photographic Archives of the National Milk Propaganda   98
    YLVA HABEL

9   Daniel Ellsberg and the Lost Idea of the Photocopy   112
    LISA GITELMAN

10 Fetal Photography in the Age of Cool Media   125
    SOLVEIG JÜLICH

11 *Expedition Robinson*, Reality TV, and the History of the Social
    Experiment   142
    PER WISSELGREN

12 History on the Web: Museums, Digital Media, and Participation   158
    BODIL AXELSSON

Bibliography   173
Contributors   185
Index   189

Figures

3.1	Visitors gathering around one of the open-air dance pavilions at the 1909 Stockholm exhibition. Stockholm City Museum.	24
4.1	Stabilizing spectators and the discourse of inspectability. Illustration from W. F. Exner, *Der Aussteller und die Ausstellungen*, vol. 2 (Weimar: Voigt, 1873).	34
4.2	Patrick Geddes and children with the Outlook Tower in the background in the 1890s. Patrick Geddes Collection, Edinburgh University Library.	38
4.3	Learning to see the city. A view from the Outlook Tower, 1900. Patrick Geddes Collection, Edinburgh University Library.	44
5.1	The Swedish missionary Karl Laman playing back cylinder recordings for an audience in Kingoyi, Belgian Congo colony, 1909. Karl Laman's Archive, National Archives, Stockholm.	50
5.2	Boys of the first class of the missionary school at the Swedish station Madzia, Belgian Congo colony, making cylinder recordings for Karl Laman 1911. Karl Laman's Archive, National Archives, Stockholm.	57
6.1	The "Lottery Villa" at the 1909 Stockholm exhibition. *Dagens Nyheter*, 18 June 1909.	71
6.2	*Lustiga Huset* (Fun House) at the 1909 Stockholm exhibition. *Aftonbladet*, 10 June 1909.	72
6.3	*Lustiga Huset* (Fun House) at the 1909 Stockholm exhibition. *Aftonbladet*, 10 June 1909.	73

viii *Figures*

7.1 The "Congo Bus" offered not only a touch of distant lands, but also a temporary intrusion of urbanity and modernity. Published with permission of the Archive of Mission Covenant Church of Sweden. 82

7.2 Hunting trophies on display at the exhibition infused the mission with adventure, exotic wildlife, danger and bravery. Published with permission of the Archive of Mission Covenant Church of Sweden. 88

7.3 Artifacts associated with traditional life styles were grouped with photographs of unnamed people, an imagery that in accordance with contemporary visual conventions illustrated ethnic types rather than individuals. Published with permission of the Archive of Mission Covenant Church of Sweden. 90

8.1 Drawing contest brochure for depicting the Milk Boy and Coffee Boy: "The Milk Boy is healthy and strong, the Coffee Boy weak and fragile." *Meddelanden från Mjölkpropagandan* 3, no. 2 (1926). 104

8.2 Milk lesson for school children at Liljevalchs Art Gallery, 1924. Courtesy of the National Library of Sweden. 107

8.3 School children at the film theater "auditorium" in Stockholm during the Milk Week in 1935. Courtesy of the LRF Archive at the Centre for Business History, Stockholm. 108

9.1 Indochina in an nth-generation Xerox (note the electrostatic traces in the left margin), from the Pentagon Papers as printed for the House Committee on Armed Services. *United States-Vietnam Relations 1945–1967: Study Prepared by the Department of Defense*, vol. 1 (Washington, 1971). 117

10.1 Sexual education in the age of audiovisual media. Ad from *The American Biology Teacher* 23 (May 1973). Courtesy of Time-Life Pictures/Getty Images. 128

10.2 "To have a child ... A lesson for life." Photographer Lennart Nilsson with school children looking at his famous images of embryos and fetuses. Cover of *Idun Veckojournalen,* 1 October 1965. Photo by Pål-Nils Nilsson. Courtesy of NordicPhotos. 132

10.3 "This is my client." Lawyer Stephen Foley was one of the members of early antiabortion groups that started to bring Nilsson's images to lectures, meetings, and debates. Photo by Art Rickerby, first published in *Life*, 17 April 1970. Courtesy of Time-Life Pictures/Getty Images. 135

Acknowledgements

We would like to thank the Swedish Research Council and the Division of History of Science and Technology at the Royal Institute of Technology (KTH), Stockholm, for their generous funding of the workshop at which the idea of co-authoring a volume on the history of participatory media was first conceived, and for supporting the work involved in preparing and editing this book. We are especially grateful for the helpful comments and suggestions of the anonymous reviewers and the editorial board at Routledge.

1 Participatory Media in Historical Perspective
An Introduction

Anders Ekström, Solveig Jülich, Frans Lundgren, and Per Wisselgren

In recent years, there has been a growing interest in issues relating to participatory media in most disciplines and fields in the humanities and social sciences. For example, literary, film, and music scholars discuss how new modes of amateur media production and collaborative media art affect long-established concepts of creativity and originality. Communication and media researchers examine how blogs, podcasting, video-sharing websites, and other media distributed via the internet are changing the relationship between media industries and consumers. Scholars in the field of cultural studies investigate the way in which fan communities reshape media content as they personalize it for their own use. Legal scholars reexamine issues of authorship and copyright law in light of practices such as digital sampling and remixing in popular culture. Sociologists and political theorists discuss the activities of online communities as an opportunity for enhancing democracy and making room for a revitalization of the public sphere. Researchers in the field of science and technology studies speculate about the ways in which participatory media might constitute new sites for emergent forms of active and scientific citizenship. Media educators explore issues of literacy in relation to the notion of a new participatory culture. All of these discussions address fundamental issues regarding how media technologies shape and are shaped by economic, political, legal, social, and cultural institutions. However, they are all too often obscured by a "rhetoric of newness" that assumes participatory media is radical and revolutionary, something unique in history.[1] But active and politically engaged uses of media are not exclusive to our times. As a matter of fact, it is fair to ask the question: Has there ever really been such a thing as a passive audience?[2]

Participatory media has also become a buzzword among business people, economists, and journalists. With the development of Web 2.0, the internet is assumed to have become a global platform for creativity, collaboration, and sharing. Sites like Wikipedia, YouTube, and Facebook are said to enable users to take a more democratic role in content production and consumption. That the line between expert and amateur, author and audience is becoming blurred is a recurrent theme in recent business literature. "Collective intelligence" or the "wisdom of the crowd" are claimed to be generated in processes of peer production, social networking, and open-sourcing. Business and marketing strategies based on models of active, participatory audiences are encouraged. Not all commentators have been equally enthusiastic about the rise of amateurism and the democratization of information, but in general these perceived changes due to the internet are hailed as being truly revolutionary in nature.[3] To move beyond such a simplistic narrative, we feel that a longer and more elaborate historical perspective is necessary.

This is not to say that historically oriented discussions about active audiences and creative media use are brand new.[4] Marshall McLuhan's much-disputed distinction between "hot" and "cool" media is one concept that immediately comes to mind. In *Understanding Media* (1964), McLuhan claimed that different media require different degrees of participation from the audience. Some media, such as films, prioritize one sense over the others, insofar as the viewer need not fill in or complement the details of the moving image to determine meaning. In contrast, television programs, and cartoons even more so, lack certain details and require a higher sensory involvement on the part of the people in the audience. Accordingly, film is said to be a hot medium that is low in participation, and television a cool one that is high in participation. In line with his historical outlook, McLuhan stated that his own time was a period of change from the hot era of the machine age to the increasingly cool era of electronic media.[5]

Although McLuhan's concept has been much criticized, several media scholars have broached similar theories and arguments over the years. However, a line can be drawn between two different approaches. On the one hand there has been a tendency to view participation as a media-specific characteristic, i.e., a quality that in different degrees distinguishes different kinds of media. On the other hand, it has been emphasized that participation is above all an issue defined by the user. In general terms this can be conceptualized as a dividing line between a perspective that stresses the materiality of media and a more culturalistic approach.

Both of these positions have been articulated in recent discussions about new media. Henry Jenkins, for instance, has suggested a distinction between interactivity and participation. In his view interactivity should be reserved for describing the opportunities offered and constraints imposed on media by technology. Participation, on the other hand, should be understood as being shaped by "social and cultural protocols."[6] In Jenkins' analysis, participation is also lent a wider and more political significance. New media are not only linked to new and more active forms of media consumption but also with the emergence of a new political culture, even new utopias.

The contributors to the present volume propose a change in approach to current discussions about participatory media by treating them as historical phenomena. The authors wish to continue exploring the relationship between the two perspectives while readdressing the issue of how the history and politics of participation can be related to the materiality of media and the cultural habits of its users. After all, how clear is the distinction proposed by Jenkins? Is there a risk that a culturalistic perspective obscures the actual opportunities and constraints created by different media technologies? How can participation be analyzed without losing sight of the asymmetry that nevertheless characterizes the relationship between media and audiences? Is there a way to emphasize the materiality of media while at the same time avoiding the kind of technological determinism associated with McLuhanism? And how, in turn, do such considerations affect the analysis of the political dimensions of participation?

A CLASSIC DIVIDE

In order to properly develop this argument, we need to address the implicit historiographies at work in the rhetoric of newness. Most important in this respect, the understanding of media history continues to be informed by classic public sphere theory.[7] Scholars such as Jürgen Habermas and Richard Sennett influentially framed the history of audiences as a history of decline by arguing that the collectively defined and responsible publics of the late eighteenth and early nineteenth centuries were successively transformed into individualized and consuming audiences in the late nineteenth and twentieth centuries.[8] This historical analysis shared many of the concerns of cultural critics as different as Frankfurt School theorists Max Horkheimer and Theodor Adorno and activist Guy Debord.[9] Working within the conceptual framework of "mass media" and "mass culture," these and other critics reinforced an analytical divide between (active) publics and (passive) audiences that has too often been translated into a simplistic narrative of a two-dimensional historical development.[10]

This conceptual and historical divide also influences the multidisciplinary discourse of media theory. For instance, Sonia Livingstone claims that it is still commonplace to understand audiences and publics as mutually exclusive. "In both popular and elite discourses, audiences are denigrated as trivial, passive, individualized, while publics are valued as active, critically engaged and politically significant."[11] However, in relation to changes in the contemporary media environment, and especially the extent to which this development is characterized by the participation of audiences and the mediation of publics, Livingstone argues that this distinction becomes increasingly blurred. In this context, the rhetoric of newness makes sense—and perhaps a rhetoric of return would make even better sense since the emergence of new media is identified with the return of audiences as publics, participants and active citizens.

However, this implies a past in which the divide between passive audiences and responsible publics was indeed an unproblematic empirical fact. But this was never so. As will be demonstrated throughout this book, there is a long and varied history of different modes of audience participation, and the mediation of publics can be studied from at least the late eighteenth century and onward.[12] This is not to say that significant changes have not occurred; they certainly have, and it is the collective task of historians to conduct an analysis of these changes. In such an analysis historical specificity is key, but it should be executed with an eye firmly fixed on contemporary developments. At the other extreme, by overstating the newness of participatory media, the history of audience activity is made invisible and the present elusively vague.

The chapters in this book draw on an expanding multidisciplinary field of research into the cultural history of media.[13] The empirical results of this research provide some much-needed nuance to the history of decline implied by classic public sphere theory. For instance, studies of early film exhibitions, the immersive techniques of wax displays, or the participation of audiences in demonstrations of early sound media exemplify some of the ways in which audiences were involved in nineteenth-century media culture.[14] Likewise, it has been shown how early twentieth-century audiences were invited to contribute to the very production of media, for instance by entering contests at exhibitions and movie houses or in popular magazines.[15] In contrast to discussions on the history of public spheres, which have been very much concerned with the politics of exclusion, these and other participatory practices call for an exploration of the politics of inclusion.

In line with this historical research we also adopt a broad concept of media. We argue that media has to be historically defined, not least to avoid the fallacies of a prehistory that follows from the tendency to equate the concept of media with twentieth-century mass media. This manner of understanding media explains why we have included chapters on museum displays and temporary exhibitions, for instance. Not only were these media of great significance in terms of distribution in the nineteenth and early twentieth centuries, they also contributed to a transmedial exchange of manners with which to address and activate audiences.[16] In relation to the theme of this anthology, the materiality of display is especially interesting since it highlights the performative aspects of participation. As discussed in the chapters by Mark Sandberg and Lotten Gustafsson Reinius, exhibitions have often been choreographed in a specific mode that invites visitors to make the room their own through strategies of familiarization or enactment. Materiality is a key issue in this analysis; Gustafsson Reinius investigates how participation is evoked by the circulation of tangible objects, and Sandberg's discussion is focused on the performative inhabitation of reconstructed milieus. What Sandberg refers to as the "theatricality of display" also calls for an exploration of the ways in which we literally learn to act as audiences, a question explicitly raised in Anders Ekström's contribution to this book. In dealing with early twentieth-century amusement areas, Ekström also discusses how the public sociability that evolved in these places was related to the ways in which various media and fun-fair attractions physically engaged audiences.

Leaving the divide between active and passive audiences aside thus enables us to reformulate the relationship between audiences and publics and to search for alternative chronologies in media history. Furthermore, discussions about today's new media have somewhat undertheorized the politics of participation. As stated above, there are certain affinities in the ways that research, business, education, and government policy conventionally refer to the empowering possibilities of new media. In some of these discussions, there is a tendency to neglect the asymmetries of participation. Despite the limitations of notions such as the interpellation or enrollment of audiences—sharing a tendency to make some historical actors appear overtly strategic while others seem not to act at all—they do work as a reminder of some of the basic conditions for the distribution of agency in the relationship between media and users. It is true that media are culturally defined; it is equally true, however, that the materiality of media precedes the making of audiences.

One way of developing a combined analysis of participation and enrollment is to focus on what Ylva Habel calls the "participatory strategies" of certain media events. In her contribution to this volume, Habel investigates the mixed-media practices of the so-called "Milk Propaganda" in interwar Sweden and argues that the success of events promoting increased milk consumption were highly dependent on the interactivity and cultural competence of their audiences. In this context, the notion of empowerment takes on a different and distinctively Foucauldian meaning of the "responsibilization" or self-government of individuals.[17] The didactics of participation is also explored in Frans Lundgren's chapter on the visual pedagogy and exhibition practices of Patrick Geddes at the turn of the twentieth century. In this analysis, Geddes's project is described not only as an effort to influence public opinion, but also as an endeavor to engineer experimental communities around the appropriation of visual media in his envisioned "civic laboratories." The intriguing relationship between different modes of audience participation and the history of public experiment is also discussed in Per Wisselgren's contribution to this volume. His chapter deals with the Swedish reality show *Expedition Robinson*, the very first adaptation of the format that was to become internationally renowned in its later, American incarnation as *Survivor*. But instead of exclusively relating this format to the "participatory turn in broadcast television," Wisselgren emphasizes the way it negotiates a long-standing history of social experiment.[18]

That the script of participation can be very detailed indeed is exemplified in many ways in this book. A case in point is Mathias Boström's analysis of the use of phonographs in ethnographic fieldwork at the turn of the twentieth century. In contrast to other media commonly used by ethnographers (e.g., photography), the phonograph required the direct participation of the informants, and thus detailed instructions were developed as to how to incite their will to participate. This points to the way in which the use of participatory media creates its own code of conduct. Bodil Axelsson's essay situates this question in a contemporary context. In her analysis of two history web sites, she shows how the users not only engage with the past but also with the distribution of expertise and status among themselves. While this case study exemplifies how participants themselves contribute to the script of participation, it also demonstrates how different "socio-technical arrangements" encourage different modes of participation.[19]

NEITHER DECLINE NOR UTOPIA

Stretching from the mid-nineteenth century to the present and dealing with media as varied as museum exhibits and xerography, phonographs, and the internet, the present work will contribute to a historically more elaborate analysis of participatory culture. As summarized below, there are four aspects in particular we believe deserve deeper consideration: the historiographies that inform contemporary discourses on participatory media; conceptual issues; that which Henry Jenkins calls "the politics of participation"; and how research in the cultural history of media can contribute to a more qualified analysis of temporal change when investigating the activities of audiences.

Different assumptions of historical change are often implicit when discussing how media facilitate or circumscribe, reconfigure, or stabilize the activities of readers, listeners, viewers, or users. It is also important to address the historiographies evolving from the media industries themselves. For instance, in Patrik Lundell's contribution to this volume he argues that the history of the press and its readership was constructed as part of the professional efforts of reporters in the nineteenth and early twentieth centuries. According to Lundell, the result was an historical narrative that served as a resource in descriptions of the relationship between the press and the public as mutually beneficial, both in terms of professionalism and civic discourse, and a narrative that also influenced the ways in which later historians were to outline the history of the press. Today's new media also write their own history. Exploring the historiographies at play in the rhetoric of newness, and especially in regard to the divide between audiences and publics, is one way of challenging the most celebratory versions of this history. The purpose of this critique is not, however, to propose an alternative synthesis of the development of audience activities in the last two or three centuries. Rather than looking for the common denominator among different perspectives, the multidisciplinary approach of this anthology seeks to investigate historiographical issues in relation to historical specificity.

It is crucial to critically examine what is meant by "participatory media" and related concepts. As already mentioned, the term "participatory media" is now being used in a wide range of areas including the media industry, business journalism, government policy, and education. Whatever merits ideas of participation bring to these fields, whether visionary or opportunistic, they still tend to be vague and far too broad. In the meantime, a number of academic disciplines have been struggling to develop and specify concepts that make the study of creative media use and active audiences more distinct. In his chapter on the model home in an historical perspective, Mark Sandberg explicitly addresses this important semantic question by discussing the different methodological frameworks implicit in concepts such as "spectator," "viewer," "visitor," "consumer," "shopper," "spectator-inhabitant," and "participant." The distinction between "interactive media" and "participatory media" put forward by Henry Jenkins may seem to offer a solution to this conceptual dilemma. However, there is a danger that this approach obscures the asymmetrical relationship between media and audiences. After all, technologies have provisions and constraints that also must be taken into account.

Furthermore, the politics of participation require a more multidimensional analysis. In current media history research, two lines of thought dominate the political characterization of audience activity: the empowerment analysis, which is most commonly associated with the field of cultural studies; and the incorporation analysis, which more often borrows concepts from Foucauldian perspectives on power. These theoretical orientations are conventionally regarded as competing alternatives. What would happen if they were instead considered complementary? Is it not possible to think of these two perspectives as part and parcel of what it means to be involved as a public, enabling collective action and at the same time stabilizing some vectors of action in particular? Then these two aspects would not be reduced to identity politics on the one hand and agenda-setting on the other, but could also explore what the constitution of publics produces in terms of legitimacy and authority. In addition to the traditional emphasis on access, exclusion, and articulation, this analysis would also focus on the politics of inclusion and how publics are composed of various kinds of political bodies, distinguished not just by their social profile, but also their ascribed values and functions.

Finally, questions of historical change are addressed throughout this book. Several chapters exemplify the ways in which contemporary media use connects with participatory practices of the past. For instance, Mathias Boström discusses how the constraints of participation are redefined when inscriptions made with older technologies are transferred to new media and new groups of users. The mixing of old and new media content, in this case the images of embryos and fetuses by the photographer Lennart Nilsson, is also discussed in Solveig Jülich's essay. However, creative uses of Nilsson's photographs can be found already in the late 1960s and early '70s. When analyzing the circulation and appropriation of these images over a longer period of time, it seems less evident that the convergence of media companies and grassroots communities is something unique for today's participatory culture. In addition, Lisa Gitelman indicates that new media not only redefine but also sometimes obscure our understanding of old media. In this particular case, Gitelman refers to the history of xerography. The ways in which the novelty of photocopying intervened in matters of copyright, self-publication, and political activism—themes that now recur in discussions of participatory media—remind us that media history is also about the retrieval of meaning. And indeed, the analyses offered by the present volume reach in two directions, retrieving historical meaning but also reconnecting media histories both old and new.

NOTES

1. It has been argued that a similar "rhetoric of newness" is indeed characteristic of discussions of digital culture at large; see L. Rabinovitz and A. Geil, "Introduction," in *Memory Bytes*, pp. 1–4.
2. *Participations*, a new online journal launched in 2003 also testifies (at least by its name) to the importance of discussions on participatory media to the multidisciplinary field of audience studies; see <http://www.participations.org/>.
3. See, e.g., J. Surowiecki, *The Wisdom of Crowds*; D. Tapscott and A. Williams, *Wikinomics*; and A. Keen, *The Cult of the Amateur*.
4. In this context, it should be noted that there is also an ongoing discussion on the more recent history of "participatory culture" comparing, for example, new and old digital practices, television and internet audiencing, etc. For some recent contributions, see H. Jenkins, "What Happened Before YouTube?" pp. 109–25; J. Burgess and J. Green, "The Entrepreneurial Vlogger," pp. 89–107; J. van Dijck, "Users Like You."
5. M. McLuhan, *Understanding Media*, esp. Chap. 2.
6. H. Jenkins, *Convergence Culture*, p. 133. In this aspect Jenkins refers to the concept of media discussed in L. Gitelman, *Always Already New*, p. 7.
7. See, e.g., R. Butsch, *The Making of American Audiences*; and the introduction in R. Butsch, ed., *Media and Public Spheres*.
8. J. Habermas, *The Structural Transformation of the Public Sphere*; R. Sennett, *The Fall of Public Man*.
9. M. Horkheimer and T. Adorno, *Dialectic of Enlightenment*; G. Debord, *The Society of the Spectacle*.
10. The negative connotations of terms such as "mass culture" and "passive audiences" established within this tradition, as well as the historiography implicit in the notion of an ongoing "mediatization of the public sphere," continues to be invoked within the overall history of media panics. See, e.g., K. Drotner, "Dangerous Media?"; C. Critcher, *Moral Panics and the Media*; R. Butsch, *The Citizen Audience*, esp. Chaps. 6–7.
11. S. Livingstone, "On the Relation Between Audiences and Publics," quote on p. 18.
12. See, e.g., M. Warner, *The Letters of the Republic*; R. Darnton, "An Early Information Society"; D. Zaret, *Origins of Democratic Culture*.
13. Several anthologies published in recent years have made a case for a more integrated analysis of media history, referring to concepts such as "media cultures," "media networks," "media industries," "media convergence," "*Medienverbund*," and "inter-" or "transmediality." See, e.g., L. Gitelman and G. Pingree, eds., *New Media, 1740–1915*; A. Ekström, S. Jülich, and P. Snickars, eds., *1897: Mediehistorier kring Stockholmsutställningen*; F.

Kessler and N. Verhoeff, eds., *Networks of Entertainment*; J. Staiger and S. Hake, eds., *Convergence Media History*; and J. Holt and A. Perren, eds., *Media Industries*.
14. M. Hansen, *Babel and Babylon*; M. Sandberg, *Living Pictures, Missing Persons*; and L. Gitelman, *Scripts, Grooves, and Writing Machines*.
15. Y. Habel, *Modern Media, Modern Audiences*; B. Griffen-Foley, "From *Tit-Bits* to *Big Brother*"; and A. Ekström, "'Showing at One View'."
16. See, for instance, relevant articles in D. Thorburn and H. Jenkins, eds., *Rethinking Media Change*. See also Ekström, Jülich, and Snickars, eds. *1897: Mediehistorier kring Stockholmsutställningen*.
17. G. Burchell, C. Gordon, and P. Miller, eds., *The Foucault Effect*.
18. G. Enli, *The Participatory Turn in Broadcast Television*.
19. A. Barry, *Political Machines*.

2 From Enlightened Participation to Liberal Professionalism
On the Historiography of the Press as a Resource for Legitimacy

Patrik Lundell

When criticizing the notion that participatory media is something new, another idea is sometimes implicitly adopted: that sharp distinctions between media producers and media consumers actually are appropriate, as far as the history of traditional mass media is concerned. Focusing on less-studied forms such as exhibitions, museums, and phonographs risks accepting traditional historiography on traditional mass media. The common role model for any discussion of "the media" is not just traditional mass media; it is rather traditional, that is, historically constructed conceptions of traditional mass media.

In what is called the "new film history," there is indeed an established awareness of the performative aspects of spectatorship and the cultural practices surrounding the medium.[1] Historical studies of the other supposedly key mass media—the press, radio, and television—still often limit their interest in audiences to simply counting readers, listeners, and viewers and identifying their social affiliation. Though no one today believes audiences to have been completely passive, their agency is seldom understood in terms of actual participation within the medium, but rather as an active adoption of media content, possibly resulting in activities carried out elsewhere and possibly having an indirect effect on future media content. As for the study of the press, this too is very much the case. There are exceptions, of course. John Hartley has argued for the view that journalism is "meaning" and "readership."[2] And Bridget Griffen-Foley has traced audience involvement and agency in periodicals from the 1880s through to magazines, radio, and television up until today, significantly observing that "media producers have been blurring the notion of the passive media consumer for more than a century."[3] In the present article, I would like to back up one more century and discuss not only this blurring but also how the notion as such might have historically emerged.

In the first issue of a Swedish newspaper launched in 1795, its editor addressed his readers thus: "The beginning of a newspaper which reflects the values of our city and our community is hereby made; it must however depend on the practitioners of Science, Literature and the Fine Arts to further my purpose!"[4] This publishing ideal had been established and practiced for decades. The newspaper editors of the Enlightenment not only opened their papers to a wide range of contributors; they also considered it their duty to print what the reading public sent them (as long as this did not offend law, religion, or good taste).

Although Swedish press history has its unique features and chronology, the point I want to make is applicable far beyond Sweden's borders. Although hitherto hardly studied, the theme can be found elsewhere. In the very first issue of the *London Daily Universal Register* (soon to be renamed the *Times*), one could read that a newspaper "ought to resemble an *Inn*, where the proprietor is *obliged* to give the use of his house to all travelers, who are ready to pay for it." Dallas Liddle goes on to compare the "humble public innkeeper" of the eighteenth century with the "authoritative public oracle" emerging in the next century.[5]

Any clear-cut distinction between producer and consumer is doomed to collapse when tested on various historically specific forms of media.[6] However, remarks stating the exact opposite—like Nicholas Negroponte's sharp distinction between "passive old media" and "interactive new media" in *Being Digital* (1995)—can hardly be explained by mere historical ignorance on a personal level.[7] Instead, we must ask from where these notions come. One recurring question asks how the passive audience of old, in fact and/or in rhetoric, has been transformed into today's participatory public. The opposite question is also worth addressing: How has a participating public, real or imagined, been transformed and/or discursively constructed into a passive audience? In other words, how have these traditional distinctions between media producers and media consumers—taken for granted by many interpreters of our digital age—been made? Who made them? When? Why?

In this chapter, I discuss only some aspects of the history and historiography of the Swedish press. The editorial ideals and practices of the Enlightenment press are presented with regard to their participatory elements. The decline of these ideals and practices during what is commonly agreed to be the era of the establishment of the modern press in the 1820s, '30s, and '40s is discussed with regard to its advocates' self-legitimating ambitions. These were carried out in various ways, including either simply ignoring their precursors or emphasizing the nonparticipatory qualities of their own enterprise. These modern editors' depictions of both past and present have had great influence on press historiography right up to the present day.

FROM ENLIGHTENED PARTICIPATION TO LIBERAL PROFESSIONALISM

In the latter half of the eighteenth century, the ideal of a civic press, a press for the citizens, was established. This ideal was not only successfully translated into practice; it was shaped and negotiated through that practice. The publishers of newspapers literally considered it their duty to publish letters to the paper, and its readers considered it their right to appear in print. There are even examples of individuals who incorrectly believed this was a legal right.[8] The newspaper, it was commonly agreed, should not reflect or represent a public discourse; it should actually be one, in order to promote a better society.

Lisa Gitelman proposes a model of media that works on two levels: as a technology that enables communication and as a set of associated "protocols," i.e., social and cultural norms and practices associated with this technology.[9] These protocols are what I have called an ideal and its practice. In a prospectus from 1793, its core was articulated thus:

> One would see such a daily or weekly open so to speak a constant conversation among the residents of the town, where everyone has the opportunity to enlighten, benefit and amuse each other, and where the most prominent as well as the most common resident enjoys equal right to raise his voice, for both public and private good.[10]

The protocols of the civic press were formed by several factors. The concept of freedom of the press as a collective freedom was fundamental, as was its view of censorship and belief in the existence of an absolute Truth. To this were appended negative notions of concepts like "opinion" and "party." Fundamental was also a rather hegemonic ideology, an apolitical politics—an all-revealing Enlightenment, borne primarily by the traditional elite of the old regime, the clergy and the nobility, which demanded that the true good citizen be actively involved in society.[11] The press was occasionally referred to as the "periodical Enlightenment"; and Immanuel Kant's appeal in his famous "Beantwortung der Frage: Was ist Aufklärung?" ("Answering the Question: What Is Enlightenment?" 1784), that it was a civic duty to make public use of one's reason, was a thought more typical for the times than original.[12] The right to participate was simultaneously an exacting duty to do so. Furthermore, the spirit of the age was by and large eclectic, and hence collective, not yet influenced by Romantic ideas of originality and individuality.[13]

On a practical level, the civic press was formed by book printers who lacked the cultural resources to write their own papers. There are examples of printers who strongly objected to being referred to as newspaper writers; they were printers or publishers. In the 1760s, when one paper was starting to show signs of decline, a subscriber appealed to his fellow citizens: "Whom shall I blame? Not the printer, for his task is to print, not to write. It must therefore be the learned and literary citizens of this city."[14]

A prerequisite for the press ideal was the limitation of the medium itself, conditioned by its historically specific means of production and distribution. As few as three or four hundred copies could be considered successful circulation, often in towns with less than 10,000 inhabitants. The papers usually lacked competition; they were the only ones on the local newspaper market. And although newspapers had existed since the outset of the seventeenth century, the papers referred to here were often understood as a new way of communicating, as a new medium.

In principle, the newspapers were explicitly open to all; in practice, however, high social and cultural barriers were erected around them, not to mention gender qualifications. The radical elements of the Enlightenment should not be exaggerated; in essence it was a moderate reform movement, religious at its core, that was acting within established structures of power. Its relatively conservative content and its socially and geographically limited scope do not, however, make the participatory elements of the Enlightenment press less true, neither as ideal nor as practice.

However, all this changed over the course of the first half of the nineteenth century. Protocols were transformed; and this transformation depended, of course, on a multitude of parameters, some of which can only be mentioned briefly here. With the French revolution and the Napoleonic Wars, the supply of and demand for news dramatically increased. Citizens were curious and articles readily available. Political radicalism and titillating profanity sold, as did war. The flood of news literally called for space, and hence other features, such as letters to the paper, had to relinquish their places. Furthermore, the selection and translation of articles (usually from Dutch and German newspapers) was generally carried out by a single person, usually the publisher himself, whose role thus became more professionalized and more intimately connected to the content of his newspaper. Hence the establishment and rapid acceptance in the 1790s of the Swedish term for "editor" (*redaktör*).

The selection of news items generally was not politically motivated. The dramatic events that were transpiring on the Continent needed no further processing in order to sell, and impartiality remained an explicit ideal. Since foreign reports were termed "political news," one can still speak of a politicization of the press. Political newspapers, as they began to be called, should be impartial by definition, odd as this sounds today.[15] However, the old understanding of politics as a field of knowledge dealing with truth and falsehood about the nature of things gradually gave way to a modern understanding of politics as ideology, concerned with views and opinions and preoccupied not by order but by change (especially given its radical content). On a conceptual level, the all-unifying Enlightenment was eventually replaced by the fragmented political isms of liberalism, conservatism, socialism. Previously shunned concepts like "opinion" and "party" gradually became charged with positive connotations.[16] The belief in the Truth, with a capital T, was vanishing.

The population grew, as did consumption and advertising. An increasing number of aspiring entrepreneurs tried their luck in a growing marketplace. Competition increased. Towns that for decades had had only one newspaper suddenly had two, even three. Although the flood of news about war and revolution eventually ran dry, the editorial role as such had been firmly established; professionalization sustained itself. Moreover, political language had changed. At the beginning of the nineteenth century, there were also some fundamental changes in the actual political terrain: Sweden experienced a (bloodless) revolution, lost Finland, and passed a new constitution. As the public became more interested in domestic affairs, another term was introduced with remarkable and swift success—*publicist*, which in Swedish refers to the editor as a self-reliant expert on public affairs. In 1825, one renowned exponent of this modern ideal, the *Argus*, actually called for the abolishment of "the *extensive* and *uncontrolled* practice of printing letters to the paper."[17] Truth-seeking conversation within the pages of the single paper was gradually replaced by debate between newspapers, or rather between newspaper editors.

This development should not be confused with Jürgen Habermas's Marxist narrative of the rise and fall of the bourgeois public sphere. The social structure of the actual public supporting the civic press had little to do with a pushing bourgeoisie; its "decline," on the other hand, can certainly be related to the rising middle class. And regardless, in an analysis limited to the printed press, sweeping statements about a single, uniform public sphere are never a good idea.[18]

THE RHETORIC OF NON-PARTICIPATION

The old, participatory ideals of the Enlightenment did not disappear overnight. On the contrary, both old and new ideals were elaborately articulated in debates on practice in the first half of the nineteenth century. To be sure, the battle lines were drawn between political interests, the conservative heirs of the Enlightenment and more or less radical supporters of liberalism. But it was just as much a struggle for power over the field of communications, a struggle not only about political views but also for professional legitimacy and status, and of course for market shares. This complex free-for-all (eventually won by the liberals, by the way) will not be accounted for here. Instead, I will attempt a brief survey of the arguments made, the more or less conscious strategies used, and the inherent logic at work in order to establish and defend the new ideals, i.e., to establish and legitimate the new, nonparticipatory protocols.

Everyone, claimed the editors of the aforementioned *Argus* in 1825, including the people who write letters to the papers, was motivated by self-interest, even if it was often "concealed even to the writers themselves."[19] The only actor actually capable of rising above self-interest was the independent publicist. As private citizens, the editors of the *Argus* were no different from any other. But by accepting the professional role of the publicist, they assumed this extremely demanding task. The publicist, and the publicist only, could educate and lead public thinking.

At the same time, however, the publicists claimed to be representatives of public opinion. This paradox was, at least partially, dissolved by a differentiating view on the population. Though a fundamentally pedagogic project, Enlightenment rhetoric normally included everyone in the concept of the citizen, from the freeholder and his farmhands and milkmaids to the monarch; peasants were rewarded for contributions to the public good, and King Gustavus III called himself the "First Citizen." In practice, however, there was never any doubt that it was the educated elite who had taken it upon themselves to enlighten the commoners. This tension was now explicitly articulated, or at least articulated in a new way. By representing the educated elite (and here there was no talk of any self-interested bias), the publicist was sanctioned (or sanctioned himself) to turn loyal subjects into true citizens, to transform the passive audience into an active and politically conscious public.[20] This civic activity, however, was never meant to be performed within the medium of the press. Furthermore, there were no dramatic increases in the number of newspapers finding their way into the hands of the lower classes (and would not be until half a century later). In fact, what happened was that an existing, participatory public was degraded to a passive audience receiving the teachings of the publicists.

To these offensive arguments other, more defensive ones could be added. Those defending the old ideals accused the new editors of misquotations, lies, and of most interest here, lack of impartiality and failing to give equal space to opponents. Occasionally—and this is perhaps what has most effectively been forgotten in the historiography—the liberals agreed. Under an oppressing regime, they argued, there was no room for "fair play"; the ends justified the means.[21] Still, such statements were scarce. When it became apparent that the liberals were fighting a winning battle, a more moderate version of this view was expressed. Conservatives began insisting on the legal obligation of newspapers to make room for rebuttal. In 1849, the parliamentary ombudsman recommended that such a law be enacted, because it would not only restrain abuse and defamation, he argued, but also strike at the core of the problem, namely, the lack of impartiality in the press and hence in public debate. Liberals including Herman Rydin, a professor of law, agreed these ideas were seemly and just—while at the same time dismissing them as unrealizable. Modern society and its infrastructure of communication were simply far too complex.[22]

Other discursive means existed (ranging from silence to exaggeration) for attaining status and establishing new ideals and practices in public thought. No definite line can be drawn between a conscious strategy and a sort of inherent logic of professionalization rapidly gaining momentum. Although the word *correspondent* can denote either a letter-writer or a news reporter, the professional correspondent emerged in Sweden in the 1830s, and soon it behooved every editor with any self-respect to employ at least one or two of them; at the start, these were often domestic correspondents, but foreign correspondents became commonplace soon enough.

Quite a few new newspapers even added this concept to their names, like *Correspondenten* in Uppsala (1830) and *Skånska Correspondenten* in Lund (1832). Promises to the readership to engage professional correspondents frequently appeared in policy statements of the time. Even large and successful provincial papers, like *Östgötha Correspondenten* in Linköping (founded in 1838), could eventually boast about having correspondents "at the Parliament and the Army as well as by the actual Theater of War."[23]

The more or less professional correspondent certainly existed. In many instances, however, it was a case of giving an established practice a new name. Remuneration for contributing to the mid-nineteenth century press is an issue with no clear answer. In the 1830s and '40s, there are examples of letter-writers, now known as correspondents, being promised compensation for their words. On the other hand, several papers began charging a fee. However, both phenomena can be interpreted as expressions of the same tendency, clarifying the difference between professional and layman, and hence strengthening the professional image of the paper. As for the participatory element per se, it is equally clear that material submitted by laymen comprised a substantial amount of newspaper content far into the nineteenth century.[24]

On a more general level, one might instead speak of a rhetorical exaggeration of the profession. In descriptive reports of a typical day at an average newspaper office, the huge offices are depicted bustling with people; the pace is described as fast, almost frantic; and the rotary press added an industrial air to the whole enterprise. In reality, most of these late nineteenth-century papers had only a small staff including the editor; the offices were furnished with one or two desks; and the most important tools were a pair of scissors and a bottle of glue.[25]

Another version of this kind of rhetoric can already be discerned in the 1830s and '40s, when quite a few elaborate surveys of the political affiliations of the contemporary press were conducted. In 1842, the Gothenburg paper *Phoenix* identified two main groups into which newspapers fell, liberals and conservatives, which numbered twenty-four and eleven, respectively. These papers were further defined as ranging from "radical" and "moderate" on the liberal side to "royalist" and "cynically royalist" on the conservative. To this was added an intricate system to determine each paper's degree of "intensity," which eventually resulted in eleven liberal and four conservative categories. The relative quantitative strength and biased terminology are certainly intent on making a strong liberal argument. It must be noted, however, that not one of the "conservative" newspapers called themselves conservative (whereas all of the "liberals" termed themselves so). No doubt any number of the "conservative" papers indeed supported "conservative" ideas; but officially they celebrated, and to a certain degree also practiced, impartial editorial ideals. Also of note are the twenty-two newspapers the *Phoenix* called "colorless," and hence did not treat at all in its otherwise elaborate exposition. According to the *Phoenix*, these papers were probably liberal, if their editors were forced to choose.[26] More accurately, I would argue, they were representative of the old, participatory type of paper. Their exclusion can be interpreted as not being acknowledged as proper newspapers. Only "conservative" papers that in some sense, or to some degree, spoke the same language as the liberal press were taken seriously. And a majority apparently did not.

AND THE REST IS HISTORIOGRAPHY

In the nineteenth century, the successors to the humble, ink-stained printers of the Enlightenment often treated their precursors like air. They claimed that no proper newspaper press existed before their own time. In a fundamental and obvious way, this is of course untrue. On the other hand, there seems to be no doubt that the press underwent a profound transformation in the first half of the nineteenth century. I would declare the rhetoric of these nineteenth-century liberals victorious; and indeed, this very chapter sings the old theme song criticizing a Whig interpretation of history.[27] The participatory elements of the Enlightenment press have been either completely neglected or seen as amateurish. Although everyone agrees that its history stretches much further back in time, *proper* newspapers only came into existence in the nineteenth century, or so the story goes. The preceding time is often literally seen as a *pre*-history and is quite anachronistically defined in terms of the absence of features to come.

Historians around 1900 who were broad-minded enough to acknowledge the existence of an eighteenth-century press (particularly if the paper had been edited by a canonized poet or other intellectual) still sneered at its amateurish elements and poor quality. A highly regarded illustrated history of Swedish literature informs the reader in 1927 that the pages of *Dagligt Allehanda*, one of the most widely circulated and long-lived Stockholm papers (founded in 1769), were filled by its own readers: "Thus, *Dagligt Allehanda* was a very inferior newspaper, though a newspaper that paid its own way."[28] In 1945, the Swedish Press Club arranged a grand exhibition celebrating the 300th anniversary of the Swedish press. However, its visitors were taught that the contemporary press had little in common with its seventeenth-century ancestor, despite dubbing itself a "symbol of continuity, of tradition."[29] A recently published lavish four-volume history of the press refers to the participatory qualities of the early nineteenth-century press not in terms of participation but of editorial "cunning and tricks."[30]

At the same time, the positive connotations of openness, dialogue, and civic engagement have been ascribed to the liberal press of the early nineteenth century. And its conservative critics are usually described as men of almost medieval dispositions. A popular textbook intended for the upper-secondary school level informs students that a free and open debate was established with the founding in 1830 of one specific liberal newspaper,

Aftonbladet. They are also told that conservatives of the day rejected liberty of the press out of hand. The same narrative recurs of course on the newspaper's website.[31]

The success of a medium is always conditioned by inattention or blindness to its supporting protocols.[32] Nowadays, this narrative is a part of a confirming tradition, "invented" in the nineteenth century. And this tradition is also maintained beyond the press itself. Politicians, scholars, novelists, and other intellectuals and artists have joined in the chorus.[33] Obversely, the mass-media and overall mass-cultural critical approach developed during the twentieth century from (say) Karl Bücher and Walter Lippmann onwards has generally been consistent with and confirmed the internal stories of professional media institutions.[34] Together these narratives have been so overwhelming that the professional and basically nonparticipatory aspect of the press is seen (at least implicitly) as media specific. Participatory elements, which could easily be traced up until today, are downplayed. Or rather, literally not seen.

NOTES

1. For an introduction, see J. Chapman, M. Glancy and S. Harper, eds., *The New Film History*.
2. See the introduction to J. Hartley, *Popular Reality*.
3. B. Griffen-Foley, "From *Tit-Bits* to *Big Brother*," p. 545.
4. *Linköpings Bladet*, 3 January 1795, quoted in P. Lundell, *Pressen i provinsen*, p. 23. The present article develops results from this thesis; references are henceforth only given for quotations. All translations are by the author, unless stated otherwise.
5. D. Liddle, "Who Invented the 'Leading Article'?" pp. 5–6. The professionalization of the press during the period is also discussed in L. O'Boyle, "The Image of the Journalist"; J. Retallack, "From Pariah to Professional?"; and P. Dooley, *Taking Their Political Place*.
6. L. Gitelman, *Always Already New*, p. 15: "the very categories of consumer and producer are inadequate to explain fully the deep definition of new media." I would argue that they are inadequate to explain fully the deep definition of *any* media.
7. N. Negroponte, *Being Digital*, p. 54. See also, e.g., S. Livingstone, "The Changing Nature of Audiences"; H. Jenkins, *Convergence Culture*; M. Deuze, "Participation, Remediation, Bricolage."
8. O. Sylwan, *Svenska pressens historia till statshvälfningen 1772*, p. 108.
9. L. Gitelman, *Always Already New*, p. 5.
10. Prospectus for *Örebro Weckoblad* 1793, quoted in B. Mral, "Två tidningsstarter i Örebro," p. 111.
11. On the Enlightenment as a politically moderate and elite phenomenon see, e.g., R. Porter, *Enlightenment*; J. Knudsen, *Justus Möser and the German Enlightenment*; J. Christensson, *Lyckoriket*.
12. C. Gjörwell quoted in *Upfostrings-Sälskapets Allmänna Tidningar*, 30 April 1787; I. Kant, "Beantwortung der Frage: Was ist Aufklärung?" *Berlinischen Monatschrift*, December 1784.
13. On the collective element of pre-Romanticism (and its return), see M. Woodmansee, "On the Author Effect."

14. *Norrköpings Weko-Tidningar*, 19 September 1767, quoted in Lundell, *Pressen i provinsen*, p. 23.
15. See, e.g., J. von Schwarzkopf, "Ueber politische Zeitungen und Intelligenz-Blätter in Schweden," *Allgemeiner Litterarischer Anzeiger*, no. 6, 1800.
16. For the era as one of conceptual change on a general level, see R. Koselleck, "Einleitung"; see also E. Hobsbawm, *The Age of Revolution*.
17. *Argus*, 1 October 1825, quoted in Lundell, *Pressen i provinsen*, p. 125.
18. A discussion of how this relates to Jürgen Habermas's "public sphere" is offered in Lundell, *Pressen i provinsen*, passim.
19. *Argus*, 1 October 1825, quoted in Lundell, *Pressen i provinsen*, p. 125.
20. See also C. Rosengren, *Tidevarvets bättre genius*; H. Edgren, *Publicitet för medborgsmannavett*.
21. See, e.g., J. Rosén, *Kritik öfver brochyren "Dagens händelser bedömde af en landtman"* (Stockholm, 1838), p. 14.
22. Parliamentary Ombudsman S. Theorell, *Rikets Ständers Justitiæ-ombudsmans Embets-berättelse för år 1849* (Stockholm, 1849), p. 9; H. Rydin, *Om Yttrandefrihet och Tryckfrihet: Försök till belysning af Svenska Press-Lagstiftningen* (Stockholm: L. J. Hjerta, 1859), p. 107. Rydin actually referred to laws of this kind in France, Austria, Prussia, and Belgium.
23. *Östgötha Correspondenten*, 20 December 1848, quoted in Lundell, *Pressen i provinsen*, p. 236.
24. E. Johannesson, "Med det nya på väg (1858–1880)," p. 227.
25. J. Jarlbrink, *Det våras för journalisten*.
26. *Phoenix*, 13 and 19 February 1842.
27. An inspiring discussion about and important corrective to Whiggish press history is offered in J. Curran and J. Seaton, *Power without Responsibility*.
28. H. Schück and K. Warburg, *Illustrerad svensk litteraturhistoria*, p. 76.
29. H. Gullberg, Director of the Swedish Academy, quoted in P. Lundell, "Det goda samhällets tjänare iscensatt," p. 175.
30. J. Torbacke, "Nu grundläggs den moderna utvecklingen (1809–1830)," p. 282.
31. L. Peterson and Å. Pettersson, *Medieboken: Massmedier*, pp. 86–87. Aftonbladet (newspaper) <http://koncernen.aftonbladet.se/koncernen/historik/article3655.ab> (accessed 14 December 2007).
32. L. Gitelman, *Always Already New*, pp. 6–7.
33. On the construction and communication of the self-image and ideology of the press, through various media forms and by various actors, see P. Lundell, "The Medium is the Message." See also A. Jones, *Powers of the Press*; M. Hampton, *Visions of the Press in Britain, 1850–1950*.
34. From K. Bücher, "Die Anfänge des Zeitungswesens," in *Die Entstehung der Volkwirtschaft*, vol. 1, 10th ed. (Tübingen: Laupp, 1917), pp. 257–58, stems the idea of the press developing from a news-based medium via an opinion-based one to being advertisement-based (a schedule adopted in, e.g., J. Habermas, *Strukturwandel der Öffentlichkeit*.) In his own time, Bücher saw the newspaper as an enterprise to produce advertising space, a product that required at least some editorial material in order to sell; see, e.g., K. Bücher, *Gesammelte Aufsätze zur Zeitungskunde* (Tübingen: Laupp, 1926), p. 31. W. Lippmann views the press as a means for transmitting information from professionals to the mass public (see W. Lippmann, *Public Opinion*); Lippmann's main concern is the standard and skills of those professionals, and he argued for the importance of scholarly influence on the journalistic body.

3 Knowing Audiences, Knowing Media
Performing Publics at the Early Twentieth-Century Fun Fair

Anders Ekström

At the turn of the twentieth century, large amusement areas had become a key feature of European and North American world's fairs. Exhibition experts in various countries viewed this development in different ways. Whereas some argued that the amusement areas would distract attention from the more serious exhibits, others stressed that it was only by offering amusements that it was possible to attract an audience that was suffering from acute "exhibition fatigue."[1] As a consequence, the early twentieth-century exhibitions presented their visitors with a summary of contemporary developments in an emergent and increasingly transnational entertainment industry. In addition to a wide range of new and old media, theaters, and traditional fun-fair attractions, these venues were characterized by an almost endless variation of panoramas and multimedia reenactments of scenes from war, natural disasters, and the exotic colonies. One of the most remarkable examples was the Pike, the amusement area of the 1904 St. Louis World's Fair. In all, the Pike offered its visitors more than 500 amusements and concessions, many of which created the illusion of movement in time and location.[2]

In a series of four temporary exhibitions organized in Stockholm between 1866 and 1930, it was not until 1909 that one of these exhibitions would include a separate amusement area. In selecting amusements for this event, the organizers referred to their experiences from visits to previous exhibitions in various countries.[3] The Pike was an obvious inspiration for their efforts, and although the amusement area at the 1909 Stockholm exhibition was much more limited, it displayed a similar mix of attractions. The most spectacular theatrical attraction at the Stockholm exhibition was a reconstruction of the devastating flood in the American city of Johnstown in 1889, a display that combined visual techniques, sound effects, actors, and lecturers to create its illusionary effects. The organizers also introduced the water chute and a spiral helter-skelter to local audiences, new amusements that offered thrills as well as uplifting views. Among the many pavilions in the area, one offered visitors a full-scale printing works and another displayed statistics in a figurative and visually innovative way.[4]

However, the most contested amusements at the 1909 Stockholm exhibition were two open-air dance pavilions located close to the restaurants, theaters, and helter-skelters. In one of these pavilions, an orchestra led by the conductor Theodor Pinet introduced a dance called the Boston. This soon became the most popular venue of the exhibition as a whole and attracted more than 250,000 visitors over the whole season, from June to September.[5] Many came to dance, but even more came to watch others dance. In the eyes of some spectators, the dancing couples' movements and physical closeness was an unambiguous sign of the moral decline caused by popular culture. Looking back at the event, one visitor claimed it was truly remarkable that adults were allowed "to dance with each other" in public at the 1909 Stockholm exhibition when only a few decades earlier "the children at an orphanage in Stockholm had been advised on moral grounds only to 'jump' around the Christmas tree."[6]

Other visitors considered the dance pavilions socially progressive and argued that the amusement area as a whole led to greater democratization of public space. On the dance floor, one reporter proclaimed, there were "no misgivings, no class-distinction"; on the contrary, by dancing in public men and women as well as people from different classes, professions, age groups, and regions could "happily" and "naturally" mingle. According to the same reporter, this was also true for the social interaction that developed among the crowds that gathered around the water glide. This site also attracted a lot of people watching others hurtling down the slope, an audience that was enthusiastically reported to consist of "children and servants" as well as "wholesale dealers and managers and earnest civil servants and white-haired ladies."[7] Thus, according to these reports, people of different financial and social standing were fortuitously united by the exhilaration of the occasion; the onlookers who gathered around the helter-skelters "had so much fun, laughing and conversing although they were complete strangers to each other, becoming lively and talkative."[8]

The tendency to equate the consumption of popular entertainments and media with the emergence of alternative publics was fairly common in the early twentieth century. Early film, for example, was sometimes promoted as a universal language able to bridge various social, cultural, and geographical differences. This notion of film as a "democratic art" also very soon became a powerful resource in the marketing strategies of the early twentieth-century film industry.[9] Today, similar perceptions appear in discourses on television and digital media. In particular, attention has been directed toward the ways in which audiences are enabled to participate and become visible in new media, and how this might relate to the emergence of more active modes of citizenship.[10]

The purpose of this chapter is certainly not to suggest that fin-de-siècle audience activities can be conceived of as a prehistory to a more fully developed participatory culture. Too often, the history of popular culture and its publics is anachronistically constructed as being more or less in tune with certain democratic values. My aim is rather to highlight the performative visibility of the audience positions that were developed at the early twentieth-century fun fair and amusement grounds. More specifically, I would like to suggest that a particular kind of sociability evolved in these places that, more than anything else, was a result of the ways in which the attractions physically engaged the audiences. Thus, the analysis is focused on the physicality and performative address of fin-de-siècle entertainments and media, not primarily on issues of empowerment or the production of counterpublics.[11] On a more general level, I also argue that these audience positions point to the centrality of incorporation and embodiment of the cultural practices by which we learn how to act as audiences.

The sociologists Nicholas Abercrombie and Brian Longhurst have argued that the everyday interaction with media in contemporary societies means not only that individuals are more often part of an audience than before but also that social interaction in general is becoming increasingly performative. Put simply, they suggest that by continuously interacting with various media, people learn to act as if they were in front of a camera or an audience themselves: "People see others as performers and come to see themselves as performers."[12] Abercrombie and Longhurst conceive of this process as historically cumulative, being an instance of an ever more media-saturated world. There is much to support such a view, but it is not easily evaluated in a longer historical perspective. It is clear from research, however, that a rich and varied history of participatory and performative audiences existed prior to twentieth-century "mass" media or today's "new" media.[13]

In pursuing the history of audiences, we also need to move away from too narrow a focus on issues of the circulation or appropriation of media texts. By proposing a broader history of *media sociability* rather than a history of media consumption, this chapter is sketching out an approach that focuses just as much on the physical interaction between audiences and media as on how the members of an audience interact with each other. Stressing the materiality of these interactions is also a way of highlighting the myriads of gestures, movements, rhythms, and sensory activities that audiences are drawn into and collectively create. In this respect, the chapter is oriented toward exploring fundamental aspects of how our way of physically engaging with media affects the very choreography of public space. I suggest the particular sociability that arises from these interactions is—just as in dancing—the combined result of physical restrictions and "moments of inspired improvisation."[14]

MOVING VIEWS, GLIDING EYES

The entertainments at the 1909 Stockholm exhibition were centered in large part around one organizing principle: the production of motion. This was, for example, true of both the frequent representation of movement in the pavilions and the many attractions that literally aimed to set the visitors' bodies in motion. This provided the area with a distinctive rhythm that emphasized the visitors' physical involvement with the amusements. In turn, individual bodies in motion were exposed to the other visitors in an enhanced way, for example, while dancing or on the helter-skelter. A number of amusements also directed attention toward the individual's own body and its physical performance, for example, by demonstrating the plasticity of perception, playing with bodily proportions, or focusing on the reaction of the senses to effects and thrills.

On the whole, the mediation of movement was a more general characteristic of the aesthetics of attraction that developed in relation to nineteenth and early twentieth-century entertainments and media. For example, from the early nineteenth century onward, dioramas and panoramas were used to create the sensation of motion and virtual travel. In fun fairs and temporary amusement grounds, an economy of the senses emerged that profited from the effects of vertigo and speed. Also, a number of mechanical or electrical rides were introduced at the midways in late nineteenth-century world's fairs, entertainments that translated the ideology of technological progress to immediate physical sensations. In short, this aesthetic therefore adds in many ways to the notion of modernity's fixation on motion, speed, fluidity, shifts in perspective, and the displacement of time and space.[15]

But the movements of the body in public were also socially and morally controversial, which made the physical constitutive of the very meaning attached to public performance. What some people in fin-de-siècle societies considered to be an exaggerated, too lively, or uncontrolled way of exposing the body was construed as a distinguishing feature of groups regarded as socially or culturally inferior. The aesthetic of the amusement area, on the other hand, was all about setting the visitors' bodies in motion, evoking sensory shocks and perceptual effects. These social and moral contexts obviously added to the thrills of watching others dancing or hurtling down the water slide or helter-skelter. Again, visitors came to these sites not only to perform but also to see others perform, thereby contributing to an exchange of glances that when transferred to the exhibition at large made the audiences even more visible than the objects on display.

Much of the commentary in newspaper reports and official publications from the 1909 Stockholm exhibition testifies to the widespread interest in watching others perform in the amusement area. In this material, the exhibition is repeatedly and humorously described as an open stage, crowded with visitors whose eyes constantly scanned the area. According to the official report of the exhibition, for example, "the public" gathered around the dance floors "as onlookers" that subjected the dancing couples to a "controlling gaze."[16] Another review applied similar metaphors in describing the active eyes of the audience at the helter-skelter: "there is no end to the interest in allowing one's gaze to glide down [the tower]." Even when the slide was closed, this reporter continued, visitors came so that their

24 *Anders Ekström*

Figure 3.1 Visitors gathering around one of the open-air dance pavilions at the 1909 Stockholm exhibition. Stockholm City Museum.

"gaze could trace its spiral line," which turned the site into an attraction.[17] One of the older amusements at the exhibition, a camera obscura, was also advertised for the way it enabled its users to watch the visitors, in this case without being seen by others.[18] In another review, the camera obscura was compared to an "observatory" that allowed visitors to adopt the position of a spy and their eyes to scan the exhibition area: "Perspectives change, every corner and spot and bush is turned inside out."[19]

Consequently, this was an aesthetic of attraction that focused on the visual, which thereby fostered a form of sociability to a large extent organized by the ways in which visitors visually interacted with each other and the amusements. At the same time, many of these amusements engaged the entire body, often in a very tangible way. This was obviously the case with the helter-skelters and the dancing, but there were several other examples as well, among them a rotating open-air café (to which I shall soon return). In addition, a number of attractions shared a tendency to address the visitor's senses and bodily proportions, a technique that focused attention on how individuals regarded themselves and playfully negotiated the self-reformative aspects of performance.

For example, at the amusement area in Stockholm, visitors were presented with distorted images of their own bodies in the mirror hall of the fun house.

In the same pavilion, they could also have their perceptual habits dislocated in a room literally turned upside down (see figures 6.2 and 6.3 in Sandberg's contribution to this volume).[20] A popular addition to the entertainment market in central Stockholm in the 1890s was the Oriental Maze, which also positioned the visitors in front of distorted images of themselves.[21] By the use of various mirror installations and shifts in scale and proportion, these attractions were all organized around the production of grotesque effects and optical illusions, but they were also interrelated in the way they invited the visitor to perform in front of the mirrors. According to the official report of the Stockholm exhibition, the success of the fun house was that it offered new ways of seeing the body in "grotesque shapes" and "piquant situations." The review concluded: "never before had a larger collection of deformed human beings been seen in Sweden."[22] All of these attractions invited the visitors to perform not only in front of themselves but also in front of the strangers that were simultaneously strolling through the pavilions. And I argue that by thematizing issues of bodily proportions and gestures, these performative encounters seem to have promoted an enhanced awareness of the physical aspects of public sociability among the visitors.

Another pavilion at the amusement area in Stockholm deliberately designed to engage the visitors in self-reflexive comparisons and shifts of perspective was the Statistikon, a popular display of figurative representations of statistics.[23] It was invented by the Swedish architect Ferdinand Boberg and contained a series of three-dimensional miniature scenes that were all set in motion by electricity. In this "statistical machinery," as it was referred to by the architect himself, a series of societal processes and contemporary statistical relations were presented that in some way or another also included the visitors to the pavilion. For example, one of the moving miniature scenes demonstrated the chemical elements of the human body and compared the quantities with other uses of the same chemical material. According to one of the many visitors to the pavilion, it was "a great attraction."[24]

The mediation of motion defined the statistical displays. Several of the scenes were centered on media and communication technologies, for example, in moving representations of the frequency of railway travel, telephone calls, and the traffic of post and telegrams in contemporary Sweden. During the exhibition season, the public was invited to contribute in a contest that aimed to renew the pavilion by introducing statistical representations proposed by the participants. Several of the entries to the competition also focused on the representation of movement and communication technologies. For example, one participant proposed that Sweden's international trade should be statistically represented in a three-dimensional map with miniature ships and trains "in perpetual motion." Another competitor suggested a series of "living pictures of different speeds from a messenger boy to a swallow." Of the many entries that were centered on the representation of various media and communication technologies, one suggestion was to visualize the number of spoken words transferred by the trans-Atlantic cable. As part of their efforts to enhance interest in the pavilion, Boberg and the organizers of the amusement area eventually implemented several of these suggestions. In one of the additions, the movements of the visitors at the exhibition were also turned into a statistical attraction. Following the suggestion of a participant in the contest, a model of one of the two open-air dance floors was created on which moving figures performed to a phonographic version of Pinet's music. Also, a model of a tram in motion represented the amount of physical energy consumed by the dancing couples.[25]

We can only speculate on how the sound from the electric installations and the movements in the statistical miniatures interacted with the presence of the visitors and how it all contributed to the pavilion's specific rhythm. Again, the particular sociability that developed in these places was not only the result of the interaction between the members of the audience but also of the individual encounters with the displays. The shifting of perspectives that on the one hand focused attention on new ways of seeing oneself, and on the other hand, encouraged a more distanced view of how other visitors interacted with the displays was a characteristic that the Statistikon shared with the fun house and several other amusements.

LEARNING TO ACT AS AUDIENCES

In general, the amount of intermedial exchange and cross-referencing in nineteenth and early twentieth-century popular visual culture and media is striking. The ingenuity of individual entrepreneurs can in this respect be traced in numerous practices that travelled between different countries and exhibition contexts. Thus, when Boberg chose the name Statistikon it was a way of connecting to related attractions: for example, it most certainly invited local audiences to look for similarities with the Swedish Panoptikon, the wax museum that was opened in central Stockholm in the late 1880s. Various techniques to prolong interest in their amusements were also exchanged between different entrepreneurs and media. One example was the contest organized in connection with the statistical display, an invention that was explored in relation to various media in the early twentieth century. Not only did the contest enable the visitors to participate in the production of new attractions, it also invited them to take an interest in and develop an informal expertise in relation to this kind of display. That those who chose to participate were "in the know" about the ways in which the display related to other amusements seems to be confirmed by their choice of subjects. In fact, several entries to the competition in some way or another remediated other amusements at the exhibition. The miniature model of the dancers and their energy consumption was but one example of this tendency.

Scholars such as Ben Singer, Peter Bailey, and Gerry Beegan have all discussed how fin-de-siècle audiences developed forms of media consciousness or "knowingness" in relation to the topics that circulated in various media and popular entertainments.²⁶ In a recent study of illustrated periodicals in Victorian London, Beegan importantly stresses the communal and conversational character of this shared knowledge.²⁷ However, this knowledge was not confined to the topical events that circulated in various media but also included an emergent expertise in the way different media worked and were interrelated. I argue that these aspects of early twentieth-century media sociability were especially highlighted by audiences who took an interest in aspects of intermediality or aspired to participate in the production of media.

Some of the pavilions at the 1909 Stockholm exhibition were in fact intended as educational exhibits relating to contemporary media. One example was a full-scale printing works that produced a daily paper from the exhibition. Exhibition journals had been produced in connection with the previous exhibitions in Stockholm in 1866 and 1897, and in the latter case, one of Stockholm's leading dailies had commissioned its own pavilion.²⁸ In 1909, however, the exhibition journal was not only written and distributed but printed on site. According to the announcement of the paper, the readers would thereby have daily updates of news and events from the exhibition at the same time as the visitors were offered a public demonstration of how a modern newspaper was produced.²⁹

The printing works thereby exemplifies how the production of media was turned into an attraction at the exhibition. As in the statistical display, different ways of mediating the visitors to the exhibition was also explored by the exhibition journal. The first issue of the journal contained an extensive list of the celebrities who had visited the exhibition's inauguration. In the following issue, a large number of more anonymous visitors were publicized in the same manner with their name, title, and place of residence printed in the paper. The visitors could also have the relevant issue of the journal sent to friends and relatives, thereby broadcasting to wider circles their visibility at the exhibition.³⁰ Judging from the length of the lists that continued to appear in the journal during the season, this became a very popular way for the visitors to announce that they had (been) seen (at) the exhibition.

The lists of names in the exhibition journal also reinforced the performative interplay between being watched and watching others that the visitors were continuously drawn into when interacting with the displays. Like the demonstration of how the journal was made, the invitation to the visitors to appear on its pages also focused attention on the artifactual nature of representation. Indeed, some of the defining characteristics of the exhibition medium itself further strengthened this attachment to the materiality of media. This was especially true in relation to displays that incorporated the audience in entire milieus, an immersive technique that was meant to characterize the 1909 exhibition at large in contrast to its Scandinavian predecessors.³¹ In sum, by being able to playfully perform in public, experience the visibility of celebrities, and participate in the production of new additions to the amusement area, these audiences most certainly developed a sense of agency in relation to their media encounters. And it was precisely by fostering a certain reflexivity that these interactions facilitated a prolonged and more intimate relationship between audiences and the emergent media and entertainment industry.

As we have seen, many of the amusements at the 1909 Stockholm exhibition deployed a similar aesthetic of attraction, copying each other and competing for the visitors' attention. In its insistence on addressing the audience physically, this aesthetic more than anything else focused on the production of motion. Basically, there were two ways to accomplish this: one was to set the visitors' bodies in motion; the other was to present them with moving views or techniques that produced illusions of motion. (Obviously, the area also included a cinema; however, that did not attract very much attention. For over a decade, entertainment entrepreneurs had been travelling across borders to demonstrate the film medium in ways that gave priority to the show rather than to the films, but the interest in these shows was diminishing by the time of the exhibition.)[32] However, there were also techniques that combined these two ways of mediating motion and produced moving views by setting the spectators in motion. In the nineteenth century, this approach was most prominently explored in the history of moving panoramas, especially in the kind of rotundas that added motion to the views by exposing the audience to various shifts and rotations of their enhanced position.[33]

The rotating coffee shop was one amusement at the 1909 Stockholm exhibition that produced moving views by setting the spectator in motion. From this open-air pavilion, visitors could contemplate the surroundings in a 360-degree panorama view without themselves having to move. In slow review before their eyes (too slow, according to some visitors) came the adjacent sea, some of the amusements, and the people strolling the grounds. In a way, this meant that the rotating coffee shop produced a moving view that used the actual surroundings as props. In contrast to a moving panorama, in which the audience was encapsulated in the scene, the rotating coffee shop only provided the visitors with a frame and a particular way of seeing, that is, the moving view. However, from their slightly enhanced position, the coffee shop's guests could in fact see one of the main attractions of the exhibition: the other visitors. And it was precisely in this double position as both spectator and performer, on the stage as well as in front of it, that the visitors to the amusement area were positioned.

In opening this chapter, I quoted a visitor as saying that the public dancing was the most remarkable thing about the 1909 exhibition. In the same review, the rotating coffee shop was dismissed as "almost foolish" albeit culturally significant: "The idea that you should not sit still even when having a cup of coffee has something occidental, almost American to it."[34] The rotating restaurant was in fact congenial to the overall aesthetics of the amusement area. In every corner people were moving their bodies, dancing, coming down the slides, or enjoying the vertigo induced by perceptual distortions and illusionary techniques. Contrary to the assumptions of a long-standing tradition of cultural critique, there were no "passive" audiences in these places. The aesthetic that developed in relation to these entertainments was to a large extent centered on the interaction and bodily presence of the visitors. As a particular kind of public space, the amusement ground therefore encouraged a performative sociability, in which the individuals alternated between being spectators and performers, developing and sharing knowledge of the amusements in the process.

TRANSMEDIAL PRACTICES

A number of practices emerged in the nineteenth and early twentieth century that encouraged audiences to try out various participatory and performative subjectivities. Throughout the nineteenth century it was fairly common for members of the audience to be asked to participate in the exhibition of new media. When demonstrating the phonograph, for example, exhibitors often invited people from the audience up on stage to have their voices recorded.[35] Similarly, and in close relation to the tradition of public experiments in science, spectators entered the stage to participate in fin-de-siècle demonstrations of x-ray pictures.[36] A somewhat different example of the exploration by early audiences of new media was when onlookers that gathered at recordings of film actualities returned a few days later to see themselves appear in the local theater.[37] Yet another example was the contests in which the public was called upon to suggest or co-produce various media texts. Early instances of such practices evolved in relation to newspapers and popular magazines, but as we have seen they were also explored, for example, in connection with temporary exhibitions. Very soon, contests of various kinds also became a staple in the fan culture supported by the early twentieth-century film industry.[38] In addition, the intermedial circulation of representations showing "naïve" spectators interacting with, for example, wax displays or film in unintended ways further enhanced the visibility of audiences in fin-de-siècle amusements and media.[39]

The way these practices evolved between different media and contexts emphasizes why it is important to focus the analysis on transmedial relations rather than individual media.[40] How to engage an audience was undoubtedly an issue of great commercial importance as individual entrepreneurs were constantly looking for new ways to create interest in their products. The visibility of audiences also played an important role in the marketing of new media at the turn of the century. Histories of audiences fashioned by Habermasian critique typically construct modern audiences as passive and yet absorbed by the experience. More recent discussions on participatory media, on the other hand, describe how contemporary audiences are empowered by being involved in the production of media content. In this chapter, I have proposed a slightly different approach to these issues, arguing that audiences are incorporated in a particular media sociability exactly by being able to participate and develop an interest in media production. In relation to the 1909 Stockholm exhibition, I have also stressed the extent to which the amusement area engaged the visitors physically, which fostered a public sociability characterized by its performative address. The learning processes involved in these interactions worked in at least two ways: While the visitors were exploring how to act as members of an audience, the entrepreneurs refined their knowledge of the visitors' expectations and ways of reacting to the attractions. Being of an informal and conversational nature, I suggest these learning processes were in fact crucial to the cultural organization of early twentieth-century media and entertainment industries.

This chapter was written as a part of an ongoing research project entitled "Publics on Display: A Cultural History of Audiences and Publics, 1866–1930," which was funded by the Swedish Research Council.

NOTES

1. On "exhibition fatigue," see A. Ekström, *Den utställda världen*, p. 49.
2. For statistics on the Pike, see Y. Condon, "St. Louis 1904," p. 183. The profusion of media for virtual travel at the Pike are discussed by T. Gunning in "The World as Object Lesson."
3. B. Carlsson, "Nöjesafdelningen," in C. Bendix and E. Folcker, eds., *Allmänna svenska utställningen för konsthandtverk och konstindustri i Stockholm 1909* (Stockholm, n.p: 1910), pp. 201–2.
4. A. Ekström, "'Showing at One View'."
5. B. Carlsson, "Nöjesafdelningen," pp. 205–6.
6. C. Laurin, *Minnen: 1908–1918*, vol. 4 (Stockholm: Norstedts, 1932) pp. 30–31. All translations are by the author, unless stated otherwise.
7. "Utställningslif i Stockholm," *Bonniers månadshäften* 3 (1909), pp. 502–8.
8. B. Carlsson, "Nöjesafdelningen," p. 206.
9. M. Hansen, *Babel and Babylon*, pp. 76–78.
10. See, e.g., H. Jenkins, *Convergence Culture*.
11. M. Warner, *Publics and Counterpublics*.
12. N. Abercrombie and B. Longhurst, *Audiences*, p. 99.
13. The most commonly quoted example is the colorful history of early nineteenth-century (predominantly male) theater audiences. See, for example, R. Butsch, *The Making of American Audiences*, Chap. 3. But as discussed by M. Bellanta and others, various forms of "audience interaction [were] a key feature in late-nineteenth century popular theater." Melissa Bellanta, "Voting for Pleasure." Also, there is a particular history of audience participation in the early twentieth-century noncommercial theater; see D. Chansky, *Composing Ourselves*, pp. 8–10.
14. N. Thrift, *Non-Representational Theory*, pp. 14, 21.
15. See, e.g., S. Kern, *The Culture of Time and Space 1880–1918*; M. Berman, *All That is Solid Melts into Air*.
16. B. Carlsson, "Nöjesafdelningen," p. 206.

17. "Hit och dit på utställningen: 'Intellektuell åskådning'," *Svenska Dagbladet*, 23 June 1909.
18. B. Carlsson, "Nöjesafdelningen," p. 206.
19. "Hit och dit på utställningen."
20. Cf. A. Ekström, "'Showing at One View'," p. 41.
21. On the Oriental Maze in Stockholm, and a similar attraction in late nineteenth-century Copenhagen, see M. Sandberg, *Living Pictures, Missing Persons*, pp. 129, 136–39.
22. B. Carlsson, "Nöjesafdelningen," pp. 203, 206.
23. I have discussed this kind of statistical display at length in A. Ekström, "'Showing at One View'".
24. "Hit och dit på utställningen: Hvad människokroppen duger till," *Svenska Dagbladet*, 25 July 1909.
25. "Statistikons pristäflan," *Nyheterna från Konstindustri-utställningen*, 7 July 1909; "Utställningsnytt," *Svenska Dagbladet*, 8 July 1909; "Utställningsnytt," *Svenska Dagbladet*, 14 July 1909; "Hit och dit på utställningen: Dansande statistik," *Svenska Dagbladet*, 22 August 1909. Also cf. A. Ekström, "'Showing at One View'," p. 43.
26. See, e.g., B. Singer, *Melodrama and Modernity*, p. 185; P. Bailey, *Popular Culture and Performance in the Victorian City*, Chap. 6; G. Beegan, *The Mass Image*, pp. 21–24.
27. G. Beegan, *The Mass Image*, p. 22.
28. P. Lundell, "Pressen är budskapet," pp. 47–82.
29. "Anmälan," *Nyheterna från Konst-industriutställningen*, 4 June 1909.
30. Ibid.
31. See, e.g., H. Cassel, "Konstindustri-utställningen 1909," *Svenska Dagbladet*, 4 June 1909.
32. M. Hansen, *Babel and Babylon*, p. 99. Cf. T. Gunning, "An Aesthetic of Astonishment"; and T. Gunning, "The Cinema of Attractions."
33. On the history of moving panoramas, see S. Oettermann, *The Panorama*; B. Comment, *The Panorama*.
34. C. Laurin, *Minnen*, pp. 25–26.
35. M. Boström, "Den falske kungen i den sanna återgivningen."
36. S. Jülich, "Media as Modern Magic."
37. P. Snickars, *Svensk film och visuell masskultur 1900*, pp. 166–77.
38. B. Griffen-Foley, "From *Tit-Bits* to *Big Brother*"; A. Ekström, "'Showing at One View'," pp. 43–44; Y. Habel, *Modern Media, Modern Audiences*, p. 22, passim.
39. Film historians have discussed the learning processes involved in the performance of spectators in early film; see M. Hansen, *Babel and Babylon*, pp. 25–30. On similar discourses and exhibition practices in relation to wax museums, see M. Sandberg, *Living Pictures, Missing Persons*, pp. 106–8.
40. The term "media culture" in relation to transmedial developments in the late nineteenth century is further elaborated in A. Ekström, S. Jülich, and P. Snickars, "I mediearkivet." For related discussions stressing the importance of the interconnectedness of early twentieth-century media and entertainments, see, e.g., F. Kessler and N. Verhoeff, eds., *Networks of Entertainment*; J. Holt and A. Perren, eds., *Media Industries*; J. Staiger and S. Hake, eds., *Convergence Media History*.

4 Civic Media
City Exhibitions and the Visual Culture of Community, c. 1900

Frans Lundgren

When opening the Tenement House Exhibition in New York in February 1900, Governor Theodore Roosevelt urged the public to study the material on display since it so strikingly showed the effects of the degrading living conditions of the poor in the city, "which eat at the body social and the body politic."[1] The exhibition, with its display of more than 1,000 photographs, models of city blocks, series of distribution maps, statistical charts, and a great deal more was open for only two weeks before it was taken on tour to Chicago—and later to the social economy section of the world's fair in Paris—but was nonetheless a great success. It was soon understood by the organizers as a defining moment in their efforts to bring about reform in building regulations and advocate model tenement houses in New York, an impact both they and commentators attributed to the new and thoroughly ambitious ways of representing the problems that the issue involved. As a campaign vehicle, the exhibition's mediation of the city was considered to triumph all other means of communication as it "told more in five minutes than could be obtained in a library in five weeks" and provided a comprehensive understanding of the problem "that could not have been given in any other way."[2]

Many efforts were made in the United States and in Europe at the turn of the century to exhibit the city to a general public. This new genre of exhibitions included both articulations of reformist projects and official celebrations of things accomplished, but they were all designed to direct the public's attention to some set of issues regarding the future development of urban life. They also offered novel ways to view cities, in a similar way as a number of new visual media had been used throughout the nineteenth century: the panorama, the stereoscope, and moving pictures, to name but a few. However, the political nature of not only the subject of city exhibitions but also of each event in itself raised some pressing issues: Who were supposed to see, how and to what effect? As the example from New York shows, these exhibitions often formed part of endeavors to gather a public: a body of civic-minded and well-informed people attentive to specific political issues. And the means to achieve this were provided by the visitors' engagement with the representations at hand. Thus, the city exhibitions offer an opportunity to analyze how publics were to be made and to investigate what alleged qualities set this medium apart from other media. What made the exhibition effective in fostering civic participation and commitment?

The primary focus of this chapter is the visual pedagogy developed by Patrick Geddes in his efforts to exhibit the city in the late 1890s and early 1900s. Although his project as such cannot be described as typical of the new genre, he explicitly discussed the exhibition as a medium, the pedagogical issues it raised, and other ways to visualize the city. By using Geddes's considerations and ways of arguing as an example, it is thus also possible to discern a broader set of problems to which the city exhibition was an answer. In particular, the pedagogy that Geddes advocated involved discussions on how techniques of representation and aligned modes of observation could be used to reform social life. Hence, my analysis will focus on how the exhibition as a medium was understood and utilized as means for civic training and the making of self-reflexive and engaged publics, ready to participate in the reform of society. Although Geddes's multimedial Outlook Tower in Edinburgh is often described in studies of his work, it has most often been characterized as an isolated phenomenon and primarily analyzed in the biographical context of his development as a sociologist, city planner, and theorist of regional development.[3] By focusing on the less studied pedagogic considerations in his writings—scattered in pamphlets, short essays, and manuscripts—and by placing these in the history of exhibition didactics and the burgeoning but little studied landscape of city exhibitions of the period, it is possible to discuss how media, publics, and modernity were interrelated issues in critical social discourse of fin-de-siècle Europe.[4] The cultural diagnoses articulated by canonized early sociologists such as Gustave Le Bon or Georg Simmel are often repeated in the literature, but have less frequently been considered in dialogue with contemporary reform efforts. Was the city exhibition a new way to bridge the growing social distance and dislocation in modern cities? If so, what were the crucial elements that it provided; and what societal problems in terms of perception, attention, and social adhesion did these qualities address? How could media publics become communities?

CRITIQUE AND REFORM: EXHIBITION FATIGUE AND NEW PEDAGOGICAL IDEAS

In the final decades of the nineteenth century, the growth of large temporary exhibitions had given rise to a substantial literature on their organization, economy, and pedagogy. These issues had also become a matter of much concern among the growing number of museum professionals. Despite the resources spent on these institutions—the new grandiose buildings for public museums that were being constructed in almost all large cities and the ever-growing scale and multiplication of major exhibitions—this literature did not merely offer chronicles of progress. If issues such as the inspectability of display cases and the classification of objects had been dominating concerns of previous discussions, didactics now became a major issue. Quite a few authors were critical of the way that large exhibitions and public museums were organized. Some even questioned their ability to provide any meaningful popular education. When in 1883 the economist William Stanley Jevons discussed the importance of museums as an instrument of social reform, he summed up the impressions visitors would take with them from the celebrated South Kensington Museum in London as a sensory maelstrom, "a nightmare of incomprehensible machines, interminable stairs, suspicious policemen, turnstiles, and staring fish." The endless objects on display at the large exhibitions, while impressive, would always create "a general mental state . . . of perplexity and vagueness."[5] The didactic problem that Jevons identified concerned the ability to direct and stimulate attention and to afford opportunities to perceive and think about objects: "the purpose of a true Museum is to enable the student to see

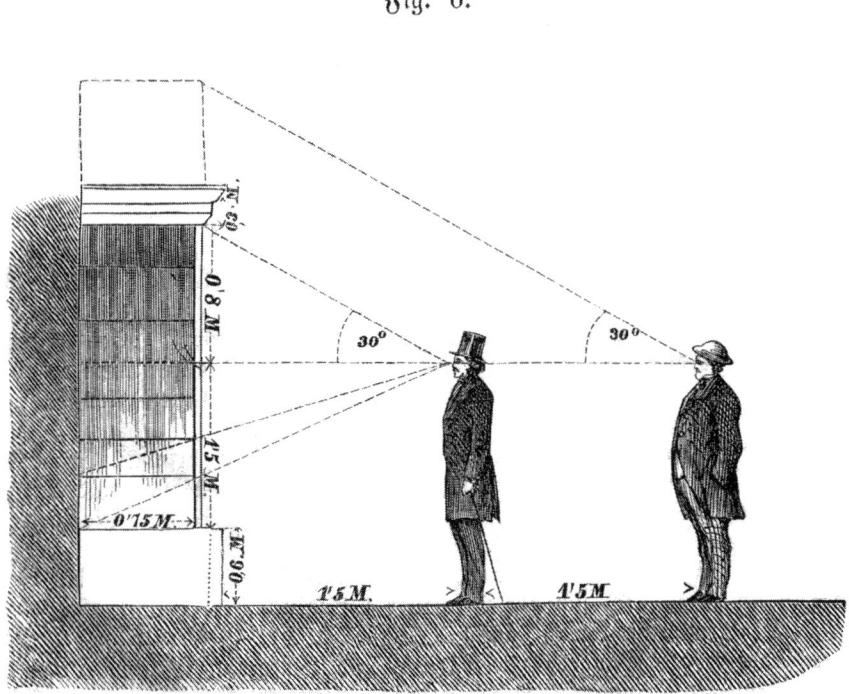

Figure 4.1 Stabilizing spectators and the discourse of inspectability. Illustration from W. F. Exner, *Der Aussteller und die Ausstellungen*, vol. 2 (Weimar: Voigt, 1873).

things and realize sensually the qualities described in lessons or lectures; in short, to learn what cannot be learnt by words."[6]

Patrick Geddes took this critical point of view when he characterized the exhibition as a medium with yet unrealized potential in *Industrial Exhibitions and Modern Progress* (1887). He used the standard rhetoric as a preamble: "there can be no better standpoint for an intelligent survey of modern progress," only to concede that most exhibitions did not bring about a retrospect of the advancements "in health and education, in social feeling and public life" that could serve as an effective education.[7] When Geddes singled out a few recent examples as models—in particular, the 1884 International Health Exhibition in London—it was because they intervened in the problems addressed: they did not "only illustrate, but further this silent and peaceful social revolution."[8] The criticism of exhibitions was thus justified, but he argued that they had to be improved as the "dawning era of scientific industrialism cannot dispense with exhibitions."[9] While Geddes provided no recipe, he argued that success had to be measured by civic effects rather than the number of visitors or economic results. If the former became the focus for designing exhibitions, this would have distinct consequences, as it would contribute to making societal development "conscious and intelligible" and thus serve as a means "to aid and accelerate it."[10] In Geddes's analysis, the task was to mediate society in such a way that the exhibition-goers became self-conscious participants in the displayed progress.

One main topic at the turn of the century was the sensory effect of the vast displays on visitors, what Geddes summed up as a kind of overindulgence comparable to the "ennui of the tourist, the apathy of the student."[11] This critique often referred to an increasing "exhibition fatigue" to describe how the visitor's enthusiasm and curiosity became replaced by weariness and a dulled mind. But the concept also expressed how the flood of exhibitions made people tired of the whole phenomenon.[12] The antidotes suggested by critics like Jevons and Geddes were attractive and pedagogically ambitious exhibits on serious issues. Much attention in the debate was given to the staging of entire milieus like habitat dioramas, period rooms, and full-scale environments, and representations such as working models, graphic statistics, or moving images. Instead of novelty mass displays of industrial products, exhaustive series of natural specimens, or halls of cabinets with cultural artifacts, the models praised were based on strict selection, careful staging with realistic allure, and the pedagogic use of perspective and scale. This didactic also drew on the field of commercial popular entertainment, for example, wax museums, panoramas, and lantern shows—what reformers such as Geddes at the same time criticized and described as distinctly "low" components at exhibitions.[13] The tension can be illustrated by the Tenement House Exhibition, which to a large degree depended on the attention attracted by Jacob Riis's media campaign on the slums of New York during the 1890s. In his articles, books, and lectures, Riis skillfully blended the police reportage of the popular press and the lantern shows of entertainers by dramatizing encounters and individual life stories. This tradition of social work that aimed to stir compassion among the audience was absent in the later exhibition, even when the very same photographs that Riis used in his performances were on display.[14] The emotionally engaging, immersive, and virtual travel qualities of several late nineteenth-century media attractions were resources that social reformers wanted to harness at exhibitions, but without the taint of sensationalism.

On several occasions in the 1890s and early 1900s, the novel genre of exhibiting the contemporary city became a model for new didactic ideals. The host cities of large exhibitions manifested themselves in a special pavilion or section where historical development, municipal projects, and welfare institutions were displayed. It became possible to see the city, not only as a sight, but also by carefully studying local phenomena and institutions. The city's pavilion in Stockholm 1897, for example, won praise because it combined abstract mapping of various relationships and facts with highly realistic exhibits, such as a full-scale city street in cross-section that allowed visitors to move between street level and the modern infrastructure below ground.[15] And in the city of Paris pavilion in 1900, visitors passed through large statistical displays on issues regarding education before entering a dark room where cinematographic projectors simultaneously showed activities on six different levels of the school system.[16] Many such exhibits became included in permanent museums, which further naturalized this type of display. In St. Louis in 1904, lessons from the social economy section of 1900 on the importance of using appropriate visual "machinery" were cited in the design of the social exhibits. Among them was a "model street" of public institutions that included a playground, a hospital, and a municipal museum; the latter did not merely exhibit displays on social and civic issues but also itself as an integral part of a modern city.[17]

What Geddes envisioned in his prolific writings and practical efforts regarding exhibitions around 1900 was a public institution of this kind, an integrated part of local social life. His critique of many existing exhibitions was that they represented a continuation of the social fragmentation and visual disorientation instead of being a solution to these conditions. The focus on the exhibition as media might seem a strange preoccupation, but many shared Geddes's analysis. Although he is better known in other contexts, Georg Simmel was one of them. While it is true that Simmel was neither a social reformist nor an advocate of exhibition didactics, exhibitions were a recurring theme in his texts. One example is the 1903 essay "The Metropolis and Mental Life," which was a public lecture held in connection with the large German Municipal Exhibition in Dresden and published as a contribution to this occasion.[18] Although Simmel primarily discussed other topics, he connected the effects of modern city life on the individual and of exhibitions on the visitor in a similar way as Geddes. In an article on the Berlin Trade Exhibition of 1896, Simmel argued that the excess of heterogeneous merchandise and objects on display had drastic effects on the visitor: it paralyzed the senses and created "a veritable hypnosis." His naturalistic analysis described exhibitions as a sociation into commodity culture and also as a distillation of the sensory stimuli that caused the distanced, unresponsive attitude of city life.[19] Geddes's didactic project, on the other hand, was to design an exhibition experience that focused the attention, directed the inquiry, and stimulated the civic commitment by taking "the psychology of the average visitor" into account.[20]

PATRICK GEDDES'S VISUAL PEDAGOGY: THE CORE OF THE SCIENCE OF "CIVICS"

While Patrick Geddes worked as a professor of botany, in the 1890s and early 1900s much of his time and energy was focused on projects outside the traditional scope of natural history. He would gradually give precision to his discussions on visual pedagogy and city exhibitions as a coherent program called "civics." At the time, this concept usually referred to a body of knowledge on local public institutions, but Geddes's civics was a comprehensive knowledge of the city as a social environment and as a community. Even more important, he described it as "applied and concrete sociology," the science of how to stimulate and reinforce good communal development. Geddes described the relationship of civics to sociology by comparing it to how the science of hygiene was applied bacteriology.[21] This also meant that the scope of phenomena and institutions that civics encompassed was very wide; anything that concerned local social patterns or had an effect on these would be included.

Geddes's civics integrated his many ideas on social reform into a general framework. And when he began to use the concept around 1905, the project had been under way for more than a decade. At the core of this process was an institution that Geddes in the late 1890s named the Outlook Tower—a permanent exhibition, what he called a "social museum," designed for the pursuit and teaching of this new knowledge. The physical space for the exhibition was not conceived as a grand scheme from the onset; it gradually took shape after 1892 when Geddes acquired the lease for a property in a slum area of central Edinburgh. This building on Castle Hill had housed a commercial exhibition of scientific instruments and mechanical displays and during the 1890s became not only a place to house the many activities Geddes organized—geographic exhibits, summer schools, current events clubs, and much else—but a didactic vision and the symbolic center of his work. The practical details of this exhibition, which was never fully realized, will not be discussed here, but the Outlook Tower is considered a focal point for his writings on exhibitions and as an ideal.[22]

During the late 1890s and until the world's fair in Paris 1900, Geddes was engaged in several projects related to the development of exhibitions

Figure 4.2 Patrick Geddes and children with the Outlook Tower in the background in the 1890s. Patrick Geddes Collection, Edinburgh University Library.

as a medium. Apart from organizing his own museum in Edinburgh, he traveled extensively to promote the building of a giant globe at the 1900 exhibition and also initiated an international association for the pedagogic development of exhibitions. Although the globe was never completed, the project took him on tour in the United States and into direct contact with many leading social reformers and social scientists. Some of them had also visited his exhibition in Edinburgh, described as the world's first "sociological laboratory" in an 1899 article in *American Journal of Sociology*.[23] Geddes's social analysis offered a perfect fit with the Spencerian paradigm of early American sociology, and his projects on university extension, social settlements, and popular education also found enthusiastic counterparts.[24] But his vision extended beyond delineating specific sites of social ills or remedies for these, the rationale that many organizations for social reform operated by. In fact, Geddes repeatedly contrasted his approach to such perspectives: he argued that the knowledge to be pursued was of "normal" social phenomena in the city rather than, for example, discerning "pathological or aberrant individuals" in the manner of Francis Galton.[25] Geddes's objective was to reform the fabric of the community by providing new means for the public at large to develop a comprehensive understanding of their city. This difference in perspectives also had consequences for exhibition didactics. When Geddes contributed pictures to the Tenement House Exhibition in New York, opened during his American lecture tour, the organizers valued the material as less relevant: "while intensely interesting in its general aspects [it] does not bear sufficiently on our particular problem . . . , there being only a few of the photographs which illustrate model tenements in Edinburgh."[26] In contrast to Geddes's approach, the exhibition in New York displayed material along the lines of a bureaucratic structure and provided arguments for technical solutions to the specific problems revealed.[27]

What visual machinery should be assembled in the kind of exhibition Geddes advocated, and what should it produce? In his discussions of the social exhibition as a genre, the need to teach methods of making sociological observations was a recurrent theme. His approach to the issue was very much modeled on the exhibition as an educative tool in natural history. Sociology was, Geddes explained, in the same way "grounded in observation, inductive methods and the process of working from the concrete towards the abstract" and hence "literally field-naturalist." However, sociological observation should not be mistaken as a simple common-sense procedure, although some of the skills and procedures involved were "incipient in everyday life."[28] The necessity of establishing training grounds, i.e., "observatory-laboratories for social science," was thus just as crucial as "observatories, laboratories, and museums" had been in each of the natural sciences.[29] But Geddes took care to distance the project from other modes of naturalistic observation in sociology. The science of civics was not a study of community as an "aggregate," what he exemplified with Galton's eugenic project, but as an "integrate, with material and immaterial structures and functions, which we call the city."[30] As this project of teaching observation had to provide new approaches to the already familiar, developing methods to study the city was a problem inextricably linked to the question of how to mediate it.

A THEORY OF MEDIATING CITIES

Geddes was greatly interested in the impact of the physical environment of cities on communal life, but he stressed that civic development was "no mere external matter" as when "Haussmannising" city streets; it was a product of the local culture that had to be nourished by an institution like the Outlook Tower.[31] In his vision, the social exhibition was a medium for organizing comparisons, what might be described as an experimental community where participants enhanced their skills and capacities to observe, analyze, and understand the city and its "crowded phantasmagoria of life."[32] But this purpose was also to be achieved through contributions by the participants to the ongoing survey of the city. Everyone already had material for the science of civics, Geddes argued, but these impressions were "still [at] too many and differing levels as of the child, the man in the street, the general reader, the traveler and scholar," and the challenge was to develop "all these observations towards exactness and order."[33] A place for simultaneously pursuing scientific observation and civic training was needed, "a type of institution which will be found of service alike to the sociologist and the citizen."[34]

In order to bring the many possible approaches to a city into an organized general framework, a common platform for carrying out visual training was needed. Geddes gave significant weight to the literal outlook from above and the associated panoramic qualities.[35] The fact that the very first panorama was made in the late eighteenth century from Castle Hill was cited as a proof of the qualities of the field of vision afforded by this specific viewing position. In his visual pedagogy, this viewing position provided immersive experiences as well as distancing, reflexive opportunities, and an extended field of vision was something he associated with the synoptic view that a social survey provided.[36] In his line of reasoning, seeing was not a straightforward sensory capacity that was already present and could be relied upon among specialists or the general public; it was a skill that needed to be carefully trained for the project of civics to succeed.

How should the exhibition mediate the city in order to become an effective training ground? Geddes discussed this issue only briefly and in different contexts, but even so the rationale can be discerned. He repeatedly referred to the Outlook Tower as "a laboratory," a concept often used in early sociology and social work, albeit with slightly different meanings. In the American context, among Geddes's contacts in Chicago, university sociologists described the city as a laboratory where the ongoing social interaction provided "experiments" to study while those involved in the social settlement-movement could use the same vocabulary to describe their initiatives, but also with negative connotations to distance them from the abstract and detached academic production of knowledge.[37] In Geddes's use of the term, it was impossible to separate abstraction and practical solutions. The social exhibition/laboratory was to become a site for the production of new knowledge, a school for teaching methods to study the city, a museum for disseminating existing knowledge, and a center for organizing civic reform initiatives. If anything, abstraction was a necessary prerequisite to make the participants realize a common purpose and to discover opportunities to shape the ongoing processes in the city. Depending heavily on the terminology of the French exhibition theorist and sociologist Frederic Le Play, Geddes favored the mapping of abstract concepts and classificatory systems as a tool for stimulating further investigation and discussion.[38] But these diagrams were also necessary to aid the "emancipation from the tyranny of detail."[39] In order to further develop the methods available to study the city, the institution needed to combine conceptual development and the innovation of viewing devices and visual representations.

Critique of text-based education was a central theme in Geddes's discussion of exhibition didactics. In an unfinished manuscript on the general "museum problem" from the early 1900s, Geddes singled out Jevons' 1883 article and more recent essays by Brown Goode at the Smithsonian as the most insightful writings on the matter. He particularly highlighted the latter's characterization of each specimen in the exhibit as the equivalent of a type at the printer's office that could be combined to make almost any idea intelligible. According to Geddes, a true museum should thus literally be an "Encyclopaedia Graphica" where each entry consisted of a label and the specimen or, if not possible, an image or model of the latter.[40] Just as Jevons argued any true museum should teach what could not be learned by words, the integration in Geddes's didactics of graphic representations and devices for seeing was an extension of the pedagogy of object lessons.

According to Geddes, many components should be included in a city exhibition showing "things in their mutual relations."[41] He often praised the pedagogic potential of contemporary realistic attractions, such as the panoramas, dioramas, and reconstructed historical streetscapes at the Paris exhibition of 1900, but he was equally enthusiastic about new modes of making abstract representations of the city, for example, the statistical maps in Charles Booth's recently published survey of London.[42] Different visual media offered complementary resources for studying the city, and the exhibition would be effective as long as it gave ample opportunities to alternate, literally, between different points of view or to combine various analytical temporalities, for example, that of the geographer and the sociologist.[43] But the rationale of the city exhibition was the interaction and engagement with the material and devices on display, an activity that was to be extended into the city and other public repositories of relevant material, for instance, libraries and museums. Although it would always have to rely on the capacities of other institutions and could never become comprehensive in itself, the purpose of the civic laboratory was to be the central nodal point in the organization and accumulation of opportunities to study the city.[44]

The pursuit and dissemination of civics was very much a matter of organizing heterogeneous resources in a way that stimulated discussions among those involved. Geddes criticized initiatives to make civics part of school curricula both because of how the subject matter was rendered and how the teaching was hierarchically organized: this educational "machinery" would shape "the future citizen in the image of the perfect schoolboy" rather than as someone participating in public matters.[45] Furthermore, and in contrast to much social criticism at the time, he argued that popular culture was not a distraction from serious issues but an important resource in the pursuit of a well-organized science of civics. The detective of popular fiction could serve as an example of the "active science" that the "applied sociologist" should pursue, and the abundance of picture postcards on display in the newsagent's shop window could be approached as the start for a photographic survey of the city. The skills of observation and of connecting different phenomena to the larger civic and social whole could be pursued by stimulating the habit of collecting and discussing artifacts of popular visual culture, for example, in schools.[46]

The underlying premise of Geddes's ideal city exhibition was that society had to be studied and understood by visual means. However, teaching the general public to read the city depended on intense visual stimulation and activity. The central problem of his didactics was how to make those participating in the project actually see phenomena. He argued that this capacity, "the art of seeing," was very rare, as the intellectual training of most people and their associated faculty of vision only enabled them to see what they already knew. In fact, they were "hypnotized" by their previous education and especially by knowledge acquired from reading rather than firsthand study of the world. Thus, an opportunity to pursue self-reform in these matters was needed, what Geddes characterized as "a kind of convalescent hospital for those who have lost the power of observation and have to be brought up again from the beginning."[47]

EDUCATING THE EYE

Observational skills were central in most museum projects of the late nineteenth and early twentieth century. Collections were formed and exhibitions designed on the basis of taxonomic characteristics, signature aesthetic qualities, or broader cultural patterns. But some critics argued that many exhibits did not provide good training in making observations, and they especially associated the problem with new exhibition techniques such as the habitat diorama. The immersive qualities of carefully staged realistic milieus risked turning the spectator into a lazy consumer of spectacles rather than a careful student discriminating between different classes of specimens or artifacts.[48] Geddes's strong emphasis on visual sensations rather implies a reversal of this analysis. The endeavors to develop scientific observation and to provide popular education were not necessarily different projects. Making "Social Museums more advanced and more developed" for specialists did not preclude allowing them to become more accessible to the general public.[49] The primary risk was not that realistic mediation or visual devices distracted the visitor from serious purposes. In fact, such components were a crucial resource for discussing everyday modes of seeing. Realistic attractions could activate new ways for the public to see the world, and Geddes was optimistic that the complex subject matter of civics could be made decipherable to most people.⁵⁰

However, teaching visitors at the Outlook Tower to observe the city without being bound by cultural conventions and habits was not a straightforward process. In a historical city such as Edinburgh, argued the organizers, the "empire of routine" was especially strong, and for this reason the "education of the eye" needed to be pursued with even more energy.⁵¹ Designing an effective exhibit hence involved considerations both of what people were accustomed to in their everyday life and when visiting exhibitions. The first problem was to direct visitors' attention toward objects and social phenomena themselves, as if seeing them for the first time. They were instructed to approach the exhibition in a new way: "I want you . . . not first to read the label and then see the thing as people often do."⁵² But what was to be achieved by interacting with the material was nothing less than "the untraining of the eye," as the goal was to make the visitors "get rid of all prejudices, habits, and conventionalities of vision."⁵³

This process of unlearning had to operate by several didactic strategies. One prominent feature of the tower was that it literally changed the visitor's point of view, made them consider "familiar ideas and facts from some wholly new angle."⁵⁴ This could be achieved by painting a large map on the floor, for example, or by geographical devices such as an episcope or a hollow globe.⁵⁵ Another approach considered effective was making the participants engage with the specific qualities of different media. When, for example, someone contributed to the accumulation of local photographic surveys, the work would by necessity include "criticism and selection" and a developed habit of making distinctions between essential and unimportant aspects of the material. The argument seem to be that those involved in the process would become familiar with different modes of selection, for example, on the basis of aesthetic or sociological merits and hence also be able to shift between such perspectives.⁵⁶

The effects of such new forms of interaction with media—what could be described as a form of literacy—was also discussed with regard to specific media technologies in the exhibition. Geddes took extra care to explain the pedagogy of the camera obscura on the roof, as it was often mistaken for a "mere infantile show."⁵⁷ He argued that it was very valuable in teaching the art of seeing because the moving images of the surrounding city provided the "ordinary observer" with a sensation of seeing the familiar in a new way, a difference that proved what "habit has made commonplace" and the need to start "observing the things immediately around us" in new ways.⁵⁸ The limited range of sounds, light, and colors offered an even more valuable lesson when the visitor alternated between the views inside the camera and the terrace roof below, as this gave opportunities to consider possible ways to extend the "direct observation of our surroundings." The

44 *Frans Lundgren*

rest of the exhibition provided many examples of how different sciences approached the city in their respective analysis and the associated outlook by which each of them operated.[59] By comparing and varying perspective through the use of different media and modes of observation, the participant in civics would extend his capacity to observe firsthand, but also to discuss the different options available.

Figure 4.3 Learning to see the city. A view from the Outlook Tower, c.1900. Patrick Geddes Collection, Edinburgh University Library.

The idea that the general public's vision and observational capacities needed to be restored was based on the idea that any useful understanding of the city depended on studying it at length. By being involved and engaged in the processes of observation, the visitors should realize that they were agents in society. In short, the problem was not merely to distribute descriptions of the city and make people aware of these, but also to engage as many as possible in the discussion of how to make sense of the development of society and the possible actions to guide this development. Therefore, the "education of the eye" also had a clear moral: it was not supposed to be "purely spectacular . . . merely a refinement and enlargement of the lust of the eye." Everyone involved should realize they had a responsibility for the development of the city and its civic culture. The organizers underlined that they should not allow considering themselves—in either sense of the term—merely as "onlookers."[60]

CIVIC MEDIA: COMMUNITIES MADE OF MEDIA PUBLICS

The city exhibition was a new and expansive genre at the turn of the century, and such displays were organized by a variety of political rationales, pursued by different pedagogic ideas.[61] Their primary objective could also differ: to mobilize support for a specific political agenda, to promote an organization, to enhance accountability, and many others.[62] But although the project Geddes pursued was more far-reaching and ambitious than most other initiatives, it was not untypical. The common strategy of these efforts was to exhibit contemporary society in order to influence it. And the components of Geddes's project are very similar to other city exhibitions of the period: the strong emphasis on the necessity of visualizing social phenomena, the importance of assembling comparative collections of examples by different media, and the necessity to activate the general public through the design of the displays. Geddes enthusiastically referred to many such exhibitions, and he also advised existing museums to incorporate exhibits of contemporary society to attract more people and to become more relevant.[63] In his vision, the city exhibition was a kind of community-making mechanism that could be incorporated into many different institutions.

As the examples in this study have shown, the nature of this mechanism is difficult to understand without references to a notion of media publics and their participation in the project. The civic exhibition and laboratory was a sort of media platform; the exhibition can be understood as a specific way to organize, combine, and engage with several different media. This interaction and participation should not be understood as a substitute for accessing the exhibited phenomena from some more privileged position, for example, as an eyewitness or as a participant observer. The mediation was not something that should ideally be eliminated; instead it was an important pedagogical resource for fostering skills in observation and for stimulating cooperation.

Among the desired outcomes was a new sort of literacy, the ability to read the city. The ideal exhibition should be a collaborative project where each person would be not only a member of a public, informed and ready to participate in common matters; everyone should also be involved in the development of the exhibition and its associated activities. In contrast to many other similar social reform efforts at the time, the rationale of the exhibition was not only to influence public opinion, but also to expand and intensify involvement in the project by making each participant self-aware of their participation and its possible effects. Although it would be stretching the concept to describe Geddes as an engineer of social media, his city exhibition in many ways resembles the way in which recent new media have been characterized. In his case, participation and the making of community was what motivated the project in the first place.

This chapter has been written as a part of an ongoing research project entitled "A History of the Social Museum: Mediating the Public and Political Subjectivities through Scientific Communication, 1880–1950," funded by the Swedish Research Council.

NOTES

1. "Gov. Roosevelt on Tenement Reform," *New York Times*, 11 February 1900.
2. Ibid.; L. Veiller, "The Tenement House Exhibition of 1899." *Charities Review* 10 (1900–01): 19–25.
3. The biographic literature on Geddes and his work is substantial; see H. Meller, *Patrick Geddes*. Few studies have primarily focused on Geddes's visual pedagogy and exhibition didactics, but aspects are discussed in several; see esp. ibid., Chap. 4; A. Ponte, "Building the Stair Spiral of Evolution"; and N. Burton and H. Fraser, "Mirror Visions and Dissolving Views."
4. These short writings of Geddes repeat the same general discussions, although they are often expanded on some particular aspect of the project. When I consider other contemporary writings on the Outlook Tower, these will also be considered as part of Geddes's discussion as they explicitly reproduce his descriptions.
5. S. Jevons, "The Use and Abuse of Museums," In *Methods of Social Reform and Other Papers*, London: Macmillan, 1883. p. 60.
6. Ibid., pp. 61–62, quote on p. 66.
7. P. Geddes, *Industrial Exhibitions and Modern Progress*, Edinburgh: David Douglas, 1887. pp. 1–2.
8. Ibid., pp. 7–8.
9. Ibid., pp. 14–16.
10. Ibid., pp. 56–57.
11. P. Geddes, "Educational and Social Uses of Museums," fragment of manuscript ca. 1900, Patrick Geddes Papers, 5/1/6, University of Strathclyde Archives, Glasgow (hereafter cited as PGP).
12. See, e.g., the discussion of the concept in Paquet, A. *Das Ausstellungsproblem in der Volkswirtschaft*. Jena, Germany: Gustav Fischer, 1908, chap. 13.
13. A. Griffiths, "Media Technology and Museum Display," pp. 381–85. Geddes repeatedly criticized wax museums and other midway shows but praised their

didactic qualities; see, e.g., P. Geddes, "Comments of the Paris Exposition of 1900," fragment of manuscript, PGP, 6/1/3; and P. Geddes, "A Suggested Plan for a Civic Museum (or Civic Exhibition) and its Associated Studies," *Sociological Papers* 3 (1907), p. 232.
14. M. Stange, *Symbols of Ideal Life*, Chap. 1; G. Jackson, "Cultivating Spiritual Sight."
15. F. Lundgren, "Social samling," pp. 309–37.
16. J. Bennet et al., *1900: The New Age, A Guide to the Exhibition*, p. 49.
17. J. Brown, *Health and Medicine on Display*, pp. 152, 156–59.
18. D. Frisby, *Cityscapes of Modernity*, Chap. 3.
19. G. Simmel, "The Berlin Trade Exhibition." In *Simmel on Culture: Selected Writings*, ed. D. Frisby and M. Featherstone. London: Sage, 1997, pp. 255–58.
20. P. Geddes, "Educational and Social Uses of Museums."
21. P. Geddes, *City Development: A Study of Parks, Gardens, and Culture-Institutes*. Edinburgh: Geddes and Co., 1904, p. 221.
22. On the particulars of the exhibition in Edinburgh, see H. Meller, *Patrick Geddes*, Chap. 4; and P. Kitchen, *A Most Unsettling Person*, Chap. 8.
23. C. Zueblin, "The World's First Sociological Laboratory." *American Journal of Sociology* 4 (1899): 577–92.
24. F. Giddings, one of the first professors of sociology in America, solicited the essay "The Relation of Physical Environment to Social Evolution and Character" for a book project; see F. Giddings to P. Geddes, 23 March 1899, PGP 3/6/19. On the paradigmatic status of Spencer, see D. Breslau, "The American Spencerians"; and C. Renwick, "The Practice of Spencerian Science."
25. P. Geddes, *Education for Economics and Citizenship; and the Place of History and Geography in This*. Manchester: Co-operative Printing Society, 1895, pp. 20–21. On the prevalent one-sidedness when analyzing the "evils of the city" and the need to survey and understand the "normal," see P. Geddes, "Civics: As Concrete and Applied Sociology, Part II." *Sociological Papers* 2 (1906), pp. 95–96 (hereafter cited as "Civics II"); and P. Geddes, "A Suggested Plan for a Civic Museum," p. 222.
26. L. Veiller to P. Geddes, 27 January 1900, PGP, 9/282. However, it should be noted that Geddes soon was mobilized as an authority on social museum initiatives in New York; see J. Reynolds to P. Geddes, 8 March 1901, PGP, 9/333; J. Paton to P. Geddes, 18 June 1902, PGP 7/9/256; J. Strong to P. Geddes, 10 July 1902, PGP, 7/9/257; J. Strong to P. Geddes, 12 December 1902, PGP, 7/9/200.
27. M. Stange describes the "gridlike" or "dossiered" mode of organizing information at the exhibition; see M. Stange, *Symbols of Ideal Life*, esp. pp. 44–45.
28. P. Geddes, *Synopsis of a Course of Lectures for the Second Term, Spring 1904: Observation and Method in Sociological Studies*, London: School of Sociology and Social Economics, 1904, pp. 1–2. Cited here is a copy of the pamphlet in PGP, 3/4/17.
29. Ibid.
30. P. Geddes, "Civics: As Applied Sociology." *Sociological Papers* 1 (1905) (hereafter cited as "Civics"), quote on p. 104.
31. P. Geddes, "Civics II," p. 103.
32. P. Geddes, "The Survey of Cities," *The Sociological Review* 1 (1908), p. 74; see also P. Geddes, "Civic Education and City Development." *The Contemporary Review* 87 (1905), pp. 416–17.
33. P. Geddes, "Athens in London," fragment of manuscript, ca. 1900, PGP, 1/7/11.
34. P. Geddes, "Civics II," p. 92.
35. P. Geddes, "A Suggested Plan for a Civic Museum," p. 203.

36. See for example P. Geddes, "Civics," pp. 103, 105, 107, 110. On his reference to the first panorama, see P. Geddes, "A Suggested Plan for a Civic Museum," p. 227.
37. M. Gross and W. Krohn, "Society as Experiment," esp. 66–70.
38. See P. Geddes, "Civics II," esp. 66–72.
39. *A First Visit to the Outlook Tower* (Edinburgh: Geddes and Co., 1906), p. 5.
40. P. Geddes, "Museums: Actual and Possible," esp. Chaps. 4 and 6, PGP, 5/1/10. The manuscript was never finished, but chapters 6 and 8 have been published as P. Geddes, "The Index Museum: Chapters from an Unpublished Manuscript," *Assemblage*, no. 10, 1989: 65–69. On the ideal of a graphic encyclopedia showing not "simply organized data, but mutually related facts," see also C. Zueblin, "The World's First Sociological Laboratory," p. 585.
41. P. Geddes, "The Edinburgh Outlook Tower." *Report of the Sixty-Eight Meeting of the British Association for the Advancement of Science*. London: Charles Murray, 1899, p. 945.
42. P. Geddes, "Civics," pp. 104–5; P. Geddes, "Civics II," p. 62; and P. Geddes, "The Museum and the City: A Practical Proposal," *The Museums Journal* 7 (1908), p. 373.
43. See, e.g., *A First Visit to the Outlook Tower*, p. 23; and J. Kelman, *The Interpreter's House: An Exposition of the Ideals Embodied in the Outlook Tower*. Edinburgh: Oliphant, Anderson and Ferrier, 1905, p. 17.
44. See, e.g., A. Ponte, "Building the Stair Spiral of Evolution"; and P. Geddes, "Museums: Actual and Possible."
45. P. Geddes, *Education for Economics and Citizenship*, pp. 3–5. Cf. P. Geddes, "Civic Education and City Development," pp. 413–17.
46. Ibid., pp. 415–16.
47. P. Geddes, "On the Art of Seeing," fragment of manuscript early 1900s, PGP, 7/4/5.
48. A. Griffiths, "Media Technology and Museum Display," p. 383; compare B. Comment, *The Panorama*, Chap. 11.
49. P. Geddes, "A Suggested Plan for a Civic Museum," p. 230.
50. Ibid., pp. 226–27. Here Geddes alluded to the often-quoted maxim regarding museums that "whoever walks may read" but gave it a specific outlook reference: "so that whoever climbs may read." Compare the discussion of this maxim in T. Bennett, *Pasts Beyond Memory*, pp. 97–98.
51. J. Kelman, *The Interpreter's House*, pp. 12–13.
52. P. Geddes, "On the Art of Seeing."
53. J. Kelman, *The Interpreter's House*, p. 15.
54. Ibid., p. 17.
55. *A First Visit to the Outlook Tower*, pp. 13–15.
56. P. Geddes, "Civic Education and City Development," p. 416.
57. P. Geddes, "On the Art of Seeing"; and *A First Visit to the Outlook Tower*, p. 9. Cf. C. Zueblin, "The World's First Sociological Laboratory," pp. 585–86.
58. *A First Visit to the Outlook Tower*, p. 10.
59. Ibid., pp. 11–12.
60. J. Kelman, *The Interpreter's House*, pp. 30–31.
61. The city exhibition can be characterized as a sub-genre of what Geddes and many other contemporaries understood as "social museums." I have discussed participation in this context further in an as yet unpublished essay, "The Politics of Participation: Francis Galton's Anthropometric Laboratory and the Making of Civic Selves."
62. See, e.g., F. Lundgren, "Social samling"; and D. Frisby, *Cityscapes of Modernity*, Chap. 3.
63. See, e.g., P. Geddes, "Civics II," pp. 109–10; and P. Geddes, "The Museum and the City," pp. 372–73.

5 Creating Audiences, Making Participants
The Cylinder Phonograph in Ethnographic Fieldwork

Mathias Boström

When thinking about media participation and participatory media in an historical perspective, the ethnographic use of the cylinder phonograph—the first medium for the inscription and playback of sound—is a fitting point of departure for illustrating the complexities of creating audiences and making participants. Furthermore, use of the cylinder phonograph in ethnographic fieldwork from the 1890s to the 1950s has been poorly covered in the literature of the history of recorded sound; and in ethnomusicology, a discipline for which the invention of the phonograph was a prerequisite, little attention has been given to the media-participatory aspects of early field recordings. Participatory media studies have generally focused on media technologies first introduced in the 1950s and later; the histories of sound recording have generally focused on the commercial production of phonograms (performers, repertoire, technological developments, and corporative changes); and ethnomusicological historiography has mostly addressed the development of research methodology and theory.[1] In the latter instance, one reason for the lack of attention to media participatory aspects might be that the publications based on early cylinder phonograph fieldwork are seldom explicit about the circumstances in which the recording technology was used.[2] It is also likely that interaction with the cylinder phonograph has been overlooked due to a strict separation between the roles of "audience," "performer," "demonstrator," and "collector." Drawing on my research on the making and uses of ethnographical cylinder recordings by Swedish collectors from the early twentieth century, I will present and discuss how the introduction of a new medium with which informants were asked to interact actively created situations wherein the positions were not set, but shifting; some users oscillated between being audience and performer, others between being collectors behind the machine and demonstrators and performers in front of it.

THE CYLINDER PHONOGRAPH IN THE FIELD

Figure 5.1 shows a photograph taken on 2 February 1909, in the border region between the French and Belgian Congo colonies (today the Republic of the Congo and Democratic Republic of the Congo, respectively). Boys from the village Kingoyi on the Belgian side have gathered on the ground around one of the huts. Three white men dressed in khaki and sporting pith helmets are seated on wooden boxes under a tarp in front of the hut. They are in Africa in the service of the Swedish Missionary Society, and the man in the middle operating a cylinder phonograph is Karl Edvard Laman. The machine is a German-made Excelsior phonograph, a small and light but sturdy, spring-driven model recommended for use in the field. On the table next to Laman are several cylinder boxes featuring recorded material.

An entry in the diary of the Kingoyi missionary station made on this day reads, "Laman let the boys hear his phonograph. Much cheering and tremendous surprise."[3] What surprised and excited the youngsters was most likely not a novel way of hearing the Gospel preached by means of a new mechanical media miracle, but rather Laman's recordings of something much more familiar—the voices of their relatives on both sides of the colonial border performing traditional songs.

Figure 5.1 The Swedish missionary Karl Laman playing back cylinder recordings for an audience in Kingoyi, Belgian Congo colony, 1909. Karl Laman's Archive, National Archives, Stockholm.

In addition to depicting one important aspect of media interaction in fieldwork with the cylinder phonograph—the demonstration of the apparatus for an audience, to which I will return in the following text—another reason for reprinting this photograph is that it illustrates a significant difference between phonography and photography, the two most common mimetic media for documentation in ethnographic fieldwork at the turn of the twentieth century. However, unlike photography, phonography required the informants' consensual participation.

With the exception of two boys looking straight into the camera, the audience focuses its attention on the performance of the phonograph, as if unaware they were being photographed. Whether or not the photograph was staged is beside the point; the cooperation of its subjects was not a prerequisite for the production of photographic evidence. Although many informants did not mind being photographed, or at least could be persuaded to participate, it is not uncommon to read accounts by early twentieth-century ethnographers of how they outsmarted unwilling informants.[4]

This difference in documentary approaches between phonography and photography at this time was based on technology, not on divergent methodological ideals. Whereas dry-plate cameras that could take snapshot photos from a distance were readily available, the corresponding apparatus for sound recording was yet to appear; a recording technology that could surreptitiously capture sound was for the time being only a figment of scholarly fantasy and a feature in popular fiction.[5] In practice, the sound source had to be very close to the phonograph's horn to make useful recordings of playback quality. The necessity of spatial proximity between performer and phonograph is stressed in instructions for making field recordings in the 1910s issued by the Museum of Ethnography in Stockholm: "One speaks, sings or plays as close as possible to the horn without in any way touching it even the slightest. In the same way, the musician places his instrument as close to the horn as possible."[6]

The unfamiliarity of the informant with the cylinder phonograph, the required intimacy between performer and apparatus, and the attitude of the collector toward using the machine in the field created a setting that might affect performances. This possible impact ran contrary to the epistemological view that the use of mechanical inscription devices would provide more objective, and thus more scientific, material. Based on his own experience in front of the recording horn of an expedition sent to Sweden from the Phonogram Archive of the Austrian Academy of Science, Professor J. Lundell, the doyen of traditional folk-culture collecting in Sweden in the early twentieth century, criticized the use of sound recording technology in its current state in 1914:

> It is, however, quite difficult for anyone to speak fully naturally in their everyday language into a gramophone horn; it is even harder to get a peasant to speak into the horn . . . If we are to get to the point where we

can record the words without in any way affecting the speaker (preferably without their noticing it), as one can now shoot with a camera—then it would be different. At present one can only get prepared samples with the gramophone.⁷

Whereas Lundell feared that the use of the available sound recording technology would render traditional material inauthentic, other writers on methodology were less concerned about possible negative aspects and instead stressed other experiences encountered in the field. Also in 1914, budding folklorist C. von Sydow—himself an occasional cylinder phonograph user in the 1910s—in a similar article on folklore collecting emphasized the performative aspects of the cylinder phonograph in enhancing results:

> The best thing is to use a cylinder phonograph when a good traditional singer has been tracked down, because the melody will be exactly recorded with all its peculiarities. As the cylinder phonograph usually highly interests the peasant population, it is furthermore of great help when it comes to encouraging singers to retrieve their songs from memory.⁸

Although the interpretation of the phonograph's impact on the recording situation differed between collectors, they could agree that it was not neutral. Add to this the fact that the machine often broke down or failed to produce acceptable inscriptions, and folklorist Erika Brady's description of the cylinder phonograph in her important study of its early ethnographic uses by American collectors is apt: "The result must have been very much like the introduction of a third stubborn, sometimes uncooperative, and slightly deaf, presence into what otherwise would have been a normal conversational or performance dyad. The machine insistently and quite literary called attention to itself in ways that could be both diverting and frustrating for the operator."⁹ In other words, the cylinder phonograph can itself be seen as a kind of participating media, an "actant" in an actor-network theoretical sense, with potential agency in interaction with its users.¹⁰ With this in mind, I will proceed to examine the collectors' and informants' interaction with the cylinder phonograph.

CREATING AUDIENCES AND PARTICIPANTS

Bringing phonographs and cylinders on an ethnographic expedition not only added weight to collectors' luggage but also added new tasks for them. In addition to creating ethnographical data together with their informants, using a cylinder phonograph in the field entailed a number of performative actions and interactions with the phonograph itself. The collector had to serve as a recording technician maintaining the machine, a demonstrator of the technology, and a performer on the recordings.

As seen with the advent of many new technologies, the phonograph was at first an attraction in itself—regardless of whether it was used in urban Western or rural non-Western areas.[11] The apparatus's fascinating and enchanting ability to play back speech, song, and instrumental music of almost any kind through its immobile metal horn was sure to attract an audience. The perceived wonders of the sound technology were not only useful to attract potential performers but often also functioned as a catalyst for collectors to make contact with locals and build relationships in the field, which was especially important in cross-cultural settings. Even when ethnographers had no intention of making field recordings, bringing sound technology could prove very useful. For example, in the late 1920s, Swedish ethnographer Erland Nordenskiöld brought a gramophone (without recording capabilities) on an expedition to Central America, with surprisingly good results:

> On the upper Baudo [River] . . . we were very well welcomed as always, not the least thanks to the gramophone. Night and day my wife had to wind up the scary thing, which attracted Indians to us even better than our bartering goods. The Indians liked the songs the best, and these they wanted to hear again and again.[12]

In the aforementioned recording instructions from the Museum of Ethnography in Stockholm, playing prerecorded cylinders was recommended as a way to rouse the locals' interest in performing for the phonograph, which was the main purpose of bringing a cylinder phonograph to the field in the first place: to turn this newly created audience into participants.[13]

A variety of strategies were employed to enroll audience participation. In cases where reluctance was encountered, hearing familiar songs emanating from the phonograph could persuade listeners to perform themselves. Selma Laman accompanied her husband on his 1911 trip, during which Karl Laman made recordings at newly founded missionary stations at Madzia and Musana in the French Congo. Concerning recording efforts at the Musana station, she wrote,

> Apart from linguistic studies, Karl also wanted to get some of their tales and songs, but how to do this when they were so terrified? In the beginning we went to the village and talked to them about anything that did not involve God, because they were very angry with Him. It was He who killed them [by sending smallpox]. So Karl let them hear how they could sing at Madzia and now their interest awoke. It was after all their own songs and melodies, and after they later recorded a song and then got to hear their own voices, their amazement knew no limits.[14]

Another way to persuade informants to record was to play recordings of music from the collector's own musical culture to challenge the informants to perform for the phonograph. Ethnographer Gustaf Bolinder offers a colorful account of this recording tactic used with Ijca Indians in Colombia in 1920:

> One of the last nights we managed to arrange a music session in our hut. The Indians played good old music on the flute and pan flute into the phonograph. Our old friend *mama* [medicine man] Froilán did not want to at first. Finally I played a cylinder with [Swedish baritone John] Forsell and told him that this is how beautifully people sing in my country, at the same time expressing doubt that an Ijca Indian could equal that. This insulted the old man's honour. 'Do you call that song?' he exclaimed. 'No, listen to this.' And he sang a wild, old magical song and then kept on singing as long as the cylinders lasted and longer than that. It was hilarious to see the delight with which he heard his own rough voice from the horn when we played back the recorded pieces.[15]

The collector's role as phonograph demonstrator was not limited to introductory displays. During recording sessions it was customary to play back the recordings to check the quality of the inscription by listening together with the informants, which of course also served to entertain them (see the following). At the end of the ethnographers' stay, it was not unusual for phonograph concerts to be arranged, with the newly recorded cylinders played for a larger audience. The diary of the missionary station in Madzia informs us that after Laman's sermon on 25 June 1911, "whites and blacks alike gathered in the school to hear phonograph records made by Laman, which was highly interesting. It was really entertaining to watch the blacks, when they listened to some of their most known and beloved melodies."[16]

THE COLLECTOR AS PERFORMER

When listening to ethnographic cylinders, one is likely to encounter not only the informants' performances but also to hear the collector participating on the recording, announcing its contents or performing as a musician. As observed with many new media, potential performers were not always immediately willing to participate in a recording session upon first contact with the phonograph. To demonstrate how the sound recording medium worked and coax listeners to perform, collectors sometimes first had to make recordings of themselves, a practice encouraged in the recording instructions from the Museum of Ethnography: "It is recommended to first record a speech or song, so that the natives can get an impression of how to behave in front of the apparatus."[17] Ethnographer Yngve Laurell, the probable author of these instructions, followed the advice when he made recordings with Australian aboriginals in the Buccaneer Archipelago in northwestern Australia in 1911. Laurell's first recording contains a couple of tunes performed by him, which he presumably played back for the audience before recording a song by a group of aboriginal men on the same cylinder.[18] Similarly, Sámi music collector Karl Tirén on at least one occasion had to demonstrate how the cylinder phonograph worked by making a recording himself to persuade a potential performer. During a 1913 expedition to collect *yoiks* (traditional Sámi song) in northern Sweden, Tirén and his entourage met two young Sámi women, one of whom "with some hesitance and [after] persuasion sings some tunes into the phonograph horn." On the cylinder Tirén first sings a *yoik* melody he had earlier notated by ear, followed by the Sámi performer.[19]

The announcement of the contents of an ethnographic recording on record, a kind of internal labeling of the phonogram, was a practice taken from the commercial production of recorded cylinders, where due to difficulties in labeling the wax surface it long remained standard.[20] But in the case of the Swedish ethnographers discussed here, by the time they started to make recordings around 1910, disc phonograms (without internal labels) had taken over the lion's share of the phonogram market. The ethnographic recording practice featuring an announcement and a reference tone (to facilitate playback at the correct speed) was adapted through contact with the Berlin Phonogram Archive, probably the most important European institution for the collection and study of traditional music on phonogram in the early twentieth century.[21]

Not all ethnographic collectors followed this practice, but when they did, the announcements are made without exception by the collector, never the informant. In cross-cultural ethnographic recording sessions, there were of course practical linguistic reasons for the collector to make the announcements in his language in order to facilitate future identification of the recordings. In this sense, the announcements point to the future trajectory of the phonogram collection as part of a Western memory institution. This is illustrated by Karl Laman's decision to refrain from making such announcements on his second collection of Congolese music for the Berlin Phonogram Archive. Since he was not proficient in German, Laman instead left some room on the wax cylinders for the archive staff to record the appropriate announcements later, based on his notes in English.[22]

Aside from the practicality of these announcements, a desire to assert his or her status may have also motivated the collector. The preserved collector's voice thereby essentially becomes the "master's voice" and may be indicative of a need to demonstrate authority—both to the present performers and future listeners. With the use of cylinder phonographs, collectors no longer had to mediate the sounds they heard through their bodies into written notes. It is therefore not unlikely that the collectors were busy securing their status by asserting their role in the creation of each recording. For this reason, and probably also reflecting gender issues in fieldwork, Frances

Densmore, one of the most diligent American music collectors, wrote to a prospective collector: "The singer must never be allowed to think that he is in charge of the work. A strict hold must be kept on him."[23] The voices of the collectors announcing the recordings can be seen as a desire to be acknowledged as the creators of a phonogram whose contents they sanctioned and had ethnographic authority over.[24]

This phonographic ritual of science, as Michael Taussig has so appropriately described it, at the same time paradoxically undermined one of the strongest arguments for the use of the mechanical inscription technology—the objective, transparent, and authentic representation of performance, ideally by informants unaware that they were being recorded. The announcements instead highlighted the cultural construction of ethnographic recordings and obliterated any hope of the listener enjoying a "fly on the wall" position. The collector's repetitive speech between every recorded piece could also affect the performers, forcing them to wait for him/her to finish before they could begin. On several of Karl Tirén's recordings of Sámi *yoik*, the informants simply could not wait for him to finish his announcement before bursting into song.[25]

THE ROLES OF THE INFORMANT

As previously mentioned, the rationale for taking a bulky cylinder machine on an ethnographic field trip was to turn the audience into participants. The informants seem generally to have been fascinated by the workings of the phonograph—and collectors seem to have had a never-ending fascination with that fascination, as Michael Taussig has pointed out and several quotes here illustrate.[26] Not surprisingly, listening to their own performances and their own voices reproduced by the phonograph was the most thrilling event for the informants.

They were not always the most willing of performers, however; as previously shown, persuasion was sometimes necessary before a recording could be made; in other cases it was not possible at all, and recording in secret was not a feasible option. Concerning his 1912 recordings made among the Akamba in British East Africa (now Kenya), Gerhard Lindblom writes that "the men were pretty willing [to be recorded], but the women were impossible, although I asked those that I had been in daily contact with for months and whose confidence I enjoyed."[27] Karl Laman encountered similar problems while recording at the Musana station. Although he used songs recorded at a neighboring station to try to persuade the locals to record, he only managed to get children from the missionary school to perform for the phonograph. In a letter to the director of the Berlin Phonogram Archive, Erich von Hornbostel, Laman explained that the adults at Musana were too "superstitious" to make recordings. Similarly, while recording in Brazzaville, Laman had to record from outside of the hut

Creating Audiences, Making Participants 57

in which the musicians played, because they could not be persuaded to perform as close to the recording horn as he wished. The longer distance between sound source and recording horn inevitably resulted in cylinders of inferior sound quality.²⁸

In other cases, the informants became so interested in interacting with the phonograph and enjoyed the recording session so much that the collector could step back and allow the informants some measure of control over the process. This is illustrated by some of Karl Tirén's recordings among the Sámi between 1913 and 1915. Author and folklorist Karl Erik Forsslund accompanied Tirén on a couple of his *yoik* collecting trips and has given a detailed account of the collecting process. Tirén's first trip in 1913 took him to the annual winter market in the town of Arjeplog, where he set up his phonograph in the home of Maria Persson, his key informant on Sámi music culture, who invited people to come over and record. This arrangement—together with the cylinder phonograph's ability to instantly record and play back the performances—allowed Tirén to let his informants take charge of the direction and content of the recording session, albeit without letting them actually man the phonograph or make the announcements. Forsslund describes how the informants insisted upon which cylinders be played back as newcomers arrived: "Lars

Figure 5.2 Boys of the first class of the missionary school at the Swedish station Madzia, Belgian Congo colony, making cylinder recordings for Karl Laman in 1911. Karl Laman's Archive, National Archives, Stockholm.

Nilsson Ruong . . . sings a yoik to the grouse with a perfect imitation of its call—kabáu-kabáu-njao-njao—and it draws a special cheer. That cylinder is requested again and again as each new group arrives."[29] In addition, the choice of repertoire seems to have been effected by the presence of the phonograph as opposed to when Tirén collected by ear. The result was more *yoiks* about individuals: "When a new guest arrives, one of those present might whisper with a twinkle in their eye, 'Now I will sing his (or her) yoik!' And then there it is, and everyone listens, smiling with recognition, not least the subject itself."[30]

Whereas some performers were enthusiastic participants, in the Swedish cases presented here there is no evidence that the informants expressed any interest with regard to future (empowering or emancipatory) uses of phonography in their community or asked any favors of the collector regarding the use of the recorded cylinders. Elsewhere, even when such wishes were expressed, the performer had no control over the use to which the recording might be put. After Frances Densmore had recorded music among the Native American Ute for the Bureau of American Ethnology in Washington DC, Chief Red Cap asked her in return to let him record a speech airing his grievances about the local Indian Affairs agent. Densmore promised to play the cylinder for the commissioner of Indian Affairs, but presented it in the commissioner's office without an accompanying translation, thus rendering the chief's speech unintelligible for the audience.[31]

THE POLITICS OF MEDIA PARTICIPATION

In the participatory culture of media, not all participants are created equal, as Henry Jenkins has observed.[32] This inequality is highlighted in the cross-cultural ethnographical usage of the phonograph discussed here, wherein collectors controlled the means of media production and its access and later uses, and the recorded informants had limited, if any, access to and influence over the recordings other than the times they were played back during fieldwork.

Nevertheless, collectors hardly had sole control of the actual act of inscription. Informants could refuse to participate and since it was almost impossible to make quality recordings in secret, the collector would leave empty-handed. Once the informant was situated close to the phonograph horn and the recording needle began to cut the wax cylinder, the collector could exercise no further influence on the performance being recorded. As a way to counteract this mechanical representation work independent of the collectors and reinstate their ethnographic authority, a particular framing of the recording event was often introduced. This framing, an aspect of the politics of media participation, turned the collectors into active participants on the same phonograms as their informants—and not only for demonstration purposes—announcing contents (and sometimes the performers' names) before sounding a reference tone. This part of the recording process was never delegated to the informants, even on occasions when the collector otherwise seems to have let his informants have a larger say about the repertoire to be documented, as with Tirén's Sámi recordings. Not all media participation in ethnographic recording situations was considered desirable, and documentation had to be monitored, especially if the collector wanted to assert their scientific value.[33]

Discussions about participatory media have often focused on newer communication technologies from the second half of the twentieth century and onward; Jenkins suggests the photocopier as the starting point of participatory media, followed by home video, sound recording tape technology, and so on to the internet.[34] Participatory media have been characterized by the users' personal access to the means of media production—allowing them to become producers themselves—and their opportunities for distributing the media products in many-to-many communication. However, a strong emphasis on the peer-to-peer networking side of participatory media risks historical blindness toward participatory aspects of earlier media, an oversight not necessarily due to the profound differences between earlier and present-day media, but rather to their different historical contexts. For example, I see no fundamental technological difference in the participatory opportunities offered by the cylinder phonograph and the compact cassette and the resulting "cassette culture" of the 1980s, which included circulating homemade tapes among fans. Almost all cylinder phonograph users could make their own recordings and make copies either by pantographic (mechanical) or moulding techniques, and cylinder collections—at least ethnographical ones—regularly changed hands through the mail in the first half of the twentieth century.[35] On the other hand, access to privately-owned cylinder phonographs, in particular machines for making copies, was never high in the early twentieth century, and financial aspects and youth culture differed significantly.

In the salvage anthropology paradigm that dominated early twentieth-century ethnography, the idea of repatriating material to communities of ethnographic Others was seldom discussed. A widely held belief among ethnographers at the time and a prime motivation for ethnographic pursuits in the first place was that many traditional cultures were on the verge of becoming extinct due to contact with the West, and that there would thus be no one to repatriate material to in the near future. Whereas some ethnographers developed their photos while still in the field and used them to barter, a similar exchange with phonograph cylinders, which required hardware to use, is not documented.

Instead, these ethnographic cylinders found new and different audiences at lectures and museum exhibits or were used in research. In Stockholm, field recordings were played at several exhibitions at the Museum of Ethnography in the 1910s, and Karl Tirén used his Sámi recordings as evidence of the highly developed level of Sámi music to counter the belief that it was the expression of a primitive culture. In Berlin, the director of the Phonogram Archive, Erich von Hornbostel, included several of Laman's cylinders in his early 1920s anthology of traditional music from around the world—known as the *Demonstrations-Sammlung*—which was for sale and intended for scholars, museums, schools, and the general public, whereas his successor Marius Schneider used Laman's recordings in his chronicle of the different stages in the evolution of polyphony.[36]

Fortunately, in most cases the situation for traditional cultures has not turned out as catastrophically as predicted, and over the last few decades a movement has gained momentum among indigenous peoples and minority communities to seek access to and full or partial control over the use of ethnographic material collected from their ancestors for Western memory institutions.[37] With the recent media convergence, to use Jenkins' term, or migration of the contents of earlier media formats (including phonograms) into the digital realm, the accessibility of the material has increased and hence also the opportunity of effortlessly repatriating copies of recordings. Karl Tirén's Sámi cylinder collection is today partly available on a commercially produced CD and has been incorporated into the Swedish Sámi Museum's virtual "Yoik Archive." It is furthermore not unusual to hear interpretations of *yoiks* collected by Tirén in contemporary performance.[38]

Thus the original media participation that resulted in the ethnographic cylinder collections has not been lost to us today. These early recordings are still relevant and often in demand, as they represent the informants' more or less framed, direct interaction with the participatory mechanical media rather than mediation through a collector. These often wonderful musical performances, their potential for cultural revival, and the still enchanting experience of listening to the phonograph's mimetic faculty—representing media participation a full century ago—are all good reasons for listening.

NOTES

1. See, e.g., "standard" narratives like R. Gelatt, *The Fabulous Phonograph, 1877–1977*; W. Welch and L. Burt, *From Tinfoil to Stereo*; and H. Myers, ed., *Ethnomusicology*. See also entries on "ethnomusicology" in the *New Grove Dictionary of Music and Musicians*, 2nd ed. (London: Macmillan, 2001); and *Musik in Geschichte und Gegenwart*, 2nd ed. (Kassel: Bärenreiter, 1994–2007). The best discussion of the cylinder phonograph in fieldwork is E. Brady's *A Spiral Way*.
2. E. Brady, *A Spiral Way*, pp. 60–64.
3. Diary 24 April 1904–20 March 1909, entry 2 February 1909, Swedish Missionary Society Archives, series F, no. 1, SMF Kongo/Zaire—Kingoyi Station, National Archives, Stockholm. All translations are by the author, unless stated otherwise.

4. For examples of Swedish ethnographic photos of unwilling or unaware informants, see, e.g., G. Lindblom, *Afrikanska strövtåg* (Stockholm: Bonniers, 1914).
5. For Swedish scholarly ambitions for using the phonograph in secret, see J. Lundell, "Om uppteckningar av folkmål: Anvisningar och råd," *Svenska landsmål och svenskt folkliv*, 1914, pp. 5–45; and C. Hartman, "The Photographone," in F. Heger, ed., *Verhandlungen des XVI. internationalen Amerikanisten-Kongresses. Wien, 9. bis 14. September 1908* (Wien & Leipzig: A. Hartleben, 1910), pp. 563–68. For popular fiction dealing with sound recording in secret, see examples in C. Marvin, *When Old Technologies Were New*.
6. The instructions are reprinted in G. Ternhag, "'Ett fonogramarkiv för svensk folkmusik'," 100–1.
7. J. Lundell, "Om uppteckningar av folkmål," pp. 27, 36.
8. C. von Sydow, "Råd och anvisningar för insamlande av folkminnen," *Folkminnen och folktankar* 1 (1914), pp. 35–36.
9. E. Brady, *A Spiral Way*, p. 43.
10. See, e.g., B. Latour, *Pandora's Hope*.
11. See E. Brady, *Spiral Way*, Chap. 2.
12. E. Nordenskiöld, "Folket utan hövdingar: Med kamera och grammofon hos Choco-indianerna," *Dagens Nyheter*, 2 October 1927.
13. G. Ternhag, "'Ett fonogramarkiv för svensk folkmusik'," p. 101.
14. "Lamans språkarbete i F. Congo," pp. 5–6, Swedish Missionary Society Archives, Selma Lamans arkiv, National Archives, Stockholm.
15. G. Bolinder, *Indianer och tre vita* (Stockholm: Bonniers, 1921), pp. 165–66.
16. Diary 5 January 1909–31 December 1918, entry 25 June 1911, Swedish Missionary Society Archives, series F, no. 1, SMF Kongo/Zaire—Madzia Station, National Archives, Stockholm.
17. G. Ternhag, "'Ett fonogramarkiv för svensk folkmusik'," p. 100.
18. V78–0366, Department of Audiovisual Material, National Library of Sweden. The cylinder box is labeled "Music by Laurell and Song by Natives."
19. K.-E. Forsslund, *Som gäst hos fjällfolket* (Stockholm: Nordiska bokhandeln, 1914), pp. 105–6. The cylinder is kept in cylinder nos. 19–22, Tirén Collection, Department of Dialectology, Onomastics and Folklore Research, Umeå.
20. See L. Gitelman, *Scripts, Grooves, and Writing Machines*, pp. 156–60.
21. For the connections between the Museum of Ethnography, Stockholm, and Berlin Phonogramm-Archiv, see M. Boström, "The Phonogram Archive of the Stockholm Ethnographic Museum (1909–1930)." For the Berliner Phonogramm-Archiv, see A. Simon, ed., *Das Berliner Phonogramm-Archiv 1900–2000*.
22. K. Laman to E. von Hornbostel, 20 September 1911, Berliner Phonogramm-Archiv, files concerning the Laman cylinder collections, Ethnologisches Museum, Berlin.
23. Cited in E. Brady, *A Spiral Way*, p. 91.
24. Cf. L. Gitelman and G. Pingree's question, "How do they [media] acquire and carry epistemological authority?" in L. Gitelman and G. Pingree, eds., *New Media, 1740–1915*, p. xv.
25. Tirén phonograph cylinder nos. 24, 42, 309–10, National Collections of Music, Stockholm.
26. M. Taussig, *Mimesis and Alterity*, pp. 194–98. About the trope of the "alien naïf" in the encounter with the phonograph, see also L. Gitelman, *Scripts, Grooves, and Writing Machines*, pp. 121–25.

27. G. Lindblom, *The Akamba in British East Africa: An Ethnological Monograph* (Uppsala: Appelberg, 1920), p. 417.
28. See note 22.
29. K.-E. Forsslund, *Som gäst hos fjällfolket*, p. 98. For a monograph of Karl Tirén as Sámi music collector, see G. Ternhag, *Jojksamlaren Karl Tirén*.
30. Ibid., p. 98.
31. E. Brady, *A Spiral Way*, p. 93.
32. H. Jenkins, *Convergence Culture*, p. 3.
33. See K. Tirén, *Die lappische Volksmusik* (Stockholm: Nordiska museet, 1942) for a study that uses the cylinder recordings to deflect criticism of his representations of the songs in musical notation; and E. Emsheimer, "Drei Tanzgesänge der Akamba," *Ethnos* 2 (1937), pp. 137–43, for an analysis of some of G. Lindblom's Kamba cylinders, marred by the lack of reference tones on the recordings.
34. H. Jenkins, "Quentin Tarantino's *Star Wars*?," p. 286.
35. For "cassette culture," see K. McConnell, "The Hand-Made Tale," pp. 163–64.
36. See M. Boström, "The Phonogram Archive of the Stockholm Ethnographic Museum (1909–1930)," on the use of the cylinders in exhibitions; K. Tirén, *Die lappische Volksmusik*; M. Schneider, *Geschichte der Mehrstimmigkeit*; E. von Hornbostel, "Phonogramm-Archiv des Pshychologischen Institut der Universität," pp. 97–105.
37. See E. Brady, *A Spiral Way*, Chap. 5; and several contributions in G. Berlin and A. Simon, eds., *Music Archiving in the World*.
38. *Samiska röster: Karl Tiréns fonografinspelningar 1913–1915*, Svea fonogram SVCD 9, 2003; for Åjtte Sámi Museum's "Yoik Archive Project," see <http://www.ajtte.com/>. For contemporary performances of *yoiks* collected by Karl Tirén, hear, e.g., Krister Stoor's *To yoik is to live*, UMUFCD-002, 2003.

6 The Interactivity of the Model Home
Mark B. Sandberg

Early in 2003, a pair of IKEA commercials aired on American television. Created by film director Wes Anderson, both of these offbeat, postmodernist television spots featured the same quirky concept.[1] In the first, entitled "Kitchen," a man and woman are caught on camera in the midst of a difficult marital confrontation in a modern kitchen as the wife accuses the husband of being "out there prowling the streets" while she is "stuck in here like some prisoner." As the argument heats up, an off-screen voice interrupts with a tentative "So . . . " As the camera pulls back to reveal the larger setting of an IKEA showroom, the salesperson comes in from the right edge of the screen and continues " . . . what do you guys think?" Quickly shifting tone, the couple responds with "It feels good," and "Yeah, we'll take it." The second ad, "Living Room," shows a similarly uncomfortable (if clichéd) family scene, with a pregnant teenage daughter breaking the news to her parents. As accusations get tossed around and the argument heats up, the same inquiry comes from an off-frame salesperson. This couple also reports that the model living room works just fine, and they decide to buy it. Each of the ads plays with the difference between a mode of participatory performance in which each family momentarily goes too far in making the room its own, and that of a more detached consumerism, the level from which the viewer watches and the sale is made. That difference left some viewers confused: Lewis Lazare, reporting on the upcoming ads for the *Chicago Sun-Times* in 2002, called the ads "ill-conceived" and added, "The new spots probably will leave you thinking the world is one big, hugely unhappy and terribly dysfunctional family unit. An odd way to sell household goods? You bet."[2]

As it turns out, the overly eager mode of consumer participation depicted in these ads is not limited to Wes Anderson's imagination alone; there seems to be something about IKEA's mode of display that encourages such fantasies of immersion. A much more elaborate version of the concept was played out by American comedian Mark Malkoff, who convinced the IKEA corporation to allow him to move into one of the model bedrooms in its Paramus, New Jersey store for one week in mid-January 2008, to live and sleep there around the clock while filming the experience. The result is a series of twenty-five episodic videos that can now be found on Malkoff's official website documenting the experience, "Mark Lives in IKEA."[3] Using a hybrid form of site-specific comedy and installation art, Malkoff interacted with the real IKEA employees and customers for a week, mostly playing out the main joke of what happens when one *really* makes oneself at home in IKEA's surround-style simulated interiors and tries to live there ("And to make matters worse," Malkoff confides to the camera, "the plumbing doesn't work. Fake toilet! Fake sinks! Fake bathtub!").[4] He also plays extensively with the imagined boundaries of his newly domesticated space, the one bedroom display suite that he chose from the many in the store; he insists, for example, that visitors entering his new home are either neighbors, houseguests, or interlopers ("Next time you come over here, knock!" and "Is there a reason you guys are in my house?").[5]

Malkoff's weeklong performance of IKEA inhabitation attracted extensive media attention in everything from blogs to mainstream news outlets. The store, of course, sensed the promotional possibilities and even made a special sign for the week with the typical IKEA logo pointing to "Mark's Apartment" (the online Mark Malkoff website store continues to sell T-shirts and mugs emblazoned with the same). Less predictable than the store's own promotional efforts, though, was the participatory playfulness of the visitors and IKEA employees, who joined in pillow fights on his bed, brought him housewarming gifts, and helped him shave in the fake sink in his bathroom. One article in the *Washington Post* offered an explanation: "People come to visit Mark in Ikea because it makes sense to them. Not the older people; they come because they want a spectacle. But the Web gen visitors, they come because they wonder why they didn't think of this first."[6] Although the same writer compares Malkoff's stunt to "a people exhibit in a zoo," it is logically speaking something more than a zoo, which typically is more careful about demarcating the difference between the animal displays and spectator space. Malkoff's experiment showed that IKEA visitors were in fact willing to play house with him at the drop of a hat.

These various advertising fantasies highlight a particular convention of public consumer display put under pressure—the delicate behavioral balance between spectating and immersive participation that is required of visitors to model homes and furniture showrooms. Today this is an inconspicuous but essential part of a shopper's behavioral repertoire, a sort of basic cognitive skill: When trying out a new mattress in a showroom, one does not simply observe it from a distance, nor does one go so far as to fall asleep on it. Instead, the usual response falls somewhere in between: potential buyers either give the bed a tentative bounce or two or, at the very most, take off their shoes and lie down for a few awkward moments. That moment of hesitation is precisely the interesting conceptual area worth exploring in this article, however, because the perceived ambiguity signals an internalized sense of boundary that is much more complex than the actually physical barriers separating viewers from objects. Shoppers in showroom situations are technically invited inside a scene, yet their relation to the space is in many ways tentative. It is the realm of pre-ownership, which is to say, the liminal space of modern consumer culture more generally.

The IKEA showrooms are especially well known for encouraging this kind of consumer performance with their powerful scenic logic: The individual furniture pieces are gathered in whole-room groupings, stage sets of the possible worlds and styles one might inhabit. Here is where The Teenage Boy might live; over there is clearly The Young Professional Couple's living room. Like a theater or film set, the model-home interiors at IKEA propose a fictional world complete with traces of human presence. (In IKEA stores in the United States, this identification with the space is of course complicated by a dynamic that encourages multicultural American shoppers to imagine themselves living in a room that is also foreign in subtle ways—to judge from the Swedish books that are often placed on the bookshelves in these model living rooms.) The most familiar trademark of an IKEA showroom, in fact, is that the rooms look lived in, which encourages shoppers to think in complete-room units. The desire to inhabit such a space tugs at the viewer's imagination, and if not for the herds of other shoppers flowing by each display, one might in fact be more tempted to give the rooms an authentic tryout, even if stopping short of staging a practice family fight or spending the night. The fact is, however, that almost every IKEA shopper imagines at some level the inhabitation of the display space.

This process probably seems quite natural to modern consumers, but we should not take our familiarity with the practice to mean that it is historically constant. One might well wonder: When and where did this particular kind of housing theater begin? Few would be surprised to hear that the period of cultural emergence for the model home—the time before which the practice did not quite make sense, and after which it began to seem perfectly natural—was the late nineteenth and early twentieth century. Not every aspect of this story is equally predictable, however, and the task of this article is to examine some of the more interesting aspects of this genealogy.

A CULTURE OF SCENIC IMMERSION

The first of them is an unexpected formal connection between model homes and another strand of display practice in the late nineteenth century, namely that of popular museology. In *Living Pictures, Missing Persons* (2003), I examined in detail the scenic logic in turn-of-the-century Scandinavian visual culture, a logic that similarly oscillates between detached voyeurism and participatory immersion. In the tableau aesthetic of mannequin displays at wax and folk museums in Scandinavia, one finds evidence of not only a detached spectating position similar to that of the film viewer but also of a spectator experience that was always on the verge of crossing over into participation. The carefully arranged tableaux of these museums were so appealing in their physical detail that they activated a desire in viewers to cross the invisible fourth wall and immerse themselves in the space. The discourse generated by these museums contains many anecdotes whose main point was to explore in humorous form the permeability of that boundary—serving very much the same function as these IKEA ads or the Malkoff comedy sketches, in fact.

The various Nordic folk museums (like Skansen and its equivalents in the other countries) took this immersive logic to the greatest extreme, eventually developing a display technique that has been extremely influential in ethnographic museums around the world: namely, the fully furnished, walk-in interiors that gave late nineteenth-century museum visitors a palpable sense of inhabited space. For all its subsequent success, however, the fully staged and fictionally activated museum space was at the time a new and contested development within museology. It required that visitors to the museum should learn a new set of spectating skills; they had to internalize the rules about how to be in the space without completely making it theirs.

There is clearly a morphological similarity between this folk-museum experience and that of a visit to a model home, despite the diametrically opposed cultural intentions of each practice (the emerging consumer culture encouraged by the latter was in fact the primary reason that the preservation of traditionally crafted folk materials was first perceived to be necessary). The fact that theatrically staged interiors could be put to such different uses, however, suggests that we are dealing with a culturally innovative moment in which several different kinds of public space turned to immersive displays. What these spaces had in common was the idea that as spectators entered, they would perform a kind of temporary attachment, in essence a sort of "participatory non-participation." Seemingly invited inside the display to encounter the compelling materiality of the space, spectators were nevertheless expected to continue observing more subtle and invisible boundaries. Real ownership or inhabitation of the display space was simply deferred, and in the evacuated foreground space, a new kind of performative spectating developed and flourished.

The interest of these early housing exhibitions is that public behavior in a model home had not yet become routine and conventional; one can see more clearly what was at stake when the practice was still noteworthy and mentionable by commentators. Clearly, each new spectator must continue to be socialized to the conventions of this kind of spectating, even today. Even after many years of development, when the practice had become widely familiar, there were of course always new spectators to train. But at this early stage, there are both practices and viewer commentary that stand out more clearly than they do when the model-home idea became integrated into mainstream consumer culture.

Counteracting this kind of "mentionability" in source material is another factor that is typical of architectural history, however; namely, that documentation of that history is rarely interested in the inhabitants and users of the spaces in question. One quickly realizes this when looking at existing visual sources. The historical spectator of housing exhibitions is in fact both literally and figuratively missing from most of the visual record, which in its photographic form typically focuses on conveniently empty rooms that offer the most unobstructed view of their design and contents. Spectator bodies, after all, just get in the way. For serious architectural discourse, the behavior of actual spectators in the space is clearly understood to be a contingent rather than essential feature of the display. Why would any one person's reaction matter? This was especially the case in the model homes of early functionalist design, where it was important that the clean-line aesthetic operate more efficiently without bodies interrupting the concept. (Of course, one senses here the seeds of a powerful critique, namely, that for many theorists and designers of modern model homes, the eventual inhabitants of the space were equally contingent and ultimately uninteresting, even though their potential needs were ostensibly the point of the design.)

These missing persons make this kind of study difficult, of course, since one has to constitute this spectating experience indirectly through other means. Newspaper reports from the various Swedish exhibitions do contain comments that demonstrate that some spectator reactions were in fact seen as interesting enough to mention. But another means of approaching the question is to turn to popular entertainment practices at the margins of official housing exhibitions. Here one can see how the mainstream ideas get commented on in a secondary or subordinate discourse of housing. In the imaginative, playful response to the prescriptive "modeling," that is, one gets a hint of a broader reaction to new housing concepts as they were being introduced, one that might in fact have more participatory (and less prescriptive) overtones.

FUN-HOUSING AT THE 1909 STOCKHOLM EXHIBITION

There are many good reasons to pursue this argument primarily within a Scandinavian or even specifically Swedish cultural historical context, at least as a point of departure. Although Sweden did not invent the model home (there were precursors at other mid to late nineteenth-century American and European expositions, for instance), housing exhibitions became something of a cultural specialty in Scandinavia that in many cases rivaled the same kind of popular interest as that attracted by the living-history folk museums. This was due in large part to the special role that architecture and design policies played in the early formation of the welfare state in the 1920s and '30s, which would eventually give the Swedish model home special social and political stakes. The model home was often the imagined tool for transforming the nature of social relations. It is of course debatable whether the prescriptive architectural vision of cultural radicals was in fact the experience that actually got taken up in practice by the general public, but there is no question that at an official cultural level, there developed a political urgency attached to the model-home showroom that did not exist in the United States at the time.

The breakthrough of modern functionalist design is usually tied to the famous Stockholm exhibition in 1930, but there were housing exhibitions of many kinds before that date, beginning in 1899 with one of the earliest displays of model interiors to the public in Sweden. That year, Ellen Key published her landmark collection of essays *Skönhet för alla* (Beauty for Everyone), which argued that beauty in the home was a basic human need and would have a positive effect on members of all social classes.[7] As a practical illustration of the principles therein, she arranged two display rooms at the Worker's Institute in Stockholm the same year, rooms that encouraged workers of limited means to attempt nevertheless simple design improvements in their surroundings. According to Key, 5,000 people visited the displays that summer and fall.[8] From this early effort, the idea of display homes as the source of ideas and practical solutions to housing problems got its first strong impulse in Sweden.

The 1909 Stockholm exhibition, the "Industrial Arts Exhibition," was the real breakthrough for the model-home idea in Sweden, however, and this discussion will thus concentrate on material from that event. This is not the best known of the Stockholm exhibitions; the fairs of 1897 and 1930 have drawn far more critical and historical attention. This exhibition as a whole was sponsored by the *Svenska Slöjdföreningen* (The Swedish Society of Arts and Crafts) and was intended as a follow-up to the successful Swedish efforts in applied-arts displays at the 1897 Stockholm exhibition and the 1900 World Exposition in Paris. Though from the start it was limited in scope as a specialty exhibition, the 1909 Industrial Arts Exhibition aimed high by emulating the architectural style of the 1893 World's Columbian Exhibition in Chicago: in Stockholm, there also arose a "White City" for the duration of the summer.

Several Swedish commentators of the day made clear that by 1909, the idea of an exhibition was nothing new: "Our age does not infrequently claim to be a bit blasé about these constant revues showing [original switches to German here] 'how wonderfully far we've come.'" Continuing, he writes, "We have gotten our experts in this airy art of construction, whose material is plaster, boards, and whitewash, and organizers of the energetic variety who with a magic wand can conjure forth white summer cities on marshy fields . . . "[9]

As was the case at all such exhibitions, the overall logic of the site was that of temporary housing; viewers were encouraged to imagine as substantial the building façades that they knew to be scheduled for demolition after the fair. But in fact the popular success of this particular exhibition prompted a general discussion in the press about the possibility of preserving *Den hvita sommarstaden* (the White Summer City) past the scheduled closing date, in effect suggesting that they make the temporary housing permanent.[10] The general agreement, however, was that the Summer City's construction plans never included calculations for a Swedish winter, and that past experience had showed that buildings held over from exhibitions of this sort rapidly fell into decay and disrepair.[11] The logic of the overall exhibition, then, was as liminal as the model home itself; most of the buildings were never really intended to be fully used. In this sense, this exhibition resembled it predecessors in the late nineteenth century.

What was new for Sweden in 1909, however, was the consistent attention to the display of fully staged domestic interiors. Swedish newspaper commentary on the exhibition makes quite clear that this was the first Swedish design exhibition that consistently placed domestic display objects in contextual groupings (chairs grouped around tables with other furniture in a whole-room display concept). In addition, some newly designed model villas actually were intended for actual inhabitation after the fair (when moved to a new residential location). The furniture groupings were arranged in simulated room interiors in the main halls, and five villas were constructed as model homes (three for middle-class incomes and two for workers) down in the entertainment district adjacent to the enclosed arcade of buildings on the exhibition grounds.

These villas drew on the *egnahem* model of housing development (an early twentieth-century Swedish movement encouraging individual home ownership) and thus did not represent any radically new housing reform in content or urban planning. But their presentation in contextualized scenes at the exhibition was seen as a significant departure in display strategy for this kind of public event:

> We knew in advance that the fully equipped and furnished interiors would turn out to be the exhibition's 'clou.' Judging from appearances, however, reality looks as if it will exceed expectations. These interiors, which above all else illustrate the main principle from the planning of the exhibition, namely to show the artistic production as much as possible in the surroundings for which they are intended, can be found gathered in certain parts of the building complex and spread among the collective and special exhibits.[12]

Another saw the experiment as an attempt to "transform an exhibition site into lots of different dwelling places, each with its own special character," and notes the crucial conceptual difference in this way: "They have therefore chosen the solution of showing the owner-occupied home in several completely furnished villas, while other exhibitions have arranged things within a frame that to a certain degree is neutral."[13]

The impulse to reject previous exhibition attempts as artificially framed and distant and to embrace the newly contextualized display as more authentic and alive is evidence of a shift in attitude: the spectator-observer is being reimagined as a temporary inhabitant. The circumstances surrounding one of the villa displays provides us with a concentrated metaphor for what was at stake. This was the so-called "lottery villa," where each exhibition visitor could buy a five-crown ticket for a chance at ownership of the house after the exhibition's close (it was scheduled to be moved to a more suburban location outside of Stockholm). One journalist wrote a clever piece about his own fantasies of ownership, pretending to be generous in letting fellow visitors temporarily share what he was sure would eventually be his own:

> All the people are going around believing it's theirs. But I know it's mine, and what's more, I have put my visiting card on the door ... But it's fine if people want to have their summer illusions and hope that the lottery villa will be theirs. You are welcome to do so, gentlemen, I don't at all begrudge you the chance to come in and admire my villa—your grief will just be all the greater later.[14]

He goes on to wish that these interlopers would wipe their feet even so, and worries that if so many guests continue to visit after he has moved in he will need a higher salary from the newspaper. But he finds it fun "to promenade around incognito now and then among my guests in the rooms; they seem to be really at ease in there. Now and then I even see a covetous look in their eyes, as if they wanted to take over the whole villa. But I warn you most seriously to give it up: *You are being watched!*"[15] A quick juxtaposition of this 1909 journalist's fantasy with the Mark Malkoff comedic stunt in 2008 reveals striking similarities in tone and mode, even down to the detail of faux aggression toward those who dare to enter "his" space. It was stated earlier that Malkoff's fans wondered why they didn't think of it first; from this earlier account, we see that Malkoff was not the first to think of it either.

The image of all these potential inhabitant-spectators in 1909, with their overlapping fantasies of belonging and ownership, suggests more than the literal lottery competition. The overall logic of display at the exhibition in fact becomes a quite ubiquitous and constant aspect of consumer culture throughout the twentieth century. The individual appeal to each viewer proceeds from the combination of contextualization and evocative absence of actual owners in the space. The juxtaposition of the original caption—"*Min villa*" (My Villa)—with the depiction of other viewers as co-inhabitants simply makes clear the underlying shared spectatorial fantasy. To the same degree that each visitor imagines his or her own fit to the space, he or she must also ignore the presence of the other visitors in the space; that is one of the developing conventions of model-home spectatorship. More sophisticated spectators learned to negotiate this kind of belonging in the subjunctive mood; the visitor with the best model-home spectating skills

Figure 6.1 The "Lottery Villa" at the 1909 Stockholm exhibition. *Dagens Nyheter*, 18 June 1909. (Caption reads: "From the Summer City," above, and "My Villa," below.)

would not make the mistake of latching on to any particular space, but instead would limit the experience to a series of imaginative entrances and exits, a kind of participatory nonparticipation.

This conceptual play with housing display space spills over into other forms of imaginative mischief in the entertainment district of the 1909 exhibition. This extra space, outside the exhibition "proper," was created through the initiative of three of the exhibition's leading architects and engineers, and it included many venues that might be seen as parodic inversions of the more earnest presentation of housing models inside the main complex of buildings. One of them was a directly satiric commentary, a building named *Konstiga utställningen* (Peculiar Exhibition). This was a close pun of the official exhibition name (Konstindustriutställningen). Inside this orientalist structure visitors could find a parodic art gallery, with various paintings caricaturing the style of current artists. One sees the effort to show contextualized interiors here too, but of an outlandish

72 Mark B. Sandberg

sort quite different from the more serious furniture groups of the *egnahem* villas. Most interesting perhaps, given this early date, were the furniture parodies in the Peculiar Exhibition, since the satirized principle was a protofunctionalist notion of efficiently combined, multifunctional furniture pieces. *Herrns Möbel* (The Gentleman's Furniture Piece) claimed to be a combination of "bathtub, bed, egg-cracking machine (for breakfast), home pharmacy, liquor cabinet . . . and furthermore a clock, fireplace, clothes closet, and sofa."[16] That this was intended as a direct inversion of the serious furniture displays is clear from this writer's joke that it wouldn't be long until they also saw this furniture piece in the display windows of Nordiska Möbleringsaktiebolaget, which just happened to be one of the companies with an official furniture display elsewhere in the "proper" area of the 1909 exhibition.[17]

Figure 6.2 *Lustiga Huset* (Fun House) at the 1909 Stockholm exhibition. *Aftonbladet*, 10 June 1909. (Caption reads: "The pleasures of the exhibition: The amusement area's most entertaining section.")

The Interactivity of the Model Home 73

The Peculiar Exhibition may have been the most direct satire on the budding model-home idea at the exhibition, but in fact there were several other examples that we might call "special" forms of housing. In the market street Landskapsgatan, which ran parallel to the main set of buildings, there were booths representing goods from all of Sweden's regions. Among these one could find an unmarked, seemingly run-down structure called *Lustiga Huset*. This generic Swedish term for a fun house would also have

Det upp- och nedvända rummet i Lustiga huset.

Figure 6.3 *Lustiga Huset* (Fun House) at the 1909 Stockholm exhibition. *Aftonbladet*, 10 June 1909. (Caption reads: "The upside-down room in the Fun House.")

been used to describe that kind of attraction at a rural marketplace or fair, but the particular qualities of this fun house had extra resonance for visitors to a temporary housing exhibition such as this one. For one thing, the structure looked shaky—perhaps echoing background anxieties among the visitors about the flimsiness of the rest of the exhibition buildings? As one amused observer put it, "it is a mixture of different styles, yes such a mixture that one believes that it might all fall apart at any moment. But it holds up."[18] Another important point: the entry room of the house was upside-down, so that when one entered the structure one found a hanging lamp shooting up from the floor and furniture (and according to one account, a playful housecat) hanging down from the ceiling.

Further rooms in this fun house included one with a springy mattress for a floor, which apparently made the more genteel visitors squirm at the thought that they had stepped in something soft—perhaps another comment on the phenomenology of exhibitions, and the model home more particularly?—and a final room with a gallery of distorting mirrors. *Lustiga Huset* proved immensely popular and reportedly attracted 210,000 visitors that summer out of a total attendance at the exhibition of 767,400. Next to the dance floor, it was the most popular attraction of the entertainment district that summer.[19] The house in several ways served as the punch line for a joke about the model home, a joke set up precisely by the mode of temporary inhabitation of space, by the repeated entrances and exits made by viewers at the serious housing displays elsewhere in the exhibition.

Taken together, the varieties of "insider" experience in the entertainment district clearly functioned as counterpoint to the new housing environments built for serious exhibition. We might even be tempted to call them carnivalesque, following Bakhtin, if not for the fact that both the official displays and their inversions were designed and approved by the same governing board. If one of the associations with the idea of "participatory media" is a kind of unofficial play or self-determined use, a redirection of officially prescribed space, then these housing inversions might not qualify, since the amusement area was planned from the start as a playful comment on the main exhibits. Instead of improvised usage and empowerment, one finds in these housing "inversions" an indication of the endlessly recuperative power of consumer society to both expose and promote itself at the same time.

The combination of serious and amusing displays in 1909 underscores that this was indeed a housing *exhibition*, or rather, an exhibition on the *idea* and *possibilities* of housing. In the literal sense, the 1909 Stockholm Industrial Arts Exhibition featured the home interior and its practical possibilities. But it also featured a thoroughgoing and multifaceted enactment of the fundamental relationship between spectator and display space, and by extension, between inhabitant and home. By housing its spectators in the in-between space of the model home and the temporary exhibition, the exhibition may have planted the seeds of a different attitude toward housing, one that imagined home as a series of possibilities or alternatives instead of the traditional hearth alone. Many other social developments contribute to the diminished authority of the traditional home, to be sure, but one can see quite clearly how attendance at a model-home exhibition would reinforce and contribute to a sense of domestic contingency.

Loosened by this kind of play from more natural connections to domestic space—and again, even the model homes in the "serious" part of the exhibition could be considered a new form of role play—the visitor to this exhibition would first of all have been more favorably positioned as a potential consumer of new styles and interior design. This is the recuperative move that makes the consumer society so flexible and resilient. The appeal of this particular exhibition, that is, despite the presence of the two working-class model houses, was primarily directed at the middle class. It is especially telling that the drawings I have included here, when they show visitors at all, choose to imagine properly bourgeois spectators in respectable clothing. When confronted with the exhibition's homes in series and with the parodic inversions of housing, however, even the most middle-class visitor must have been stretched to adopt a more elastic relationship to the idea of alternative interiors.

On one level, of course, the simple act of attending a fun house would have been a toss-off moment of amusement that may not have created any lasting impressions, nor would it have been likely to translate into real social effects; it is, after all, important to retain a sensible sense of scale when speculating on the resonance of popular entertainment. On another level, however, this couple's depicted encounter with the upside-down room strikes me as evocatively paradigmatic, a concentrated expression of a fundamental shift in attitude toward the home in the early twentieth century. The exhibited house, that is, created a new set of looking relations that tested the givenness of the middle-class home by stressing the series of alternative forms an interior might take. The collateral effect might be a consciousness of one's own home as a model, to be seen from both inside and outside simultaneously, with endlessly rearrangeable furniture. This had the potential to create its own estrangement effects, not as conspicuous as those of the upside-down room perhaps, but worth consideration nevertheless. This attitude would only find further reinforcement in the increasing proliferation of housing exhibitions in the 1920s and '30s.

LIVING FICTIONALLY

Many of the subsequent housing exhibitions in Sweden continued to develop the techniques of contextualization, and by extension, of spectator performativity, although the displays of individual items continued side-by-side with the more "scenic" technique. In 1917, The Swedish Society of Arts and Crafts sponsored another large housing exhibition at Liljevalchs Art

Gallery in Stockholm, where some of the more famous Swedish functionalist architects like Uno Åhrén and Gunnar Asplund contributed model kitchen displays with more consistently simplified and practical design ideas. A series of annual exhibitions called *Bygge och Bo* ("Building and Dwelling," sponsored by the Stockholm Association of Building Engineers) followed in the 1920s, which brought construction professionals and consumers together in an ongoing education about modern housing possibilities. Not all of these exhibitions advanced the logic of immersion, and many took on the logic of a builder's fair instead, but by the mid-1920s, the idea of the model home was ready for the next conceptual step, the link with more wide-scale urban planning.

This final section of the chapter, then, will concentrate on a particularly interesting treatment of the model home, one that emerged from the *Bygge och Bo* exhibit outside Stockholm on the island of Lidingö in 1925. This exhibit took the step of creating actual model homes for sale in a centrally planned neighborhood built in a consistent style. This extended the model-home idea beyond the temporary arrangements of industrial exhibitions and their "airy construction" and opened out onto a more direct kind of model-home consumption that included the purchase of a particular housing site and neighborhood along with the home. The trend would continue; soon after the Lidingö exhibition, the Swedish housing cooperative HSB, which was founded in 1923, had its own exhibition of model working-class apartment buildings. These too were intended for actual sale after the exhibition in 1927. Both of these developments are again quite familiar to us today in the concept of model-home neighborhoods.

The intriguing consequences for spectators of this shift to model neighborhoods can be seen in a Swedish film made and shown at the time of the 1925 Lidingö exhibition. The film in question was a weekly newsreel filmed by Svensk Filmindustris Veckorevy (The Swedish Film Industry's Weekly Review) for release on 26 October 1925.[20] It was called *Så ska vi ha't!* (That's How We Want It!). This ten-minute silent film had its debut about a month after the close of the Lidingö exhibition (the housing exhibition ran from 28 August to 27 September 1925), so it is likely that it was filmed either during the exhibition or immediately thereafter, before the houses were sold to eventual buyers. That timing turns out to be important, because the charm of the film is that it manages an intriguing mix of factual presentation of housing features (not unlike a matter-of-fact inspection tour with a real estate agent) and a fictional simulation of the lives that could be lived out in the space. The model villas, that is, are populated for the purposes of the film as if every space were already inhabited and life were proceeding apace, and the film's hybrid mode thus falls somewhere between documentary and fiction.

The Lidingö exhibition itself was perceived to be perched on the cusp of actual inhabitation. The nineteen new villas, arranged in community relation to one another, were fully furnished and the gardens planted with new trees, but the overall impression visitors received was more one of potential future inhabitation. As one observer put it, "It will be very interesting to see the little town in a couple of years, which will only really exist when inhabited."[21] Another wrote, "All in all the little community seems unusually alive for a brand-new creation to which human habitation has not yet conferred its final patina."[22] Nevertheless, this was seen as something above and beyond the previous sort of model home: "On the other hand, how many of the visitors actually understand the worth of this unique exhibition, which does not have the provisional character of the usual show, but instead is already an actual community whose history has already begun, even if the tenants have not yet moved in."[23]

It is against the backdrop of many such comments that the narrative position of the newsreel film is so interesting, since its mixed mode carefully walks the line between rational design and inhabitation. It begins with a long shot of three women in modern clothing walking toward the camera down the main street of the Lidingö model neighborhood. In an intertitle, the women are named "Mrs. Landkvist, Lindkvist, and Lundkvist."[24] The naming of the characters creates the preconditions for a fictional situation, and the film then employs the visual language of continuity cinema to establish a set of intelligible spatial relations and a narrative situation, which is explained as that of three friends coming for coffee at the house of a Mrs. Lundin.[25]

After a brief depiction of a chat over coffee, an intertitle in Swedish announces, "Now it's time for a tour of the house, which the women start in the kitchen." The film then shifts to a very different mode, which is basically an analytic view of the house and its modern features, but still ostensibly couched in terms of a fictional character proudly showing her new place to her friends Mrs. Landkvist, Lindkvist, and Lundkvist. The film is especially charming for its pantomime of the different ergonomic features of the home (this was a silent film, so whatever information was not contained in the intertitles needed to be spelled out with gestures, physical demonstrations, and measuring sticks). Adding to the complex mode of address to the film viewer is the fact that the house does in fact seem to be fully inhabited; as we follow the tour group through the rooms, we find servants going about their business, children doing homework, even a baby in the bath—all the signs of routine family living. Interspersed with the apparent rhythm of daily life, however, are moments of analytic demonstration of the house's features.

Finally, at the end, comes the consumer moment as the film wraps up its little story. They have all returned to their coffee at the end of the tour, and the hostess Mrs. Lundin asks the group, "Now that we're away from the kitchen smoke, what do you think of our nifty living and dining rooms?" The final intertitle says it all: "That's what we want!" This is of course also the attitude cultivated by all model homes: the goal behind the whole enterprise is to convert the spectator into an actual consumer. This is where we

78 *Mark B. Sandberg*

see the morphological similarity with the IKEA ads mentioned at the beginning of this article: "That's what we want!" in this film is the same moment as the statement "We'll take it!" in those later advertisements.

But it is worth dwelling on the mode of this film's presentation just a bit longer. The impression one gets is indeed of a fully inhabited space, which of course it probably isn't—given the timing of the filming, less than a month after the model homes were closed to the public, I am guessing that all the people on this newsreel are to some extent acting and performing, from the kids to the servants to the next-door neighbors. They show us a provisional mode of dwelling, a performative inhabitation that *could be*, but is not yet. When the three women exclaim the film's title in unison at the end of the film ("That's the way we want it!"), they double over the potentiality of the inhabitation yet again, since in effect they as the fictional "guests" are convinced to aspire to live there like the other actor-inhabitants. This relation to the actual dwelling space is doubled over yet again for the film spectator, of course, whose virtual inhabitation of the image on screen is being relayed through the visit of Mrs. Lindkvist, Landkvist, and Lundkvist, who function as stand-ins and points of identification for the film spectator.

The makers of this newsreel could of course have simply made an actuality film instead, a sober documentary look at the Lidingö exhibition that presented the facts of the event and the detailed features of the houses. The fact that they are instead drawn into the fictional mode of presentation, or more accurately, into exactly the mode of participatory nonparticipation that typifies the model home experience more generally, is the best evidence of the appeal of this more modern kind of threshold participation. The consumer imagination is in this sense simply a special mode of living fictionally.

SPECTATOR-INHABITANT OR PARTICIPANT?

A final observation: when working with this kind of material, there is inevitably a bit of a struggle to find the right terminology to describe the person who encountered these model-home displays, because each term entails its own methodological frame. The words "spectator" and "viewer" borrow from visual media like film and television; "visitor" works well for museum studies; "consumer" or "shopper" calls up a method of economic analysis. Which of these does the model home have: spectators, visitors, or consumers? Perhaps we need a combined term like "spectator-inhabitant"?

Given the theme of this anthology, it is clear that I should give another term a try: how about "participant" instead? What happens to the spectator-inhabitant when conceived in that way? If it seems slightly odd to use that word, perhaps the semantic mismatch can tell us something about both model homes as a historical practice and about what might be hiding behind the term "participation" as a concept. Within the context of the model home, I think we would have to give up any utopian assumptions about participation as empowerment, because the recuperative power of the eventual moment of sale limits much of the dynamic of performativity and fantasy inhabitation that goes on before that point. But of course, only one person ends up the owner—only one ends up with the lottery villa. What about all that excess imaginative activity from the ones who didn't end up buying but for a moment imagined living there nonetheless? What about all those in-between modes of inhabitation that do not get recuperated for the sale, or the sort of spontaneous participant play that rose up around Mark Malkoff's IKEA stunt? The ability to "play house," in all of its extended cultural forms, has clearly become part of the modern consumer repertoire without necessarily becoming entirely purposeful. Some of it simply creates a sense of housing contingency, of a series of possibilities somewhere in the margins of the imagination.

Still, calling a visit to a model home "participatory" puts pressure on the utopian assumptions hiding in that word. If closer analysis of the phenomenon of model housing encourages us to examine the margins between terms like "spectator," "inhabitant," and "participant," it also helps us recognize the fallacy of imagining purely "redemptive" modes of reception solely in terms of agency and empowerment. True, in the Malkoff performance at IKEA, participatory play broke out within the universally standardized IKEA interior and could be promoted by Malkoff as a sly exaggeration of a universal consumer desire. At the same time, however, his performance could at some level be recuperated by the store as a marketing ploy. Even if modern consumer culture locates itself somewhere between imaginative play and prescribed response, the boundaries are nevertheless given ones.

NOTES

1. Anderson is the director of such films as *Rushmore* (1998), *The Royal Tenenbaums* (2001), and more recently, *The Darjeeling Limited* (2007). "IKEA: Kitchen" can be viewed at <http://www.boardsmag.com/screeningroom/commercials/534/>, and "IKEA: Living Room" at <http://www.boardsmag.com/screeningroom/commercials/533/> (both accessed 26 March 2010).
2. L. Lazare, "IKEA Makes Argument," *Chicago Sun-Times*, 14 November 2002.
3. Online. Available HTTP: <http://www.marklivesinikea.com/> (accessed 26 March 2010).
4. S. Cunningham, dir., *Mark Wakes Up in IKEA* (2008). Online. Available HTTP: <http://www.marklivesinikea.com/> (accessed 26 March 2010).
5. M. Dworkin and S. Cunningham, dirs., *Mark Moves into IKEA* (2008). Online. Available HTTP: <http://www.marklivesinikea.com/> (accessed 26 March 2010).
6. M. Hesse, "No Assembly Required: For Ikea's Live-in Weblebrity, Reality Comes at a Discount," *Washington Post*, 17 January 2008.
7. E. Key, *Skönhet för alla: Fyra uppsatser* (Stockholm: Bonniers, 1899).

8. E. Stavenow-Hidemark, *Villabebyggelse i Sverige 1900–1925*, pp. 93–94.
9. "Den hvita staden," *Nya Dagligt Allehanda*, 4 June 1909. All translations are by the author, unless stated otherwise.
10. See, e.g., "Bör sommarstaden bevaras som Stockholms sommarpromenad för all framtid?" *Dagens Nyheter*, 16 June 1909; and "Skall den hvita staden bevaras?" *Nya Dagligt Allehanda*, 16 June 1909.
11. "Sommarstadens öde," *Dagens Nyheter*, 19 June 1909.
12. "En vandring genom utställningshallarna," *Svenska Dagbladet*, 4 June 1909.
13. "Konstindustriutställningen 1909," *Svenska Dagbladet*, special exhibition number, 4 June 1909.
14. "Från sommarstaden," *Dagens Nyheter*, 18 June 1909.
15. Ibid.
16. "Det lustiga på utställningen," *Svenska Dagbladet*, 6 June 1909.
17. Ibid.
18. "Utställningens nöjen," *Aftonbladet*, 10 June 1909.
19. U. Sörenson, *När tiden var ung*, pp. 403, 412.
20. SF catalogue no. 492, Department of Audiovisual Material, National Library of Sweden. The film is listed as no. 7 in the "Veckorevy" of 26 October 1925, with the catalogue title of "Hur vi bygga och bo." The title on the film material itself is "Så ska vi ha't!"
21. T. Hedberg, "Det gamla byalaget åter till heders," *Dagens Nyheter*, 19 September 1925.
22. "Ett blivande idyllsamhälle på Lidingön," *Svenska Dagbladet*, 18 September 1925.
23. N. Wohlin, "Lidingöutställningen: Planeringen," *Socialdemokraten*, 30 September 1925.
24. I have been told that this draws on a popular song of the period called "Kafferepet (Coffee Clutch)." My thanks to Ingegärd Stenport for pointing this out to me.
25. The woman of the house, Mrs. Lundin, is the real-life wife of the architect responsible for the Lidingö development, C. Lundin. It is possible that his family has already moved into one of the homes, but it couldn't have been much before the film was made since the public exhibition had just closed a month earlier.

7 Touring the Congo
Mobility and Materiality in Missionary Media

Lotten Gustafsson Reinius

Years before the methodological breakthrough of fieldwork and participant observation in anthropology, Protestant evangelists gathered data and objects of everyday life from throughout the world.[1] In fact national museums, in Sweden as well as other Western countries, largely depended on this group in the creation of their ethnographic collections. There was notable collaboration between the National Museum of Natural Science in Stockholm and missionary collectors, who in the wake of high European colonialism had established their field in lower Congo.[2] These autodidactic missionary ethnographers belonged to the Swedish Missionary Society, which was founded in 1878 through the unification of several smaller groups that shared a critical attitude toward the national church and a desire to connect instead with the transnational missionary movement.[3] Considering the thousands of masks, baskets, cooking utensils, items of clothing, ancestral sculptures, weapons, jewelry, and other objects missionaries acquired and brought back to Sweden around 1900, it is surprising that it took until 1918 before the board of the society requested similar things be gathered with an autonomous missionary museum in mind.[4]

The result was a traveling "missionary ethnographic exhibition" that started to roll in 1924 and toured the nation for over a decade and brought visual images and about one thousand artifacts from the missionary field in lower Congo to small towns and rural outposts throughout Sweden.[5] With this "Congo Bus" as the focus of my case study, I will devote the present chapter to missionary media strategies in a period of self-defined crisis. The analytical focus will be on conventions and techniques of exhibition that developed within the movement and which—as I will argue—differ significantly from equivalents in contemporary museums of ethnography. How should the systematized and laborious circulation of concrete things and images from geographically distant places be understood? What constituted the affective and moral power of the traveling exhibition to its temporary audiences? Raising questions like these, I also wish to contribute more generally to an understanding of the relationship between concrete exhibition techniques and the enrolment of participants in social movements.

82 *Lotten Gustafsson Reinius*

The participatory aspects of exhibitions are at the core of Tony Bennett's well-known analysis of the "birth of the museum."[6] Exhibitions that increasingly began to open their doors in European and American cities from the late nineteenth century, according to Bennett, played a crucial role in the development of the modern nation state.[7] New kinds of spaces were created: arenas where socially stratified crowds could blend and join in the shared visual pleasures of each other and the things on display; ordered and didactic choreographies that had both disciplinary and democratic potential while they disseminated grand narratives about national history, modernity, and civilization. Following Bennett, scholars of museology and media history have gone on to explore the political and cultural significance of the concrete ways in which bodies and objects have been brought together by the medium of exhibition.[8] Museologist Barbara Kirshenblatt-Gimblett, for instance, has claimed that differing techniques of display work as "powerful engines of meaning carrying their own messages."[9] Visual perspectives as well as physical relationships established between attractions and visitors may be understood as manners of evoking differing modes of perceiving, feeling, and acting in the world. In a discussion about the media landscape in which an international exhibition in Stockholm in

Figure 7.1 The "Congo Bus" offered its natural destinations not only a touch of distant lands, but also a temporary intrusion of urbanity and modernity. Published with permission of the Archive of Mission Covenant Church of Sweden.

1897 found itself, Anders Ekström explored the didactic roles of elevations of audiences in space, whereas I took an interest in the meanings produced through manipulations of size and scale.[10]

In addition to dichotomies of high and low, enlarged and miniaturized, I turn my attention toward other significant oppositions, equally extant in shifting, literal ways at exhibitions, namely, those of distance and nearness, stability and motion, the multisensory and the untouchable.[11] As far as the latter pair is concerned, a recent discussion on the problematic and colonial aspects of prohibitions against touching in museums provides a source of inspiration.[12] The main argument of this chapter is that the *literal circulation of tangible objects* was crucial to the Swedish Missionary Society as a communicative technique engaging emotions and minds as well as bodies and senses. In particular, I would argue that *mobility* and *materiality* played crucial roles in addressing audiences, imploring them to become publics, participating in the transnational Protestant movement, emotionally, spiritually, in word and in deed.

MEDIA STRATEGIES OF THE SWEDISH MISSIONARY SOCIETY

The first official head of information of the Swedish Missionary Society was appointed in 1918, motivated by the growing concern that people were losing interest in the missionary cause.[13] Missionary leaders were worried that not only were fewer young people heeding the call but also that those who did tended to be of the wrong (i.e., female) sex.[14] Such complaints were in tune with a more general contemporary discourse on the "regrettable" domination of women in church activities and the related, supposedly weakened image of Christ.[15] Facing the dual (and possibly interrelated) crises of undermined masculinity and waning public support, Missionary Society propagandists decided to stage—nationwide and systematically—a multimedia performance focusing on its prime missionary field.

At the time, the society had three "foreign fields"—Congo, Turkistan, and China.[16] It seems that a particular emotional quality was associated with "the Congo," generally perceived as the most primitive and heathen, its peoples sorely in need of gospel and guidance. Since its founding years, a sense of adventure and heroism lingered in the central African colony, which Stanley mortgaged and which later became more ill famed. Apart from glimpses of the Holy Land and from the institution in Stockholm where children of (absent) missionary parents were raised, the film that accompanied the traveling exhibition featured images from all three missionary fields. In its selection of artifacts, however, the focus on the Congo was total.

The Swedish Missionary Society secured autonomous status in the Congo by taking over the station Mukimbungu from the Livingstone Inland

Mission in 1884, just before the international authorization of the Congo Free State (1885–1908).[17] The colonial project of Belgian King Leopold II was somewhat unusual as a colony framed as international rather than national; the rhetoric stressed that it was open to beneficial work from all civilized nations. Together with military officers, business entrepreneurs, and merchant sailors, missionaries belonged to the two hundred or so Swedes who actively partook.

When the traveling exhibition was planned, the range and cruelty of labor exploitation of the Leopoldian regime had become infamous. Violence, social change, and the often-resulting death and misery had been so intense that certain missionaries believed the people among whom they worked would become extinct within a generation.[18] According to one contemporary voice, the "labor of converting Congolese" was likened to "giving the last anointment to a dying race."[19] Prophetic movements, inspired by Protestant Christianity but fuelled by nationalistic and countercolonial visions, left missionaries doubtful about whether they had failed or succeeded in their spiritual duty and also increasingly dubious in the face of the new colonial regime, who naturally favored Belgian Catholics. Powerful objects coveted by many ethnography collectors were burned en masse by pious crowds, perceived by colonizers as subversive.[20] The decision to create collections for the mission's needs in Sweden was praised as coming just in time, a statement that made sense not least in relation to the traumatized and turbulent Congolese field.[21]

Outfitting the Congo Bus was not the society's only strategic move during these years. It ran during a period when the centrally governed propaganda machine—aimed at combining its "domestic" mission with the "foreign" one—was the topic of heated debates, deliberate reorganization, and explorative development. Martin Westling, the head of information who had formerly edited the society's periodical *Missionsförbundet*, seems to have vigorously and inventively pursued his task "to awake and sustain interest and love for the foreign mission in the homeland."[22] In the years following his appointment, minister-led tours to congregations, Sunday schools, and youth organizations began to be planned centrally and more systematically. Verbal testimony delivered by the clerics was complemented and doubled through a variety of textual, visual, and material media. Funding was granted for several traveling libraries, aimed at spreading the growing library of missionary literature throughout the nation. This initiative was justified with reference to the advantages of the borrowed book. Not only could a book thus be attained by people with sparse means, it also remained in people's homes "performing its enlightening task" longer than a real, live preacher could.[23] Postcards were similarly handy by virtue of their ability to reach and address people both literally and personally. A number of new visual motifs were printed and distributed at this time, mainly illustrating nature, village life, and convert families in the missionary fields.[24] Small folders of photographical series—recommended as prizes in Sunday schools—allowed friends of the mission to own their own pocket-size version of places and people commonly and sentimentally referred to as "ours."[25]

The new propaganda machine thus built on established conventions but intensified and elaborated them while increasing their geographical dissemination. The attempt to reach out to many yet to be received—in accordance with the Protestant ideal of individual calling—personally and with intimacy and immediacy is reflected in many initiatives. The traveling exhibition, with its ambitious touring program and combination of tangible and visual evidence from the distant missionary fields, epitomizes this development. The only subsequent feature that seems to have outshone it in popularity was the tour by Jeremia Kibangu in 1929, which marked the society's fiftieth anniversary. To judge by the contemporary enthusiasm, he was not only a real, living Christian Congolese but also a charismatic and handsome man, smartly dressed and skillful at preaching. Schematically, the forms of representation thus moved toward a gradually heightened insistence on realism, mediated through physical encounters with tangible and full-scale materiality. The intimacy obtained with the distant missionary field and its inhabitants, however, was not entirely without its critics.

MOVING IMAGES AND TANGIBLE THINGS

In the founding years of the foreign mission, a traveling preacher would typically have been a missionary on temporary leave, following a rather spontaneous tour and equipped only with his verbal testimony and possibly one of the series of sciopticon slides provided by the society.[26] Around the turn of the century such a show could still attract a thousand-strong audience. According to one lyrical report from a "Congo evening" held in Gothenburg, the effect of a blinding point of light—created with the help of a dangerously flammable blend of gases—projecting images of "black people and small huts on the huge white screen" was stunning and impressive.[27] At the end of the First World War, however, voices were raised complaining about the outdatedness of such visualizations. "No matter how beautiful and illustrative they may well be," one man wrote after returning from a series of rather poorly attended missionary lectures, "people in the cities are no longer pleased with these [sciopticon images]. Even Christians today expect so-called 'moving images'."[28]

Before the 1920s, film had been regarded with general suspicion by the members of the society, who associated the medium with the frivolous and sinful pleasures of the movie house. The fact that the Congo Bus, along with its collection of objects and photos, also had cinematographic film on board reflects a more pragmatic attitude. As a crucial cog in the accelerating wheel of propaganda, the suspect reels could be morally recoded. In the 1920s, the society's board requested new missionary films to supplement the few earlier ones.[29] In the quest to be granted sanction to employ a formally despised technique, the Lord Himself could be drafted as a media-savvy propagandist:

> God is the truly great educator. He teaches through the mediation of both *eyes* and *ears*. As he wishes to give lessons to mankind about his great wisdom and omnipotence, he uses *lucid material*. *His* media, however, are the sun, the moon and the countless hosts of stars.[30]

Proponents praised the "reality" and "lifelikeness" of filmed scenes. Using a striking number of physical metaphors, one enthusiastic report stated that audiences "had been grasped, moved and stirred into a festive mood that compelled them also to compassionate and self-sacrificing good deeds."[31] However, even the most dedicated stressed the need for strict content control and an understanding of the media as the means toward a higher end. It was suggested that prayers, Bible readings, and psalm singing should be mandatory on movie nights—a strategy meant to reinforce the original framework of religious meeting instead of the threatening alternative: an evening of pure cinematic entertainment.[32] Obviously, the medium had to go through a process of domestication and careful reframing in order to be accepted.

One scene, considered "too wild for a Swedish audience" and thus cut from the original edition of Josef Öhrneman's film from the Congo, featured a bare-breasted woman engaged in ecstatic dance.[33] The fact that a still of her—cast in daylight—passed unadulterated illustrates that it was the motion—captured so suggestively—that was considered most problematic. Scenes illustrating mass baptisms and communions were also met with heated debate. One opponent argued that "sacred actions" like these ran the risk of attaining "entertainment value and a certain likeness to machines."[34] Generally, the praised "lifelikeness" seems to have become dubious when visualizing rituals: actions considered more evocative and spiritually transformative than others. It seems to have been the very efficiency of the medium—and its related capacity to make audiences participate emotionally in what unfolded on the screen—that was considered paradoxically a danger and an opportunity.

If this was the case with moving images, then what about the approximately one thousand tangible things, brought from a distant world to the immediate physical presence of exhibition audiences? Was there a similar concern about the presence of tools from domains considered foreign, dangerous, and even demonic? Among the many collectibles the bus featured were a number of objects formerly used to communicate with spirits. On display on boards and tablets, with numbers and hand-written texts attached, ritualistic objects such as ancestral Bakuta skulls and fierce-looking *minkisi* sculptures were obviously detached from their earlier contexts and turned into isolated still lifes. Yet their literal, material presence, within reach of curious hands and eyes, mediated the absent Congo as a full-scale and multisensory reality. A telling comment appeared in *Missionsförbundet*:

> A traveling museum—would it really be capable of bringing blessings and sacred impulses to the people of the mission? Church benches would be cleared away and our beautiful Sunday home would be filled instead with idols, poisoned arrows and the swords of executioners, calabashes used for palm wine and medicine bags. I was anticipating the ill-famed exhibition with a certain anxiety.[35]

Exemplifying a selected array of objects—in missionary circles connected with violent and sinful heathen life—the author was in fact only setting the rhetorical scene for a drastic twist. From the huge omnibus, at first glance reminiscent of a "gypsy's van"—a designation freighted with culturally dubious status in the contemporary rural landscape—emerged two "hearty and cheerful men."[36] Following this was a passionate report of the author's surprise and relief when he realized the wonderful potential of the exhibition these men unloaded from "ten huge boxes." The film brought the Congo—"the land of our youth's most beautiful dreams"—closer "in a wondrous way." Thanks to its striking realism, distant realms opened for imaginary physical participation: "We were present at the moment when missionaries arrived. We wandered by their sides, over hills that were flooded by sunlight."

According to this testimony, objects added to the affective possibility. The books on display "preach[ed] with force." Several people in the audience were moved to tears, and an old man gave thanks to the Lord aloud while walking among the "idols." The message is clear: The new realism that infused the missionary media contained not only threats but also, and more so, a wonderful and maybe even God-given participatory possibility. A church attendant even testified that the atmosphere during the stop in the small community Taberg was such that a kneeling prayer meeting would have felt entirely natural.[37]

ADDRESSING TWO AUDIENCES

The exhibition addressed a dual audience: grown-ups and school children. Established but allegedly fatigued "missionary friends" were to be strengthened in their resolve through testimonies of the efficacy of prayer and financial support. The second target group was the young, upon whom hopes for the future were forcefully projected during these years.[38] Whereas the ideal response from the adults would come in the form of continuing donations, the young, possessed as they were of boundless energy rather than wealth, were invited to participate and identify on another level. As mentioned, the recruitment of male missionaries was a particular concern; the staff of the touring exhibition was entirely male. A teen assistant and a driver usually accompanied an older missionary with field experience. It was probably up to the latter—whose weathered body not only mastered new media but had traversed seemingly fantastic distances in space, faced danger and evil in the name of God and returned to talk about it—to arouse a mimetic desire of heroic masculinity: the urge to become such an exemplary man.

Differing from contemporary museums, where recently established disciplinary borders between natural science and anthropology were carefully patrolled, the mission freely combined elements from nature with objects that more clearly belonged to the realm of culture. Among the approximate one thousand items on display were teeth and elephant tails, a hippopotamus' jaw, an entire immature crocodile, and antelope and leopard hides.[39] The semantic domain of the exotic and dangerous supported the frame of heroism and bravery and made missionaries stand out as triumphant conquerors of real, live lions and snakes as well as the fauna of biblical bestiary.[40]

Other objects on display were organized according to themes of everyday labor. The anthropologist Wilhelm Östberg, who has directed attention to the missionary movement's role in the dissemination of images of Africa in Sweden, also remarked that rural and working-class audiences

Figure 7.2 Hunting trophies on display at the exhibition infused the mission with adventure, exotic wildlife, danger, and bravery. Published with permission of the Archive of Mission Covenant Church of Sweden.

(who dominated the movement) were likely to have appreciated the technical skills reflected in Congolese crafts and tools.[41] The exhibition featured tokens of numerous practical activities including construction, carpentry, weaving, pottery, hunting, fishing, engraving, carpet-weaving, basket-braiding, cooking, and cultivation.[42] By far the most dominant category, however, was reserved for the domain of "heathen" spirituality. Together with tubes that contained edible insects, swatches of a funerary shroud, and a sword attributed to an actual executioner, they made up a kind of "chamber of horrors" that likely attracted and repelled at once. A drastic contrast was thus created between the familiar and likable and that which was perceived of as deeply problematic and foreign elements of a pre-Christian lifestyle. Entries with a more or less dubious status in this context included traditional clothing, body adornment, palm wine production, musical instruments, currency, customs, and cults.

A handwritten sign framed the exhibition as a presentation of "the primitive life of the Congo Negro."[43] The introductory remark in the catalogue referred to the Congolese as

> [a] deeply sunk people, with suffocated intelligence and misguided by lack of knowledge, superstition and sensuous desires . . . It has become clear that the only sufficient means to raise this people from its depressing state is the gospel of Jesus Christ. It is also through the power of this that they have been induced to send their gods here, to our homes, as greetings with a prayer for more evangelic messengers.[44]

Despite such echoes of evolutionism, the missionary media distinctly diverged from contemporary museums of ethnography in their representation of temporalities. Whereas regular museums tended to illustrate lifestyles of the Other as primitive and static, the missionary exhibition combined such imagery with proof of radical change and development.[45] Movies showed a series of scenes depicting lifestyles meant to be understood in this context as radically reformed.[46] Recurrent visual themes included dramatic landscapes, panoramic shots of missionary stations, group portraits of Swedish missionaries, and in particular, Congolese *crowds in motion* as they gathered at churches and outdoor masses. Energetic and orderly groups of converts were also shown performing the perfect symmetries of Swedish gymnastics, singing the Belgian national anthem to visiting colonial officers, and building brick walls and Western furniture with impressive speed. Such postures and atmospheres were conventional means of visualizing progress and modernity, but against the backdrop of "exotic and primitive Congo," new and vital meanings were added. A major rhetorical theme seems to have been the "blessings of missionary labor."

One category of objects that underlined this in particular was a display of Christian literature translated into Ki-kongo and examples of handwriting and Western-style crafts made by the children attending missionary schools.[47] The many Swedish pupils who visited the exhibition could compare their own work with that of Congolese boys and girls. Rulers and pen boxes, modeled on Swedish originals, invited recognition in multisensorial ways. It does not seem unlikely that a sensitive child felt curiosity and sympathy while touching familiar surfaces and structures, aware that these had been worked at for days by children of the same age. The impression of coming closer to people so far away was further strengthened by the convention of presenting the name and age of the individual students. A tag attached to a shirt with a decorative butterfly knot, for instance, stated that it had been sewn by "Yona Nciama in the second grade at Kinkenge missionary station."[48] Short pants made out of blue-and-white striped cotton had been produced by "Sebuloni Nzau in the fourth grade at Kinkenge School, the equivalent of the second grade in Swedish elementary school." Tellingly, individualization was restricted to the display of items attributed to the "new and better ways" of life. "Idols" and traditional crafts were arranged differently, usually in symmetrical decorative groupings accompanied by photographs of traditionally clad natives, and thus illustrated ethnic types rather than individuals. It was only through mastery of Western styles of

Figure 7.3 Artifacts associated with traditional lifestyles were grouped with photographs of unnamed people, an imagery that in accordance with contemporary visual conventions illustrated ethnic types rather than individuals. Published with permission of the Archive of Mission Covenant Church of Sweden.

life that the collectively conceived Congolese could be transformed into modern individuals and personalized fellow Christians.

Beyond all colonial and paternalistic logic, these missionary messages were broached in the context of contemporary racialist conceptions. In the late 1910s, an exhibition of "Swedish folk types" had toured the country and disseminated the dubious ideas of so-called "race biology," which at the time had numerous scientific proponents in Sweden. An elitist and urban voice from the 1920s could scoff at the educability of the African and refer ironically to Swedish missionary societies as organizations "for the equipping of naked negro children with pocket-size Bibles."[49] Audiences at the Congo exhibition could perceive not solely a self-congratulatory reflection of the Swedes as superior and beneficial donors, but also a highly contested vision of a world in which everyone had the capacity to embrace modernity.

MOBILIZING AUDIENCES INTO PUBLICS

The centralized plan for the traveling exhibition featured visions of "regular routes" and "systematically covered branches."[50] People throughout the length and breadth of the country were to be reached in a personalized and physically direct way. Advocates stressed the democratic potential of this format and contrasted it not only with earlier preachers' tours, which had tended to favor individual affinities, but also with modern museums that were exclusively fixed in major populations centers.[51] Whereas scientific fields had established their respective centers and identities and safeguarded these through the conservation of huge and mainly untouchable collections of objects, the missionary movement kept its own acquisitions in continuous motion and brought collectibles directly to people in small towns and rural peripheries.

The arrival of the Congo Bus at such a destination was a highly anticipated event, a sudden intrusion of the wondrous and exotic into everyday life. Prayer houses and church halls would be cleared, unwieldy screens and heavy objects set up, and projectors flickered in the dark, if only for a couple of evening shows and a few intense days.[52] Author Margareta Strömstedt captured the gradually intensifying excitement of a wide-eyed child sometime in the late 1930s in the Bible Belt of southern Sweden:

> Within only a few weeks something is going to arrive, more exciting than anything previously shown about the mission among heathens and life in Africa. First there are posters, depicting a bus about to come to the town and its surrounding villages. Inside this bus there is a huge collection of all the most remarkable things from Africa. There is even supposed to be a real boa constrictor in it, albeit not a living one. A famous missionary is driving around to missionary homes in the whole country, telling about Africa and showing all the secret treasures he has brought from there.[53]

This literary description conveys excitement and suspense but also hints at a sense of *communitas*, experiences of social bonds created by the awareness that the bus was making a tour that included several stops, uniting people and places likely to share such sentiments.[54] The mobile media not only bridged the distance between Congo and Sweden but also that between the various peripheries summoning the imagined community of the Swedish nation. Bringing literal objects, huge and heavy things from a distant continent around the whole country—using the automobile and the road network to reach places otherwise often considered insignificant—illustrated at once the growing potentials of modernity and the energies of religious calling.

It is telling that the transnational Protestant mission commonly referred to itself as a movement. Its rhetoric was infused with images of flows, streams, and rays: metaphors typical of the time but in this context distinctly colored by pious ideology. Since the ultimate mover was divine, the Christian Gospel was in continuous motion, impossible to stop. During the founding years of the society, a particular impetus had been the conviction that all the people in the world had to be reached by "the word" before the Second Coming of Christ. By the time the traveling exhibition was rolled out in the 1920s, a sense of having come closer to that point in time could clearly be discerned:

> The situation calls for the power of prayer from the united movement. The days of isolation are over, for all people. Nations have become connected as never before and ideas disseminate and blend without hindrance. Christianity is called to make its contribution in the power of the spirit of Jesus Christ.[55]

The missionary exhibition approached and engaged minds and bodies with imperative demands for individual responses. The realization of the literal flow of objects from an almost-mythical Congo to wherever home was in Sweden was intended to inspire a literal reciprocity, where spatial distance would be overcome and confirmed through other mutual exchanges. As pointed out by Marcel Mauss in his famous essay on the logics of the gift, he who has been offered something is also required to accept it and to repay the debt.[56] According to testimony, the exhibition indeed resulted in increased willingness to support the missionary project, not least financially.[57] Although it is possible that by giving their share people reaffirmed ideas of white superiority, they also united themselves with a larger, even global (and infinitely eternal) imagined community.

The revamped missionary propaganda machine counted on basic ritual behavior to compel its dual audiences to participate not only in the spectacle right before their eyes, but ultimately emotionally, morally, financially, and literally in the grand global mission. Its evocative play on distance and proximity, repulsion and intimacy was indeed likely to arouse religious sentiment. Mystical unions of polarities—as the divine and human in the figure of Christ—have been described as religious universals.[58] The mobile exhibition may be seen as a ritual performance of the theme of voids collapsing and remote entities uniting. According to the definition of anthropologist Roberto DaMatta, "to ritualize—just as to symbolize—is fundamentally to dislocate an object from its place."[59] DaMatta approaches ritual as a matter of concrete doing and making, rather than an established and definitive type of social action. He emphasizes the role of dislocation and passage, claiming that diverse forms of ritual travel are crucial to create the heightened and shared consciousness of symbolic meaning. As things or people move physically from one realm to another—for instance, as in processions or pilgrimages—awareness of differences and borders are paradoxically created and denied.

As already mentioned, the distances spanned by the traveling exhibition were perceived as spatial, temporal, and cultural at once. The very mobility of the exhibition and its material displays simultaneously highlighted and transgressed, confirmed and denied, the real and imagined spaces between Sweden and Congo, the Other and Us; the Congo Bus's motion in space was literal and allegorical. The circulation of Congolese objects in Swedish peripheries was crucial to the missionary medium and thus (in accordance with the classic statement of Marshall McLuhan) to its message.

The society's traveling exhibition expanded the missionary field and affected visitors by offering them virtual positions as idealized evangelists, able to experience the thrills of physical proximity to realms of reality otherwise deemed the epitome of difference and distance. It also allowed for participation in cathartic and emotionally charged moments when distances collapsed into the intimacy of human recognition. An imperative to participate actively lay not only in the selection of images and artifacts but also—and maybe even more forcefully—in the modes in which they were displayed and circulated. These objects had not been sought out by audiences, as when entering a regular, static museum, but had sought them out. And whereas regular museums generally prohibit touching exhibits, the audiences visited by the Congo Bus were free to examine the displays by hand. The tangible proxies of human encounter delivered by the traveling exhibition were handmade things, capable of eliciting imaginative intimacy and identification with their former producers and owners.[60]

CONCLUSION

One of the reasons the present anthology came into being was to offer historical perspectives on the participatory and political usages of so-called "new media." The case discussed in this article illustrates the early twentieth-century propaganda strategy of a grassroots-based social movement, one that lacked neither the utopian and apocalyptic visions nor the affective and moral fervor of today's active and politically informed internet communities. Despite the fact that the Swedish Protestant missionaries' traveling "ethnographic" exhibits confirmed Eurocentric ideas, it aimed at inspiring self-sacrificing involvement and belief in worldwide progress and (ultimately transcendent) connectedness. Hopefully, this particular foray into media history will shed some light on topical issues of interrelations between virtual presences in social media and the political ideals of engaged audiences and global citizenry.

Needless to say, the issue of "social presence" in telecommunications technology has been the subject of intense discussion since at least the mid-1970s.[61] Tearing our gaze for a moment away from the analytical seductions of diverse virtual realities created through digital interface to focus on more obviously resolute media situations that involved toting unwieldy equipment along dusty rural roads may expose us to surprising continuities. Employing a generous interpretation of the concept of "media" allows for an understanding of the mobile missionary exhibition as mixed social media whose techniques touched audiences affectively and morally by offering a kind of virtual presence of distant people and places.

As discussed earlier, the ideology of the Protestant Revival movement performed its visions and related imperatives through systematic and progressive media strategies and made use of several communicative techniques that were not uncontroversial in their day, such as the moving images of black and white film. In this chapter I have taken particular interest in the reliance on literal encounters between people and things. In the Congo exhibition, which toured the northern peripheries in a period of growing crisis in European colonial ideology, handmade things from far-off lands seem to have functioned as proxies for absent people, and thus as vehicles for encounters with and recognition of both foreignness and familiarity. It seems as though the affective power of the exhibition lay in the way in which mobility and materiality joined in mediating sentiments of global connectedness and messages of urgent need. The case of the Congo Bus thus reminds us of the inescapable materiality of media techniques, which also leads to the related theme of the social and cultural agency of tangible things.[62]

This article is the result of a research project on the roles and routes of Congolese objects in Sweden. It has been supported by the Bank of Sweden Tercentenary Foundation and Stockholm University.

NOTES

1. J. Fabian refers to missionary collecting and documentation activities as "proto-ethnography" in *Out of Our Minds*, p. xii.
2. L. Gustafsson Reinius, "Exhibiting the Congo in Stockholm," in S. Knell, A. Amundsen-Bugge, P. Aronsson, eds., *National Museums*. An earlier version was also published in C. F. Ax et al., eds., *Encountering Foreign Worlds*.

3. Its name was changed in 2003 to Mission Covenant Church of Sweden (*Svenska Missionskyrkan*).
4. Historian Leila Koivunen has informed me that the Finnish Missionary Society arranged a nationwide tour in 1911–12, with a traveling exhibition that featured Chinese and African objects. To judge by archival traces it seems that similar ideas were put into practice in Sweden around 1908 by the popular educational society *Folkbildningsförbundet*. See the inventory of "Traveling collection no. 1, from the Congo," archival collection of the Museum of Ethnography, Stockholm. In Britain, however, Protestant societies had already created autonomous missionary museums in the 1890s. See A. Coombes, *Reinventing Africa*, Chap. 8.
5. Lower Congo, a region mainly populated by Bakongo, is today divided between the two Congo states, République Démocratique du Congo and République du Congo. When I refer to places, people, and objects in this article as Congo/Congolese I am aware that this might be overly simplistic and politically sensitive. It is justified by the article's focus on the ways in which these entities were imagined and mediated to contemporary Swedish audiences in the historical situation described.
6. T. Bennett, *The Birth of the Museum: history, theory, politics* (London/New York: Routledge, 1995).
7. Ibid., 60.
8. For example, B. Kirshenblatt-Gimblett, "Objects of Ethnography," pp. 17–78; M. Sandberg, *Living Pictures, Missing Persons*.
9. B. Kirshenblatt-Gimblett, *Destination Culture* (see note 8 for cross-reference to the bibliography), p. 157.
10. A. Ekström, "Det vertikala arkivet," pp. 275–308; and L. Gustafsson Reinius, "Förfärliga och begärliga föremål," pp. 83–124.
11. In this chapter attention is mostly paid to the roles of mobility. For a discussion of the opposite but symbolically related *retardation* of Congolese objects in Swedish museums, see L. Gustafsson Reinius, "Innanför branddörren."
12. E. Edwards, C. Gosden, and R. Phillips, eds., *Sensible Objects*.
13. Minutes of board meetings 29 November and 2 December 1918, Swedish Missionary Society Archives, National Archives, Stockholm (hereafter cited as SMSA).
14. J. Lundahl to J. Nyrén, 19 November 1918, concerning the appointment of a head of missionary propaganda, in minutes of the SMS working committee, 29 November and 2 December 1918, appendix no. 10, SMSA.
15. Cf. Y. Werner, ed., *Kristen manlighet*.
16. Their first, later to be abandoned, foreign (*sic!*) mission was directed at the Sámi population in northern Sweden.
17. The society's activities were concentrated on areas in lower Congo, moving from the outlet of the Congo River and the region just south of it, up to the location of Brazzaville. The first stations were founded in the former Congo Free State, but after the Belgian take over in 1908 the Swedish missionary field also expanded over the Congo River and into the southern regions of the former French colony.
18. K. Laman, *Några drag ur Kongofolkets lif från Svenska missionsförbundets arbetsfält i Kongo* (Stockholm: Svenska missionsförbundet, 1907), p. 56.
19. S. Hede, "Kongofolkets framtid," *Ansgarius* (1926), pp. 36–44. All translations are by the author, unless stated otherwise.
20. E. Andersson, *Väckelse och andra kristna folkrörelser i Kongo*.
21. M. Westling, "Hur vi arbeta för att i hemlandet väcka och stärka missionskärleken," *Ansgarius* (1919), p. 23.
22. J. Lundahl to J. Nyrén.

23. Minutes of the board, 16–17 October 1918, attachment 37, SMSA.
24. Wilhelm Östberg has pointed out that the visual conventions of the missionary movement differed significantly from contemporary erotic and exotic photography; see W. Östberg, "Brotherhood or Masquerade? Interpreting Missionary Narratives from the Congo," unpublished paper for the conference "Aesthetic and Epistemological Traces of Congo: Art, History, and Popular Culture in Central Africa," Oslo, 14–16 September 2007.
25. Advertisement for such a series in *Missionsförbundet* (1929), p. 112. On rhetorical usages of miniatures within the mission, see L. Gustafsson Reinius "Förfärliga och begärliga föremål," pp. 22–25.
26. M. Westling, "Hur vi arbeta."
27. J. Öhrneman, *Perspektiv från Kongo*, pp. 7–8.
28. A. Wandel to the SMS board, 28 May 1919, appendix to minutes of the board, 29–30 June 1919, SMSA.
29. In the case of the Congo, this task was given to missionary Josef Öhrneman who worked with the shooting for about four months in 1926–27. Filming had previously been done by Johan Hammar, an early missionary ethnographer who also created huge collections of artifacts, housed today in national museums in Gothenburg and Stockholm.
30. K. Engdahl, "Filmen i missionens tjänst," *Ansgarius* (1926), pp. 107–14.
31. Ibid., 106.
32. Ibid., 114.
33. J. Öhrneman, *Perspektiv från Kongo*, p. 70.
34. P. Selén, "Vår missionsfilm," *Missionsförbundet* (1927), p. 469.
35. E. Rimmerfors, "Bland avgudar och palmvinskalebasser," *Missionsförbundet* (1929), p. 117.
36. Ibid., 118.
37. Ibid.
38. The connection between children and utopian visions also rose to the surface in other contemporary media events, for example, in the milk campaigns (see Y. Habel's contribution to this volume) and in radio programs for (and by) children in the 1930s; see A.-L. Lindgren, "Att ha barn med är en god sak."
39. C. Börrisson, *Katalog och beskrivning över Sv. Missionsförb. Missionsetnografiska vandringsmuseum från Kongo* (Malmö: Sv. Missionsförbundet, 1925), pp. 73–75.
40. A similar, equally tactile and visual reference is exemplified by the paper covers of the pocket-size series of photographs, which imitated snake skin.
41. W. Östberg, *När Afrika kom oss nära*, pp. 18–20.
42. C. Börrisson, *Katalog och beskrivning*.
43. Object no. 1954.1.2294, Museum of Ethnography, Stockholm.
44. C. Börrisson, *Katalog och beskrivning*, p. 3.
45. J. Fabian, *Time and the Other*.
46. For this chapter I have only worked with the scenes filmed by Öhrneman that depict the Congo. A comparison between the visual conventions of differing fields is a task for the future.
47. The following examples are found in collection 1954.1, Museum of Ethnography, Stockholm. This donation was made from the Swedish Missionary Society to the museum when the traveling exhibition had stopped running. Such objects have been labeled by the museum as "items of the mission."
48. Object no. 1954.1.288, Museum of Ethnography, Stockholm.
49. Kurt Atterberg to Moses Pergament, quoted from P. Garberding, *Musik och politik i skuggan av nazismen*, p. 178.
50. Minutes of the preparatory committee, 29 November and 2 December 1918, appendix 10, SMSA.

51. M. Westling, "Missionsförbundets vandringsmuseum och missionsfilm," *Missionsförbundet* (1928), p. 747.
52. In general, stops lasted four to five days. For example, a schedule in *Missionsförbundet* (1929), p. 199, mentions Tibro 18–24 March, Skara 2–7 April, and Lidköping 4–8 April.
53. M. Strömstedt, *Julstädningen och döden*.
54. V. Turner, *The Ritual Process*.
55. "Årsberättelse för Svenska Missionsförbundet 1924," p. 16, Archive of Mission Covenant Church of Sweden, Stockholm.
56. M. Mauss, *The Gift*.
57. E. Rimmerfors, "Bland avgudar," p. 117 (see note 36).
58. M. Eliade, *The Sacred and the Profane*.
59. R. DaMatta, "Carnival in Multiple Planes," p. 214. Ritualized dislocation is also discussed by V. Turner in *Dramas, Fields, and Metaphors*, in particular Chap. 5.
60. J. Feldman, "Contact Points," pp. 245–68; C. Classen and D. Howes, "The Museum as Sensescape," p. 202.
61. J. Short, E. Williams, and B. Christie, *The Social Psychology of Telecommunications*.
62. Recent social and cultural theory features a number of interesting attempts to highlight and theorize the active role of objects and materiality. For references only within the field of anthropology, see D. Miller, ed., *Materiality*; A. Henare, M. Holbraad, and S. Wastell, eds., *Thinking Through Things*.

8 Say Milk, Say Cheese!
Inscribing Public Participation in the Photographic Archives of the National Milk Propaganda

Ylva Habel

The cultural currency of milk and its advertising has been, and continues to be, invested with deeply symbolic values that interweave images of agrarian, domestic, and national virtues. In contemporary advertising discourse, it remains a vital component of the ongoing narrative of Sweden's tranquil, pastoral past of small-scale farming—a narrative of steady and benevolent growth, unbroken by the country's late industrialization. Seen in the context of local and national dairy production, it speaks of hygiene, civilization, and rationality, and is mobilized as an emblem of mercantilist-nationalist pride and protectionism. For example, although Swedish consumers welcomed cheese and yoghurt from international markets with open arms, they adamantly rejected milk.[1] Placed within the familial realm, milk is associated with innocence, altruism, mothering, and nurturing; connected with the more vaguely defined domain of the social, it articulates the normality and stability of Swedish everyday housekeeping and meals ranging from the sturdy breakfast to the late-night snack straight out of the refrigerator. Until the discovery of lactose intolerance and the problematic of milk fat, there was no question about it: Milk was good for you.[2]

However, the cultural ascendancy of milk to one of the cornerstones of Western modernity's public health effort has entailed much negotiation about its nutritional or detrimental effects. In her sociological study *Nature's Perfect Food: How Milk Became America's Drink*, Melanie DuPuis follows the discursive transformation of milk from tubercle-infected "white poison" in the nineteenth century to the epitome of public good in the 1920s.[3] She points to four promotional strategies through which milk became associated with perfection and progress. First, by the depiction of "particular ways of life as perfect . . . and alternate ways of life as degenerate." Second, she claims those involved in the production of milk were canonized as "champions of progress." The third tactic highlighted the technology used in milk processing—and made milking machines and cream separators iconic benchmarks of progress. Last, she mentions a "thinking by graph" logic, whereby social dynamics and human action were subsumed in a narrative of impersonal forces striving toward a "perfect goal."[4]

DuPuis richly exemplifies how the U.S. public was targeted with these types of representations and draws attention to the ways in which the National Dairy Council mobilized both eugenics and nationalist sentiment in its advertising. She argues that the idea of the human body as perfectible, and of milk as the perfect food to promote this perfection, had in turn significant ramifications for imagining the progression of a perfectible society.[5] However, even if she highlights representations of ideal embodiment in milk-promoting contests and campaigns, she fails to consider the audience to which this discourse was addressed.[6]

In this chapter, I would like to elucidate the marketing strategies that the Swedish equivalent, the Milk Propaganda (1923–72), used to engage and mobilize its audiences, mainly with examples taken from the organization's own photographic documentation. During its interwar heyday, the Milk Propaganda aspired to increase milk consumption by mobilizing and depicting public participation in its promotions on a massive scale. The organization launched multifarious events via several media events, including Milk and Cheese Weeks, that entailed elaborate strategies for enthusing and activating Swedish audiences, school children in particular.[7] In the organization's current photo archives, a specific genre of images depict publics visibly committed to milk drinking—documenting their almost ritually performed gestures of joyous affirmation. These photographs, taken for both advertising and archival purposes, employ a repeated visual rhetoric by showing an amassment of milk bottles and milk drinkers, offset like ornaments by specific aesthetic and perspectival techniques. Taking my departure from the organization's intermedial promotion, I will discuss the visual rhetoric used to engage and represent mass audiences as active resources in these contexts.

THE MILK EVENT

Writing about media and media events involving audience participation partly requires analyses that renegotiate the relationship between micro and macro perspectives on history. In the interview "Questions of Method," Michel Foucault advocates the analytical strategy of "eventalization" as a way of breaking historical objects away from their given historical period in order to reconsider their meaning.[8] In accordance with his earlier critical arguments on historiography in *The Archaeology of Knowledge*, Foucault indicates the importance of resisting the impulse to link the event to causal chains of explanation; instead, he asks us to pay closer attention to the inner relationships of meaning established in relation to "a multiplication of analytical salients."[9] "As a way of lightening the weight of causality," he continues, "'eventalization' thus works by constructing around the singular event analyzed as process a 'polygon' or rather a 'polyhedron' of intelligibility, the number of whose faces is not given in advance and can never properly be taken as finite."[10] Foucault's call for eventalization is a strategy for weaving new or alternative signifying aspects into the fabric of historiography.

In a similar vein, historical research on "new media" often takes its impulse from a polygonic perspective on Western modernity, exemplifying how cultural meaning is negotiated through specific media and their immediate context of cultural critics, users, and audiences. These often archaeological approaches offer new perspectives on power and social change by virtue of their thick description of the material aspects of discursive formation. Lisa Gitelman and Geoffrey Pingree offer a useful reminder of media's unavoidably constitutive role in articulating epistemology and authority vis-à-vis their audiences and the ways in which media more generally are part and parcel of the social. They advocate analyses based on the understanding that "communication *is* culture . . . a cultural process that involves not only the actual transmission of information, but also the ritualized collocation of senders and recipients."[11] The Milk Propaganda's promotional strategy can be taken as a case in point, as it attracted and mobilized its constituency through a governmental media interface that fused media production and public reception. Through the extensive photographic documentation of public milk campaigns, the organization chronicled its own success.

Up to the beginning of the twentieth century, Swedish rural society had considered the drinking of fresh milk as squandering a dairy resource that could be put to better use in more durable products like cheese, butter, and sour milk. Milk was also a handy household remedy instilled with magical healing powers.[12] One of the early, socially informed strategies to promote milk—and reduce the rampant consumption of alcohol—was to install warm milk "automats" in public spaces in Stockholm during the winter of 1902. These milk stands, invented by Valborg Ulrich, were set up in six downtown squares where saleswomen dispensed a quarter of milk to each customer "as hot as it could possibly be had."[13]

According to the Milk Propaganda's own celebratory history, the organization's constitution, composed in late 1922, had "not come about under . . . coincidental circumstances" but as a "natural consequence of the results reached by modern nutritional physiology concerning the foodstuffs most suitable to man."[14] International vitamin research, they claimed, had found that milk products were universal remedies to the widespread malnutrition that followed the First World War. Most important, as Jenny Lee argues, the Swedish milk industry experienced a deep downturn during this period and needed to mobilize all the major actors on the market.[15] Inspired first by its American predecessor, the National Dairy Council, and later by the German, state-driven Reichs Milch Ausschuß, the Milk Propaganda set out to raise the health standards of the Swedish populace through multifarious information and advertising strategies aimed at both consumers and producers. The nonprofit organization, headed by John Scharp (1923–28), was founded in collaboration with the Federation of Swedish Farmers, businessmen, and sundry authority figures; it later came to include an interdisciplinary constellation of landowners, MPs, dairy consultants, veterinarians, professors, chief medical officers, and senior schoolmasters. The general outline for the elaborate local campaigning activities were laid down in 1925, its guiding principle being the creation of intimate networks of local organizations which, in turn, would attract members from all parts of the dairy chain: consumers, local producers, farmers and agrarian clubs, milk and dairy shops, and industry. Additionally, the organization developed collaboration and advertising programs that established networks that extended into both municipal and private sectors to contact schools, hospitals, child care and welfare institutions, housekeeping societies, housewife organizations, milk inspection societies, and individual local lecturers.[16] Within and across all these intermeshed local contexts, the Milk Propaganda magnanimously disseminated information and advertising material with the threefold purpose of elevating product quality, food habits, and sales. A broad variety of brochures, pamphlets, and posters educated farmers regarding milk hygiene and consumers regarding milk production and nutrition.

Starting in the mid-1920s, the Milk Propaganda's local or national Milk or Cheese Weeks became recurrent events that targeted both the farming community and general audiences with multimedia milk promotion, including exhibits, lectures, radio chats, and starting in 1928, film screenings.[17] Often, these campaigns entailed various forms of interaction, such as window display contests for cheese shops. A special section concentrated on school children and gave "milk lessons" in elementary schools, often combined with screenings either on-site or at a nearby cinema.[18] Such events were framed by scripted, creative activities for the children, including drawing and essay contests. Through these mixed-media strategies, which involved various forms of documented consumer participation, and their benevolent reception by the press, the organization garnered considerable attention.

When the Milk Propaganda celebrated its success in 1933, it boasted that it had come a long way, yet acknowledged that much remained to be done. Even if the broad public now recognized the nutritional value of milk, it still did not consider milk to be part of a daily diet. Similarly, it complained that cheese was regarded a delicacy rather than as "the inexpensive food it really is."[19] Throughout the decade, therefore, efforts were steadily increased to expand the organization's vast and tightly knit media interface.

MILK GOVERNMENTALITY

In Swedish research, discussions about the political processes of modern welfare and public health is often closely linked to the logic of state initiative.²⁰ Regarding the Milk Propaganda from the perspective of eventalization, I would argue, foregrounds the organization as one of several historical agents contributing to materializing welfare principles before the Social Democratic Party's rise to power. In these contexts, media-intensive, material practices were important instruments for politically independent individuals and organizations who, for example, used exhibitions of electrification technology, home furnishing, and architecture as strategic tools for gaining concrete visibility and authority on social issues. Standing in dialogical, but not symmetrical, relation to verbal discourse or policy making, media events staged images of modernity and progress before their realization.²¹

During its first decade, the Milk Propaganda quickly established communities of consumers through media-intensive campaigns. Following international predecessors, the organization mobilized and enveloped target audiences with what could be likened to governmental rhetoric. Michel Foucault defines government as the "conduct of conduct," meaning that governing others is learned and practiced through the self-control that goes into acquiring the status of autonomous subjecthood. Government, in this respect, is not first and foremost about politics proper, but about the art of government in itself. Foucault's conception of governmentality sheds light on both the specific forms of rationality that are used and invested with truth-values, and the technologies of power that become instrumental for agents and institutions involved in the process of providing a given or chosen public with guidance and education. In an interview entitled "The Ethic of Care for the Self As a Practice of Freedom," he emphasizes how individual liberty and subjectivation processes propel and are propelled by power relationships.²² In his reading of Foucault, Thomas Lemke speaks of "'empowerment' or 'responsibilization' of subjects, which forces them to 'free' decision-making in fields of action."²³

Similarly, I would claim that the relationship the Milk Propaganda attempted to establish with milk producers and consumers was aimed at inscribing an individualized, binding "ethics of care for the self" through participatory technologies energetically employed to induce farmers to perfect their milk, and consumers to perfect their bodies by drinking it.²⁴ Adapting the eugenic rhetoric of the American National Dairy Council, the Milk Propaganda promoted milk not only as the road to health but by metonymy—as health itself. These slogans from the 1920s were later recycled or rearticulated in new constellations for the purpose of creating recognition, involvement, and reflexivity among target groups.

One such example was the long-lived narrative of the Milk Boy, the Coffee Boy, and the Meat Boy that appeared in various forms, often in pamphlets targeting a juvenile audience. The characters generally appeared as a triptych of images, circulated on posters or placards or produced locally as drawings or paintings during campaign weeks. Speaking with Foucault, each boy was depicted as epitomizing a specific "nature" with racially coded looks, the tell-tale signs of their respective dietary habits. A photograph from the mid-1920s shows a truck decorated with large placards that read "The Milk Boy—Healthy, Strong"; "The Meat Boy—Fat, Dumb"; and "The Coffee Boy—Pale, Skinny." The first boy is blond and athletic; he gazes out of the picture with a sunny smile and offers an oversized glass of milk to the spectator. The two other, darker boys are depicted in profile, sullenly eating and drinking their inadequate foodstuffs.

During Milk Weeks in various parts of the country, it was primarily the Milk Boy and the Coffee Boy who played opposite each other to encourage increased milk-drinking among the public. In locally arranged exhibits and temporary milk bars, their images served as pedagogical backdrops and frameworks for various pro-milk or pro-cheese slogans. The extensive documentation of these events, moreover, shows that the local reception and production of advertising material were closely enmeshed. Here and there, local organizers produced their own images of the Milk and Coffee Boys that offered vernacular interpretation of how their respective health/race profile should be visualized. A case in point is the Coffee Boy painted for a Milk Week display in Norrköping in the mid-1920s. In accordance with the Milk Propaganda's increasingly popular advertising script, he is depicted as a sickly, skinny boy, slumped on a chair over his coffee cup; he may even appear to be dying. His face is prematurely aged and browned, and his large, drooping dark eyes look pleadingly at the spectator. The strong, flaxen-haired Milk Boy, in contrast, basks in the sun, playing with his dog. He would later reappear as the champion of sports in other narratives for children.

In several ways, the Milk Propaganda and its marketing strategy entailed constituting a demarcated, active public out of a more general audience of different ages and levels of milk-specific expertise. Borrowing Michael Warner's formulation, specific segments of the audience came together as a public by "virtue of being addressed."[25] School children, housewives, and milk farmers, regarded as in particular need of education, were those most frequently featured in and addressed by the organization's campaign material, especially the commercial/educational films. Some time after the release of the Milk Propaganda's first film, *Mjölken, dess skötsel och värde* (The Value of Milk and Its Care, 1928), a pamphlet was published addressing the issue of mobilizing the interest of both consumers and farmers in one and the same film (regarding this short as a first attempt to cater to both audiences).[26] In fact, several of the subsequent films' narratives would retain their multiple address, intermixing selling and nutrition arguments addressed to consumers with professional "quality propaganda" for farmers. More or less consistently, the organization reiterated its narrative about the development of industrialized dairy production; most of the films of the mid-1930s recycle footage from earlier ones, showing again and again the

104 *Ylva Habel*

transformation from manual to industrial work.²⁷ The narratives recurrently bridged the gap between milk farmers, dairy workers, and consumers by bringing them into the same frame, letting one visit the realm of the other. These were highly pedagogical scenes, wherein farmers taught youngsters or children about the nutritional value of milk, or farmers

Figure 8.1 Drawing contest brochure for depicting the Milk Boy and Coffee Boy: "The Milk Boy is healthy and strong, the Coffee Boy weak and fragile." *Meddelanden från Mjölkpropagandan* 3, no. 2 (1926).

themselves received advice from experts and dairy workers on how to raise the hygienic standard of their product. The Milk Propaganda's "ethics of care for the self" in these films invoked an ideal collective of healthy, responsible, and hygiene-conscious individuals.

Over time, some of the films offered an interface of elements from other media events that audiences could easily identify since they had been familiarized with them through milk lessons, the Milk and Coffee Boys, and the narrative of hygienic milk production. In its annual report to the board, the Milk Propaganda included summaries of how many Swedish children it had reached. According to its own records, in 1928 54,000 drawing contest brochures featuring the Milk and Coffee Boys were distributed to school children. Every day, an average of 250 children became more "closely acquainted" with them in this way, while about 50 youngsters a day were assigned to write essays about them in school.[28] A new record was set in 1935, when the school campaign reached 33,400 children via lectures combined with film screenings (where refreshment was offered in the form of a bottle of milk per head), milk lessons, brochures, and essay contests.[29] During the summer of 1937, yet another implement was added to its propaganda arsenal: a megaphone-equipped Milk Propaganda bus that toured southern and central Sweden.[30] This rolling "milk bar" was covered with billboards and served milk to a total of 120,000 souls. Those who gathered were treated to a paper cup of fresh milk and live entertainment, interspersed with brief gramophone-recorded lectures.[31] The tactic of communicating the virtues of milk by "going places" was intensified across all the media mustered toward the end of the decade; a case in point is the film *Studieresan* (The Study Tour, 1938), directed by Kaj Tenow, wherein a group of farmers' wives tour farms in the neighboring countryside to learn the principles of modern milking hygiene. The organization also entered into a dialogue with public service broadcasting, such as the series "The Radio Farm," where recurrent "microphone visits" were made.[32]

INSCRIBING/DEPICTING THE PEDAGOGY OF SIMULTANEITY

Michael Warner claims that a public is characterized by its relative abstraction from the mass of embodied individuals who constitute it. Being able to say both "'The text addresses me' and 'It address no one in particular,' is a ground condition of intelligibility for public language," he argues.[33] Although the same applies to the Milk Propaganda's constituency, its embodied individuation is drawn into focus through its material engagement with a foodstuff promising to reform body and intellect. In the following, I will exemplify how such a relationship could be staged during milk events.

Before turning to the Milk Propaganda's photo collection, which harbors a mass of images that depict public participation in milk events, something should be said about the organization's iconographic documentation of its campaigns. The archives amply show that promoters strongly believed in the power of the image, not only in conjuncture with other representations, but also as visual memento. Significantly, these photos, most of them taken in the 1920s and '30s, evidence an intermedial understanding of archival usage, employed on varying communicative and accumulative levels. The organization extensively documented the many other media used in its campaigns—the posters, the window displays, the sandwich-board men, the advertising trucks, and the many local stops made by the touring bus—for documentation purposes, to illustrate their monthly journal, and to gather raw material for future advertisements.

Apart from recording the many and varied ways local milk promotion was carried out and staged during milk weeks, school events, and exhibits, the multitudinous images say something about what Lisa Gitelman and Geoffrey Pingree call "the ritualized collocation of senders and recipients" in these contexts. Out of all these photos, I concentrate chiefly on those that depict and document film screenings and their frameworks. It can be observed in this rich material that the Milk Propaganda adhered to specific staging strategies for presenting and offering milk products to (primarily juvenile) audiences. Regardless of occasion and target group, promotional events were arranged to orchestrate audience participation in such a way so that the viewing and listening experience also involved a simultaneous, performative enactment of its reformed food habits. In late fall of 1924, the Milk Propaganda participated in the Martinmas exhibition at Liljevalchs Art Gallery in Stockholm. A temporary milk bar was mounted and school children were invited to receive milk lessons on site. All in all, about 3,000 children from the Stockholm area attended these events, which were staged according to this particular pedagogy of simultaneity. The children were each treated to a bottle of milk and a cheese sandwich, and while enjoying these, they received a lecture on the values of milk. A photograph of the event shows a large group of children sitting with their backs to the camera, milk bottles in hand, attentively watching the lecturer, who points at images of the Meat, Milk, and Coffee Boys. Another photograph taken in a movie theater in Stockholm about ten years later shows girls drinking milk in the foreground while the boys in the background raise their bottles in a salute to the camera.

Three compositional devices quickly became formulaic to this unique photographic genre. First, the staging of milk bottles, which were either placed in a central position or arranged as a depth-focus accentuating, mass-ornamental framework. Second, much care was taken to feature as many of the children on-site as possible in at least one of the images captured. This photographic aesthetic could be regarded as a doubly inscriptive practice whereby the Milk Propaganda celebrated the success of its

Say Milk, Say Cheese! 107

Figure 8.2 Milk lesson for school children at Liljevalchs Art Gallery, 1924. Courtesy of the National Library of Sweden.

event as it simultaneously rounded up and made a claim on the bodies won over to milk. The third compositional device was the accentuation of the whiteness of both the milk and its consumers by daylight techniques that gave the depicted spaces and faces a glorified shimmer.

Additionally, several of the photos that were staged to communicate the virtues of milk inscribe a choreography of spontaneously enthusiastic responses. Regardless of the fact that several of the images were taken by local photographers, and that this particular aesthetic is not mentioned in the organization's textual material, the photographic situations appear uniformly scripted. The large collection of images show that there was a set repertoire of specific gestures to be carried out by each group—the performative drinking, the straw indexing instantaneous reform, the smile, and the salute to the camera. The audience's enthusiastic participation was thoroughly documented and circulated to that very same and other audiences who encountered the photos as news or advertising images in the daily press or in the *Milk Propaganda Journal*—images testifying that milk, fun, and learning was had by all. In this as well as other sub-genres of the organization's campaigns, youthful audiences were used as a perpetually renewable media resource that evidenced enthusiasm and undeniable success. Along with the multitudinously repeated images of local screenings found in the photo archives, there is an abundance of prize winners, diploma recipients and, a few decades later, locally or internationally exhibited drawing contests.

Given that the Milk Propaganda's dissemination strategies and campaigns assumed the rhetoric and staging of pedagogy, the interactive milk event was also a site of mutual investment for milk drinkers and promoters. In her book *Class, Self, Culture*, Beverley Skeggs shows how the classed,

108 Ylva Habel

Figure 8.3 School children at the film theater "auditorium" in Stockholm during the Milk Week in 1935. Courtesy of the LRF Archive at the Centre for Business History, Stockholm.

gendered, and racial subject is saturated by a dynamic process in which various attributions, inscriptions, and exchanges of value take place within a culture.[34] In accordance with this claim, I would argue that the bodies that were represented, counted, and in a sense, claimed by the Milk Propaganda in these photographs were imbued with racialized conceptions of virtue and value via the documented event. Furthermore, the mediatization of the milk-drinking public was not limited to its exploitation as ornamental, raw material for future advertising; more specifically, the communion-like, eugenic framework within which these milk-promoting events took place opened up new ways of experiencing one's body and its capacities and concretized its relationship to the body politic.

CONCLUSION

The Milk Propaganda's participatory strategies were saturated with a highly celebratory and reflexive discourse on the media at its disposal in archives and in public circulation. As testified in their yearbook, the organization's promotional strategies were articulated in almost triumphant tropes, proudly displaying annual statistics on how many cities, schools, and bodies had been won over to milk drinking. In the various local contexts documented, each medium (and local narrative) was mobilized as a highly valued resource—one that not only could be, but also should be recycled and remediated repetitively. Similarly, and almost without exception, the short films released from the late 1920s to the end of the '30s made sure to cue recognition by incorporating earlier keywords and images. This, of course, was not an unconventional strategy, yet the intensity with which it was employed must have been somewhat exceptional.

In many ways the success of the milk events depended on the interaction, cultural competence, and prescribed introspection on behalf of their audiences. Especially children and youngsters were made to understand that they should take part in actively investing their bodies in building an improved health profile for the Swedish race. In campaigns directed toward school children, concentrated efforts were made to turn them into "milk propagandists," teaching them to teach "milk love" and "coffee hate" to their families. One could claim an inverted authority relationship between children and parents was hereby established, wherein the former were addressed as teachers of improved food habits to the latter.[35] Metaphorically as well as literally, the Milk Propaganda's media events and films opened the private realm of the family circle to education and normative scrutiny; the organization's call for reflection and participation was formulated as a summoning, yet enthusing challenge. This process—in which ideal embodiment was promoted and imaged as accessible—also entailed a sensitizing of the audiences' bodies, offering a new density of experience.

Regarded from the viewpoint of eventalization, the Milk Propaganda's elaborate, mediatized forms of governmentality vis-à-vis its audiences indicate alternative forms of historical agency. Yet, to make such a claim demands negotiation on several points. On the one hand, the Milk Propaganda tapped into the extant, increasingly eugenic regimes of knowledge during the interwar period and transposed into their sales rhetoric an established logic of medical, aesthetic, and moral discourse on normality and health. On the other hand, the organization's intensely participatory media practices make eugenic ideas materialize in such a way as to elucidate the rewarding aspects of the discourse. In accordance with Foucault's polygonic strategy of historical explanation, other meanings, if not radically divergent ones, can be gleaned by poring over these documented, choreographed points of reception.

The Milk Propaganda's photo archives take up about two full meters of files. Why were these Milk and Cheese Weeks, contests, and above all, myriad of school visits so thoroughly documented and collected? To borrow from Foucault, this vast collection could be read as one of the "monuments to particular configurations of power."[36] Yet, even if the compositional repetition of the imagery certainly contributes to establishing the authority of the claims to better health, they indicate an underlying anxiety. As argued, the depiction of juvenile audiences filled several rhetorical functions, two of the most important being to inscribe the importance of the event and to testify to the local commitment to milk drinking. The children drinking from straws or toasting in milk for the camera are all subjected to a specific manuscript and set of performative gestures that showed, in an indisputable manner, that they embraced the milk, whose nutritional value as "nature's perfect food" could not actually be proven.[37] Abundant visible evidence was thus needed to support the claim that the propaganda "worked" and that the product lived up to its promises.

NOTES

1. H. Jönsson, *Mjölk*, pp. 57–60. Similarly, within a U.S. historical context, E. DuPuis shows that fresh milk production is firmly local, remaining an exception to the otherwise increasingly global food production; see E. DuPuis, *Nature's Perfect Food*, p. 9.
2. According to DuPuis, two-thirds of the global population develops lactose deficiency after six years of age; see E. DuPuis, *Nature's Perfect Food*, p. 28.
3. Ibid., pp. 39–42, 68–72.
4. Ibid., pp. 44–45.
5. Ibid., pp. 117–18.
6. Ibid., pp. 103–9.
7. A discussion of the Milk Propaganda's advertising strategies can be found in Y. Habel, *Modern Media, Modern Audiences*, pp. 71–77.
8. M. Foucault, "Questions of Method," pp. 77–78.
9. Ibid., p. 77.
10. Ibid.
11. L. Gitelman and G. Pingree, eds., *New Media, 1740–1915*, p. xv. Similar arguments are put forward by D. Thorburn and H. Jenkins, eds., *Rethinking Media Change*, p. 2. See also W. Uricchio, "Historicizing Media in Transition," pp. 23–38.
12. See Jönsson, *Mjölk*, pp. 28, 31. For a discussion on preregulation problematics, see Y. Hirdman, *Magfrågan*, pp. 173–93.
13. A. Montelius, "Mjölkautomaterna," *Aftonbladet*, 24 March 1904. All translations are by the author, unless stated otherwise.
14. *Mjölkpropagandan 1923–1933: En återblick på tio verksamhetsår* (Stockholm: n.p., 1933), p. 2.
15. J. Lee, "Pastöriseringens försenade triumf."
16. *Meddelanden från Mjölkpropagandan* 2 (1925), pp. 106–8.
17. Ibid., pp. 109–11. See also *Meddelanden från Mjölkpropagandan* 3 (1926), p. 74; 5 (1928), p. 128; and *Mjölkpropagandan 1923–1933*, pp. 7–8.

18. *Mjölkpropagandan 1923–1933*, p. 7.
19. Ibid., p. 4.
20. See for example M. Runcis, *Steriliseringar i folkhemmet*; A.-L. Lindgren, "*Att ha barn med är en god sak*"; T. Forsslund, *Frisk och stark med skolradion*.
21. See, for instance, the cultural negotiations among actors and organizations around the issue of milk pasteurization in J. Lee, "Pastöriseringens försenade triumf." On the material representations of social concerns, aiming to incite civic involvement and reflection, see F. Lundgren, "Social samling," pp. 309–37. For a discussion concerning the mobilization and material representation of women's authority through household technology, see J.-E. Hagberg, *Tekniken i kvinnornas händer*. In an as-yet unpublished essay, "Hemmets radikal: Det elektriska köket," I link questions of feminine agency to Swedish electrification discourses during the 1920s and '30s.
22. M. Foucault, "The Ethic of Care," pp. 19–20.
23. T. Lemke, "Foucault, Governmentality, and Critique," p. 5.
24. M. Foucault, "The Ethic of Care," p. 19.
25. M. Warner, *Publics and Counterpublics*, p. 67.
26. *Mjölkpropagandans film: Mjölken, dess skötsel och värde* (Stockholm: n.p., 1929), p. 1.
27. For a discussion about Swedish industrial films, see M. Björkin, "Platser i rörelse," pp. 119–135; M. Björkin, "Industrial Greta," pp. 263–68.
28. *Meddelanden från Mjölkpropagandan* 5 (1928), p. 99.
29. *Mjölkpropagandan: Tidskrift för näringshygien, mjölkhushållning och jordbruk* 13 (1936), p. 82.
30. *Styrelseberättelse [för Mjölkpropagandan 1937]* (Stockholm: n.p., 1937), pp. 6–7.
31. *Mjölkpropagandan: Tidskrift för näringshygien, mjölkhushållning och jordbruk* 14 (1937), pp. 260–63.
32. "Livet på landet: Klinisk kontroll på radiogården," *Röster i Radio*, no. 21, 1938, p. 20.
33. M. Warner, *Publics and Counterpublics*, p. 161.
34. B. Skeggs, *Class, Self, Culture*, p. 14.
35. "Skolbarnen som propagandister," *Meddelanden från Mjölkpropagandan* 8 (1931), pp. 56–59; see also Lindgren, "*Att ha barn med är en god sak*."
36. Foucault quoted in A. Burton, *Archive Stories*, p. 6.
37. E. DuPuis, *Nature's Perfect Food*, p. 112.

9 Daniel Ellsberg and the Lost Idea of the Photocopy

Lisa Gitelman

In *Convergence Culture* (2006) Henry Jenkins identifies photocopied, self-published fanzines as an early gesture toward today's online sociability. Like so much Web 2.0 content, tattered old zines—whether by science fiction fans, East Village poets, or coffeehouse radicals—evidence the power and persistence of "grassroots creativity."[1]

Yet there is a lot we do not know about the ways that "old" textual duplication technologies stand as antecedents to "new" participatory media. This chapter seeks to fill in one part of that picture by offering an account, not of fans or of zines, but of the xerographic medium so many of them have deployed: What did photocopies mean—on their own terms—before the digital media that now frames them as old and analog? Historical specificity is key, for it seems clear that knowledge of things digital has worked retrospectively to alter the meanings of xerography. As one former denizen of Xerox PARC recalls, for instance, "In the late 1980s, the Xerox Corporation began to wrestle with the consequences of the upcoming technological shift" from optical to digital copying; "Informally, it was easy to see that what had been a unitary operation of 'copying' was being broken down into a series of parts: scan, store, and print; or perhaps scan, store, modify, and print; or even scan, store, modify, retrieve, and print."[2] A conceptual shift was occurring in the face of technological change.

If the idea of xerography started to crumble to pieces in the 1980s, how and when had it ever coalesced in the first place? The answer to that question involves the invention and promotion of xerographic technology, of course, but it also involves untold millions of Xerox copies and the ordinary people who made them. When Haloid Xerox (as it was known then) placed its early models in 1959, the company mistakenly believed that its technology would fill a specific niche in current office practice. It would be good for anywhere from five to twenty copies: too many for carbon paper, but too few to make a Photostat, mimeo, ditto, or hectograph master worth the trouble. Instead, Haloid customers found myriad new uses for copies, often making as many Xeroxes in a month as the machines had been designed to produce in a year.[3]

Daniel Ellsberg and the Lost Idea of the Photocopy 113

The concept of xerography came together unexpectedly, then, emerging in the early 1960s according to the varied uses of Xerox machines, according—that is—to the double xerographic subject of the day: the self who pushed the button and the self-concerning document that lay face down on the glass. While it is impossible to chase down all of the ordinary people involved, this chapter seeks to retrieve the idea of the photocopy, an idea so lately corrupted by our intuitive knowledge of things digital. To do so, it will address itself to one famous photocopy, the Pentagon Papers—copied in 1969 by Daniel Ellsberg and leaked to the *New York Times* in 1971. The Pentagon Papers example reveals the idea of the photocopy in some complexity, framed by a cultural politics of the cold war that is seldom remembered today and was rarely acknowledged then, at least outside of Russia, where xerographic reproduction remained effectively illegal until the collapse of the Soviet Union.

The copying, leaking, and publication of the Pentagon Papers occurred as part of the groundswell of popular resistance to the Vietnam War in the United States. The government invoked national security concerns and moved to bar publication of the Pentagon Papers by the *New York Times*. A federal court in New York enjoined the *Times*, but before the Supreme Court could hear the case on appeal, the *Washington Post* and other newspapers also began to publish the Pentagon Papers. The Supreme Court ultimately ruled in favor of the *Times*, making this an important First Amendment (freedom of speech, freedom of the press) case in American Constitutional law. But the whole episode had a much more tawdry side too: Government improprieties in pursuit of Ellsberg, the xerographer, included ransacking his psychiatrist's office, an operation carried out by a covert group known as "the Plumbers," who worked to plug leaks for the Nixon administration. Not only was the government's case against Ellsberg eventually dismissed on the grounds of prosecutorial misconduct, further covert operations by the Plumbers would include the infamous Watergate break-in: first in a twisted chain of events that would ultimately lead to President Richard Nixon's resignation in 1974.

If the example of the Pentagon Papers thus helps to point up the connections between xerography and free speech, then it is also a reminder that grassroots creativity has a political valence. The mainstream press may have won the day against Richard Nixon, but grassroots self-publication by any means—hand press, carbon paper, mimeograph, Xeroxes, facsimile, cassette tape, email—has long been part of the "small media" repertoire of political activism and popular participation.[4] The smallness of small media allows "the little guy" agency within the public sphere. It would be wrong, however, to think of small media as *inherently* activist or participatory, as always and everywhere David against some mainstream Goliath. The media of textual duplication, in particular, are importantly the instruments of bureaucratic control, part of and party to the repertoire of state authority and managerial capital. Activist uses, like fan uses, are

114 *Lisa Gitelman*

largely idiosyncratic. In short, "participatory media"—the subject of this volume—is always more a question of who participates and what forms participation may take than it is a question of technology.

ACTIVISM: A BIBLIOGRAPHIC ACCOUNT

The story is simply told. In October 1969 Daniel Ellsberg began to copy in installments a multivolume work with the ungainly title "History of U.S. Decision-Making Process on Vietnam Policy." He took sections of the history home from his office at Rand Corporation, returning each after it was Xeroxed. The history was bound in cardboard covers with metal tapes, which could be removed for copying. There were forty-seven volumes in all, and Ellsberg started in the middle. He was Xeroxing one of fifteen extant duplicates, produced in-house at the Pentagon at the behest of Robert McNamara, one of the architects of the Vietnam War. McNamara had commissioned the history when he was still Secretary of Defense, and a team of thirty-six authors had compiled some 4,000 pages of documents from Pentagon files and written an additional 3,000 pages of original narrative. The thirty-six authors were anonymous by design, so they could be critical without risking their careers. Their secretaries were anonymous by custom: The history employed an unknown number of Pentagon clerks and typists. It was classified "top secret," and those words appeared on every cardboard cover and on inside pages.

If its authors and their typists had managed to turn so many documents into a single history—edition of fifteen—Ellsberg was now turning one history back into multiple papers. Xeroxing was only the first step in what became a lengthy disaggregation and multiplication process. Ellsberg made two copies that fall, but it wasn't until the *New York Times* began to publish from and about the history on 13 June 1971, that it became—inconsistently at first—plural: "the Pentagon papers," and ultimately, "the Pentagon Papers," capitalized. As Ellsberg recalled in an interview the following year, he "took out the Pentagon Papers from Rand and began to Xerox them, . . . My hope was that I could get it to the—to the Senate Foreign Relations Committee for hearings, somehow."[5] Seen from the vantage point of 1972 they were plural ("Xerox them"), yet as the intentional subject of 1969 it was singular ("get it to the Senate"). Them and it, the Pentagon Papers and the History: this schizophrenia only gradually resolved itself. Even after they became persistently plural, the "papers" were at first only capitalized in headlines.[6] In news reporting, columns, and editorials the Pentagon Papers remained "Pentagon papers," lowercase, until at least that fall, after the Supreme Court decision in *New York Times v. United States* (403 U.S. 713) and after the publication of *The Pentagon Papers as Published by the New York Times* (a Bantam paperback, $2.25). Only then did journalists begin to appeal to what "is now known as 'the Pentagon

Papers,' " two capital *P*s.⁷ Common parlance emerging from public controversy had finished the multiplication process that Ellsberg began when he undid the bindings, Xeroxed the history, and collated the results into two loose sets of pages.

Despite their keen and conflicting interest in the Pentagon Papers, neither the newspapers nor the state had much explicit interest in the Pentagon Papers as Xeroxes. They cared about the Pentagon Papers' linguistic meaning, that is, to the virtual exclusion of bibliographic meaning.⁸ Nowhere in its publication of the Pentagon Papers did the newspaper report that its document/documents were xerographic copies. The copies were assumed to be identical to the document/documents, and—because—the document/documents were assumed to be self-identical with their linguistic content.⁹ Similarly, when the government finally did know Ellsberg's role, it obtained a fifteen-count indictment against him and his associate, Anthony Russo, but only the first count of the lengthy indictment contains the word "copy" (used twice) or "Xerox" (once). Instead, Ellsberg and Russo were charged with embezzlement, theft, and "conversion to their own use" of government property. They were accused of communicating, delivering, transmitting, and retaining classified documents. And they were charged with conspiring to do all of these things. Copying was mentioned only as an incidental component of conspiracy.¹⁰ Their real offenses, according to the state, were theft (six counts) and espionage (eight counts). Xerography was by implication merely an M.O., a modus operandi or technique.

Xerographic interests can thus be dramatically asymmetrical: If the newspapers and the state both lacked explicit interest in the Pentagon Papers as Xeroxes, the same cannot be said of Ellsberg or his supposed coconspirators. While it must be obvious that Ellsberg cared about the Pentagon Papers as Xeroxes—because he Xeroxed them—what is less patent is the nature of his bibliographic investment. He had a political interest in the history and in leaking it, of course, but his interest in the photocopies *as* photocopies was additionally complex and depended upon xerography as an unacknowledged form of cultural production, as a form of making, remaking, and self-making that was framed in part by the always emergent bureaucratic norms of statecraft and citizenship. Ellsberg's bibliographic interest was at once editorial, mimetic, and variously egoistic.

First, xerographic reproduction offered a way to edit or remake the "History of U.S. Decision-Making Process on Vietnam Policy" as well as to appropriate it.¹¹ Most important, Ellsberg edited out the words "top secret" wherever he could. To begin with, Ellsberg and his companions cut the words off the bottom and top margins of the photocopies, first with scissors and later with a paper cutter. Then Russo suggested they photocopy them off. He contrived a cardboard mask for the Xerox machine, so that every page of the history was copied without its margins to produce new, empty margins—at least, in theory; in practice, a lot of page numbers and lines of text were also edited out this way, and plenty of "top secret" markings evaded them. In Ellsberg's retrospective account of this xerographic "declassification" process, the words "top secret" crop up like dragon's teeth. No matter how careful Ellsberg and Russo were at the photocopier, a few of the markings still seemed to be there when Ellsberg shuffled through his piles of copies. Particularly when he later took his copies to be recopied at commercial Xerox shops, Ellsberg had to check his edit and resorted to scissors again and again to remove "top secret," so the clerks wouldn't be suspicious as the pages in question got copied and, in effect, grown back into 8 1/2 x 11-inch pages of the history.[12]

In a certain respect Ellsberg's editorial interest in xerography can be seen as both a response to and a continuation of McNamara and the Pentagon's own editorial interests. Leslie H. Gelb had directed the preparation of the history, which involved the location and duplication of documents within the files of the Department of Defense, the Department of State, and the CIA. The history was made with and out of photocopies, it seems—and photocopies of photocopies, photocopies of transcripts of cables, photocopies of hectograph copies, etc.—and the heterogeneity of the final version reflected that process when it was typed and reproduced in-house.[13] Ellsberg himself had been recruited as an author while an employee of the Rand Corporation. He worked for several months during 1967 to compile material and draft a section on the Kennedy administration's policy, although little survived of Ellsberg's draft in the final version, according to Gelb.[14] Ellsberg was now reediting the edit to which he and his subject had been subject.

If part of Ellsberg's bibliographic investment in the photocopies was editorial, another part of it was mimetic. Once he began copying, he didn't (or perhaps he couldn't) stop. He started with two copies because making more than that would take too long—the Xerox 914 machine he and Russo used took at least six seconds per copy—and because he was "obsessed" with the thought that if he were discovered, the copies would be confiscated and all of his efforts wasted.[15] Better to make two copies and store them separately. The same logic led to a giant but partial third copy, and then the additional logic of having-one's-copy-and-giving-it-away-too took hold. Ellsberg eventually gave a whole set of copies to the Senate Foreign Relations Committee, where it languished, and then he felt he wanted to replace those copies with more copies of the copies he had retained. This led Ellsberg to commercial Xerox shops in New York City and Cambridge, Massachusetts, where Massachusetts Avenue near Harvard University was called by one observer at the time the "Sunset Strip of copying": Newsstands and tobacconists, clothes shops, and other retail outlets were scrambling to add coin-operated Xerox machines as a single generation of Harvard students began effectively to download—one might say—the contents of the university libraries.[16] Ultimately, he had copies or partial copies squirreled away with different friends. Xerography was an "addiction," according to another contemporary account, and Ellsberg came close

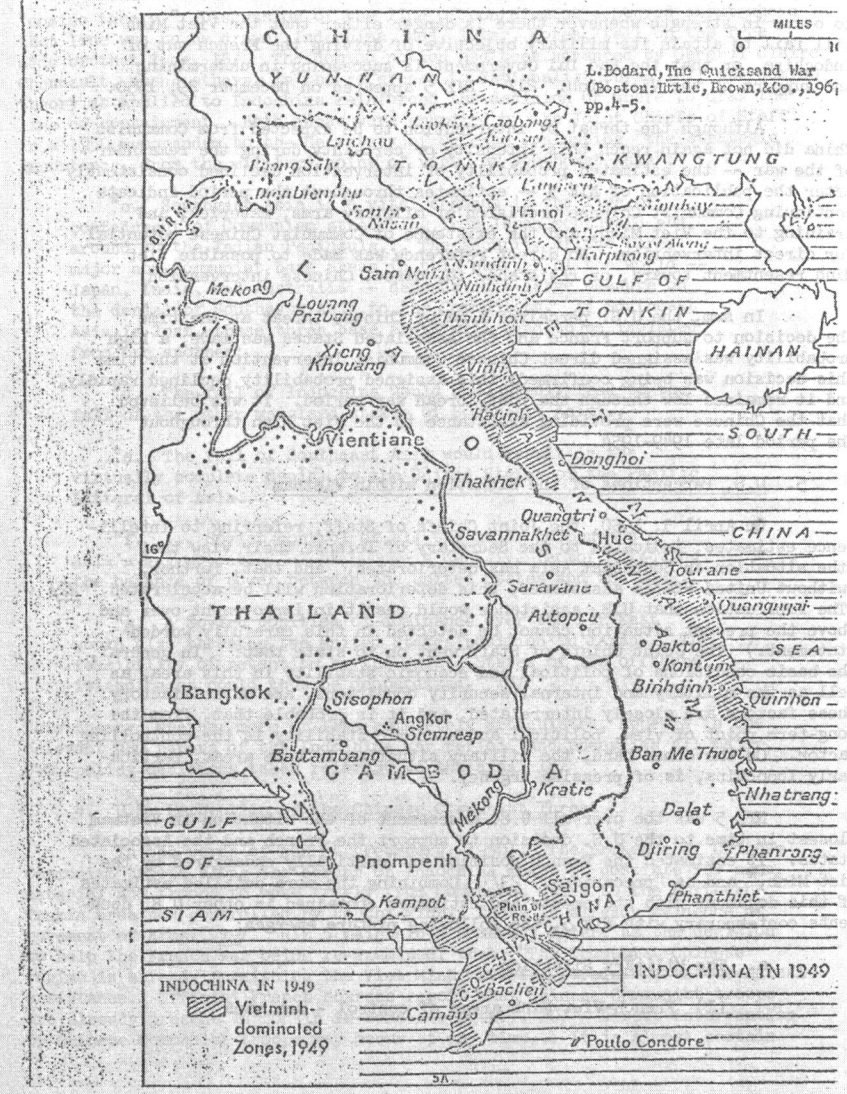

Figure 9.1 Indochina in an nth-generation Xerox (note the electrostatic traces in the left margin), from the Pentagon Papers as printed for the House Committee on Armed Services. *United States-Vietnam Relations 1945–1967: Study Prepared by the Department of Defense*, vol. 1 (Washington, 1971).

to proving the point. One of the things one did with photocopies was photocopy them: precisely what Xerox Haloid had failed to understand as it developed the technology. The result might be, the same observer worried, "the insidious grown of a negative attitude toward originals—a feeling that nothing can be of importance *unless* it is copied, or is a copy itself."[17] By this token, perhaps Ellsberg was unconsciously trying to make his copies more important—or more clearly important—by recopying them. In this he would hardly have been alone.

The year 1971 seems to have been the moment when American observers of bureaucrats and bureaucracy detected with certainty the new bureaucratic norm: "Before the Xerox era," noted an official at the National Archives, government agencies had central files: "When anyone needed information he went to that central file." By 1971, however, the government had acquired some 60,000 copy machines with predicable results: "Many a government executive prefers to maintain files in his own office ... The result is that where we used to have a limited number of central filing places we now have thousands, with endless duplication of papers."[18] A new crisis in information management loomed. Lucky, then, that the Pentagon's production of its history happened post-"Xerox Revolution" but pre-crisis, gloated historian Richard Ullman, another of the authors who worked on the Vietnam study for Gelb:

> Not only is there unauthorized reproduction and circulation (within the government usually) of even the most restricted formal documents; but also informal [ones, e.g., drafts, memos, notes] ... the like of which in a prior era would have been confined to the personal files of their writer are now reproduced and circulated to his colleagues and friends—and, in turn, are retained in their files. These informal materials ... were among the most valuable sources at the disposal of the authors of the Pentagon study.[19]

Though according to Max Weber, modern bureaucracy assiduously separates home from office, business from private correspondence,[20] the xerographic medium was helping to personalize files. Filing, that is, had become a means of self-possession.

In addition to his editorial and mimetic investments in the Xeroxes as Xeroxes, Ellsberg had other, more nebulous egoistical investments, which can only be guessed at in relation to peculiar circumstances both personal and professional. One of the oddest details of his Xeroxing is personal: Ellsberg had his two children—ages ten and thirteen—help with the copying and collation on several occasions, which struck at least his ex-wife (their mother) as appallingly irresponsible. Ellsberg retrospectively explains that he wanted his kids to be a part of things, to see that he was acting "normally, calmly," with self-possession rather than "weird" or "crazy."[21] (It is tempting to read normality in this instance as masculine and weirdness as hysterical or feminine, if only because Xerox machine operators of the day were "almost invariably" women. Ellsberg was in one sense performing his masculinity.)[22] Whatever his motivating impulse, the incident suggests that xerography—whatever else it offered—here enabled, enacted, or expressed his ego-identity at some basic level. Likewise, xerographic interests soon structured Ellsberg's professional identity as well. At the September 1970 meeting of the American Political Science Association, Ellsberg, who was then working at MIT, delivered a paper about the war entitled "Escalating in a Quagmire." He drew, of necessity, on his secret archive of Xeroxes, but he couldn't cite them. In a lengthy footnote he explains his perspective as a "view from inside" and suggestively warns that "[u]ntil more materials are made public," his conclusions "must be regarded as hypotheses whose implications can at least be analyzed, and which can be tested against the honest judgments of others who have had access to official sources."[23] At both a personal and professional level, Ellsberg's investment in the photocopies *as* photocopies helped him to position himself as an insider outside: inside his family and outside his marriage; outside of government yet in on its workings.

This position was interestingly in keeping with the outsider-inside role he had cultivated as a government employee and consultant. In a 1966 letter to McNamara, for instance, Ellsberg urged "Official reporting (including Nodis [sic] and Eyes Only, back-channel and what-have-you) is grossly inadequate to the job of educating high-level decision-makers." To really be informed, he suggested in a letter to national security advisor Walter Rostow on the same day, it was important to get "out, beyond the end of the chain of paper and electric signals, [and maybe even] out from Saigon, into a world of red dirt, green rice fields, burned schoolrooms and little, three-sided mud forts." "There is simply no substitute," he wrote to McNamara, "for long, unhurried, private conversation with the regrettably small number of people [that is, Americans] with prolonged and broad experience" out there and (as he put it to Rostow) "inside South Vietnam."[24] You could get so far outside that you were in. Sometimes the best insider was out. The inside/outside rhetoric is unstable, inconsistent in all but its binarism, and thoroughly opportunistic.

Most importantly, this inside/outside rhetoric parrots the self-authorizing inside/outside by which the Executive branch of the U.S. government routinely, if cynically, produces its own distinction. As the Pentagon Papers show with such clarity, the postwar executive branch functions as a "different world" with "a set of values, a dynamic, a language and a perspective quite distinct from the public world of the ordinary citizen," as the *New York Times* put it in framing the Pentagon Papers. Moreover,

> The segments of the public world—Congress, the news media, the citizenry, even international opinion as a whole—are regarded from within the world of the government insider as elements to be influenced. The policy memorandums repeatedly discuss ways to move these outside "audiences" in the desired direction, through such techniques as the controlled release of information and appeals to patriotic stereotypes.

The papers also make clear the deep-felt need of the government insider for secrecy in order to keep the machinery of state functioning smoothly and to maintain a maximum ability to affect the public world.[25]

In such a context, a leaked copy has the potential not only to transgress or leak across the inside/outside boundary but, importantly, has the potential to mirror—one might say to reproduce—its iteration as a form of critique. When the leaked copy is published, the sheer "incommensurability of the *locus* of enunciation and the enunciated *text*" serves as a parody or a "mockery" of the executive branch—the machinery of state—in precisely its own terms, in literally its own voice.[26] The leak thus draws lavishly on one tradition of parody: Tina Fey repeats Sarah Palin verbatim (2008), while the modern security state must create tone-deaf zones where parody can't exist. No joking at airport checkpoints: "Your safety is our priority," says the U.S. Transportation Security Administration website, "Think before you speak" (2009).[27]

OPENNESS, FROM ANALOG TO DIGITAL

If the misbegotten executive branch of today has brought the term "gulag" back into circulation,[28] Ellsberg and the Pentagon Papers, like Nixon and the Watergate tapes, in retrospect lend the term "glasnost" a certain appeal. Glasnost—openness, transparency, availability to public speech—did not become a familiar term in the West until the Gorbachev era of the late 1980s, although it was long used by authors and producers of samizdat, self-made publications—typed carbon-paper duplicates, triplicates, quadruplicates, etc.—which circulated semiprivately in the Soviet Union as a medium of dissent.[29] It can be applied in a narrow sense to the opening of Pentagon machinations and the opening of Nixonian malfeasance. When Western authors took stock of xerography, they did typically appeal to the idea of self-publication, like samizdat, but without an explicit sense of or attention to openness. Instead, as befits the Western context, their focus was usually on issues of ownership and appropriation: Now anyone can "make his own book," Marshall McLuhan pronounced, and make it out of other books.[30] Observers were quick to see the implications for copyright, and the U.S. Congress began to hold hearings on reprography as early as 1965 to contemplate its first major revisions to the Copyright Act of 1909, partly to protect publishers from Xeroxes.[31] Before Congress could act, the first major copyright case concerning xerography in North America went to trail; *Williams and Wilkins v. the United States* (487 F.2d 1345) was decided in November 1973.[32]

In one sense the Pentagon Papers example is entirely beside the point of such contests because they were government documents and therefore not subject to copyright protection. In another sense, however, Ellsberg and the Pentagon Papers precisely for this reason help to demonstrate a longer history of something like glasnost in the West. It is a history that implicitly posits openness as an opposite of ownership, rather than accept as universal the familiar antinomy of ownership and piracy/fair use. Though hardly a typical Xerox, that is, Ellsberg's Pentagon Papers help in retrospect to reveal the lost idea of the photocopy as an early locus of distinction between free speech and free beer, as the distinction is popularly drawn today in the discourse of free/open-source software. Free/open-source software—like user-generated Web 2.0 content—is "free" and "open" for skilled participants to improve upon and extend according to "a variety of motivations." Free/open-source programmers usually retain copyright on major innovations but license them freely to anyone who agrees to use them in similarly open ways.[33] The free/open-source movement confounds the ownership of public discourse—and by extension, the culture industries—via promotion of shared resources and collaborative productions. The incumbent question of motivation has consumed economists and policy makers because traditional financial incentives do not explain these sorts of collaborative productions.

What I am speculating is not just that *leaking* entails openness, but that "copying," that seemingly instantaneous push-button action and plain-paper result of xerographic reproduction, circa 1969, somehow did too. Whether the xerographer stood in the copy room of a giant corporation, at a coin-operated machine in the corner of a public library, or at the counter of a local copy shop, "making copies" may have been less distinctly a matter of "taking" copies than it was a form of localized cultural production, of self-expression if not always self-publishing. And we know from the example of Ellsberg just how variously motivated the "unitary operation" of copying could be as a performance of self, if we recall the jumble of editorial intentions, mimetic urges, and egoistic impulses that seem to have made his Xeroxes meaningful as such. We might think likewise of office workers who copy and file selected documents for their *potential* openness, items in the "just-in-case" dossiers so many of us have kept in order to prove that we knew better than—that we had some dirt on our supervisors, even if we hesitated to act outright as whistle-blowers. Or think of academics who pursue "a passion for photocopying and filing away articles," items in the self-produced archives so many of us have kept as a form of paradoxically retentive engagement with openness, as some form of partial surrogate, I suspect, for reading and for knowing.[34] What these examples help to suggest, at least by dint of the varied motivations they imply, is that photocopying has long involved contributions to public discourse, even if the contributions in question remained possible rather than actual, imagined rather than known, felt rather than acted.

Without question, recent new forms of digital self-publication have both eased the barriers to participation in public discourse and helped to modify the meaning of "copying." The Pentagon Papers of tomorrow are much less likely to be Xeroxes, first because the Xerox Corporation has no corner on the market for digital copiers/scanners/printers, but more because online self-publication now offers an alternative modus operandi for leaks. Recent failed attempts by one U.S. court to shut down the website Wikileaks.org confirm that digital copies will be virtually impossible to contain.[35] The documents on Wikileaks.org are themselves copies—provenance variously unclear—but the entire site was also "mirrored" in several places around the world after a federal judge issued his order of restraint against Wikileaks.org's host in the United States: glasnost redux.

NOTES

1. H. Jenkins, *Convergence Culture*, p. 136.
2. B. Smith, *On the Origin of Objects*, pp. 300–1.
3. D. Owen, *Copies in Seconds*, p. 223. See also E. Hemmungs Wirtén, *No Trespassing*, p. 64.
4. See A. Sreberny-Mohammadi and A. Mohammadi, *Small Media, Big Revolution*.
5. "Interview for 'Hearts and Minds' 1972," typed transcript, p. 107, Neil Sheehan Papers, box 64, Library of Congress.
6. See headlines in the *New York Times*, 25 June 1969, and *Washington Post*, 19 June 1969; see also "The Covert War," 13 June 1971, p. 38; and N. Sheehan, "Vietnam Archive: Pentagon Study Traces 3 Decades of Growing Involvement," 13 June 1971, p. 1; H. Smith, "Vast Review of War Took a Year," 13 June 1971, p. 1; and M. Frankel, "Impact in Washington; Pentagon Papers a Major Fact of Life for all Three Branches of Government," 25 June 1971, p. 21. Observations in this paragraph about usage are all based upon ProQuest searches of the *New York Times* and *Washington Post*.
7. See, e.g., W. McWilliams, "Washington Plans Aggressive War," *New York Times*, 26 September 1971, p. BR5.
8. J. McGann, *The Textual Condition*, p. 13.
9. *New York Times*, 17 June 1971, pp. 1, 18. Of course, the newspapers later covered the Ellsberg trial, so they acknowledged the Pentagon Papers were copies.
10. "On or about October 4, 1969, defendants Ellsberg and Russo, and co-conspirator Sinay operated a Xerox copy machine at 8101 Melrose Avenue, Los Angeles, California": This was one of the seven "overt acts" they had committed to "effect the objects" of their conspiracy. The indictment is reprinted as Appendix B in A. Ginger and the Meiklejohn Institute Staff, eds., *Pentagon Papers Case Collection: Annotated Procedural Guide and Index* (Berkeley, CA: Meiklejohn Civil Liberties Institute / Oceana Publications, 1975), pp. 164–71.
11. For copying as appropriation, see H. Schwartz, *The Culture of the Copy*, Chap. 6. Schwartz notes "the more instantaneous the copy, the more complete the confusion" (p. 235) between *copy* as a noun and *copy* as a verb: no wonder "Xerox" came to mean both.
12. D. Ellsberg, *Secrets: A Memoir of Vietnam and the Pentagon Papers* (New York: Viking, 2002), Chap. 20, "Copying the Papers," pp. 331, 371. See also T. Wells, *Wildman*. Wells, not Ellsberg, includes mention of lines and page numbers lost (p. 323). Ellsberg refers to this as "declassification" in scare quotes.

13. I haven't been able to determine the process used, probably photo-offset. The original photocopies—as it were—within the Neil Sheehan Papers at the Library of Congress remain classified, despite repeated publication of the Pentagon Papers. B. Westerfield notes that the edition published by the Government Printing Office was offset from "indifferently Xeroxed originals"; see B. Westerfield, "What Use Are Three Versions of the Pentagon Papers?," *The American Political Review* 69 (1975), p. 687.
14. See D. Rudenstine, *The Day The Presses Stopped*, p. 37.
15. "Interview for 'Hearts and Minds' 1972," typed transcript, p. 122, Neil Sheehan Papers, box 64, Library of Congress. Brooks gives two figures on performance, six and nine seconds per copy; J. Brooks, "Profiles: Xerox, Xerox, Xerox, Xerox," *New Yorker*, 1 April 1967, pp. 52, 55.
16. Testimony quoted in "Project—New Technology and the Law of Copyright: Reprography and Computers," *UCLA Law Review* 15 (1967–8), p. 943.
17. J. Brooks, "Profiles," p. 58.
18. Quoted in J. Dessauer, *My Years with Xerox: The Billions Nobody Wanted* (Garden City, NY: Doubleday, 1971), pp. xiv–xv.
19. R. Ullman, "The Pentagon's History As 'History'," pp. 150–56.
20. M. Weber, "Bureaucratic Authority," p. 61.
21. D. Ellsberg, *Secrets*, p. 305. He also describes working at the copying with his son, Russo, and Russo's girlfriend as a happy family scene.
22. J. Brooks, "Profiles," p. 57.
23. "Escalating in a Quagmire," typescript paper prepared for the American Political Science Association meetings, 8–12 September 1970, Neil Sheehan Papers, box 64, Library of Congress. Ellsberg was at the Center for International Studies, MIT.
24. Both letters of 8 June 1966. At this point Ellsberg was working for John McNaughton at the American Embassy in Vietnam; see Neil Sheehan Papers, box 27, Library of Congress. He was urging both McNamara and Rastow to meet with his friend John Vann for a really inside view of the situation in Indochina.
25. *The Pentagon Papers as Published by the New York Times* (New York: Bantam Books, 1971), pp. xii, xiii. This is from Sheehan's introduction.
26. S. Oushakine, "The Terrifying Mimicry of Samizdat," p. 203 for "mockery." Ellsberg's xerography may be considered as a literalized form of Foucauldian "mimetic resistance," in something of the sense that Oushakine elaborates. During the late 1960s, samizdat "became dominated by *political* documents," petitions, open letters, pamphlets, and trial transcripts, rather than the more well-known (in the West) artistic expressions (p. 195). Oushakine argues that this Soviet protest writing worked by echoing and thereby amplifying the rhetoric of the state apparatus, forming a sort of "mimetic resistance" in lieu of an oppositional discourse, which remained unthinkable in Russia until the late 1970s (p. 192). Elena Razlogova sent me this terrific article, and I'm grateful for her thinking on samizdat and xerography.
27. Slogan and instruction from TSA, "How to get through the line faster," online, available HTTP: <http://www.tsa.gov/travelers/airtravel/screening_experience.shtm> (accessed 1 January 2009). This observation about parody was made to me (pre-Palin) by Michael McKeon.
28. See L. Lynch, "The G Word," p. 1, online, available HTTP: <http://aspen.conncoll.edu/politicsandculture/page.cfm?key=546> (accessed 1 January 2007).
29. S. Oushakine, "The Terrifying Mimicry of Samizdat," p. 192.
30. Quoted in E. Hemmungs Wirtén, *No Trespassing*, p. 66.

31. "Project—New Technology and the Law of Copyright", p. 943 and passim.
32. The case concerned copies of scientific articles made by the National Library of Medicine, and the court ruled that such copying was indeed "fair use." Subsequent rulings on related cases described fair use much more narrowly. See E. Hemmungs Wirtén, *No Trespassing*, pp. 68–72.
33. See Y. Benkler, *The Wealth of Networks*, p. 63 and passim.
34. Quoted is G. Bowker, *Memory Practices in the Sciences*, p. 15, but I'm confessing my own anxieties about copying as a surrogate for reading.
35. "Stifling Online Speech," *New York Times*, 21 February 2008.

10 Fetal Photography in the Age of Cool Media

Solveig Jülich

From today's perspective it may be difficult to grasp the hype over videodiscs, audiovisual cassettes, and overhead projectors in the late 1960s and early '70s, the moment when the term "new media" came into use.[1] But Marshall McLuhan was not the only one expressing excitement about the participatory qualities that the media of the electronic age seemed to possess. According to McLuhan, television was the ultimate "cool medium" since it was low in definition and therefore required the audience to have high involvement with the televised message. At the opposite end were the "hot media" such as photography that left the viewer little to add from her experience or knowledge.[2] Others were more interested in the effects of remediation on audience engagement: how new and old media could be combined and integrated in productive ways. Educational media producers, policy makers, and practitioners promoted the mixing of media as a dynamic tool for stimulating active participation in the classroom. Also, leaders and activists of social movements invoked all sorts of audiovisual media in their efforts to turn audiences into publics. A contemporary commentator even claimed that it was cool media that "made Woodstock, Vietnam protests, black revolution, and communes."[3]

In this age of cool media and social turmoil, in 1965 *Life* magazine published a photo essay on human fetal development by the Swedish photographer Lennart Nilsson. Featuring a series of color images of embryos and fetuses, this "Drama of Life before Birth" propelled Nilsson onto the international scene and was succeeded by a long and still-active career in areas ranging from photojournalism to scientific photography. Over the years his images have been widely circulated in books, daily papers, journals, television programs, exhibitions, and on the internet. His best-selling book *A Child is Born* (1965) has been published in five different editions and in many languages. From the beginning, then, Nilsson's photographic work has been linked to new media and societal change.[4]

Feminist scholars have provided rich accounts that can help elucidate the relation between Nilsson's fetal imagery and participatory strategies of the past. In an often cited article published in the 1980s, Rosalind Petchesky used the term "public fetus" to describe the proliferation of images of embryos and fetuses in popular culture. Writing in the heyday of the Reagan era she noted that the antiabortion movement increasingly supported its claims for fetal personhood and rights with medical imagery from inside the womb.[5] In tracing the history of the public fetus, many scholars have also noted that American antiabortion activists were already beginning to mobilize Nilsson's photographs in the 1970s.[6] Most recently, anthropologist Lynn Morgan has discussed the famous pictures in *Life* magazine as one instance of the story of how dead embryos for scientific study were turned into cultural icons of life.[7] But little is known about the contexts in which Nilsson's photographs were created or how they started to circulate between diverse social arenas and were appropriated for different uses and interests. Over time, one and the same image of embryonic life can even be seen to have acquired several contrasting meanings, from progressive politics to cultural conservatism.[8] Making the public fetus has always entailed a mix of media and participatory strategies.

This essay will explore the intersection between Nilsson's fetal photography, new media (theory), and participatory practices in the late 1960s and early '70s. In particular, I wish to focus on how media companies, educational institutions, and social movements in Sweden and the United States incorporated Nilsson's images in strategies for engaging consumers and citizens. These media strategies will be discussed by relating them to concepts such as remediation and remixing, more often reserved for the contemporary media landscape.[9] My main argument is that these efforts, practices, and activities, taken together and interconnected in certain aspects, represented a vital moment in the making of the public fetus. More generally, I would like to contribute to the ongoing discussions on the materiality of media. Although McLuhan's notion of hot and cold media seems at odds with the HDTV era, his conviction that media can be categorized by specifying their characteristics have been echoed in succeeding media studies, not least in the research on the role of media in social movements and grassroots activities. By the use of terms like "small media," "radical media," "alternative media," "activist media," and most recently, "participatory media," several scholars seem to attribute oppositional or democratic qualities to the media themselves.[10] Taking these kinds of conceptual issues into account I would like to raise the question of whether the materiality of Nilsson's remediated and remixed images made any difference for their cultural uses and effects. By way of anticipating my conclusion, I suggest that the technological features of the media did matter but so too did aspects of bodily engagement and symbolic physicality.

FETAL PHOTOGRAPHY AND THE NEW MEDIA INDUSTRY

Lennart Nilsson started his career in the 1940s as a freelance photographer and worked mainly for the Bonnier Group, the largest media company in Sweden with activities in the publishing of books, magazines, and newspapers. One of the media products this company launched was the picture magazine *Se* that had been modeled on the American magazines *Life* and *Look*. Nilsson's early pictures for *Se* included everything from celebrities at parties to the daily work of a mail carrier, and he also started to contribute to photo reportages about medical events. In the early 1950s he was commissioned to take photographs for an article about opposition to abortion among gynecologists and scientists at the Women's clinic of Karolinska Institutet at the Sabbatsberg Hospital in Stockholm. The abortion law in Sweden had recently been modified so that a legal abortion could be secured for socio-medical reasons. Eventually an article featuring an enlarged photograph of a five-month-old fetus acquired through legal abortion appeared in the *Se* magazine under the heading "Why Must the Fetus Be Killed?"[11]

This reportage was the first publication of an extensive photographic project that was pursued in collaboration with gynecologists opposed to abortion and supported financially by the Bonnier Group. During the 1950s and early '60s Nilsson contributed to several articles in the press that argued against abortion. His work culminated with the photo essay "Drama of Life before Birth" in *Life* magazine in 1965, soon followed by the pregnancy guidebook *A Child is Born*. Most of the images in these publications were made possible either through surgical interventions due to extrauterine pregnancies or legal abortions. Both in image and text, the human feature of the fetus was underlined. This was achieved, for instance, by setting the specimens against an empty background, using back-lighting to give them a warm tone, and then magnifying the image several times. However, fearing public aspersions in the wake of intensified abortion debates, Nilsson, his co-workers, and the Bonnier Group accorded not to divulge how the images in *A Child is Born* had been made. Dead or dying embryos and fetuses were, then, transformed into visually appealing symbols of life.[12]

The embryological story of the beginnings of human life as promoted by Nilsson and the Bonnier Group shares many characteristics with what Henry Jenkins has termed "transmedia storytelling" to describe the movement of content across media in today's participatory culture.[13] Besides being introduced into the book *A Child is Born* as well as in the Bonnier Group magazines, the drama of human development was also extended to films and public service television programs, thereby adding sound and music to the experience of viewing the images.[14] This business and marketing strategy meant not only that the Bonnier Group reduced their production costs but also that a wider audience could be attracted by pitching the content slightly differently in different media. The Time Life publishing company adopted a similar approach when they arbitrarily launched an educational "sound filmstrip program" for the American market based on Nilsson's photographs in *Life*.[15]

128 Solveig Jülich

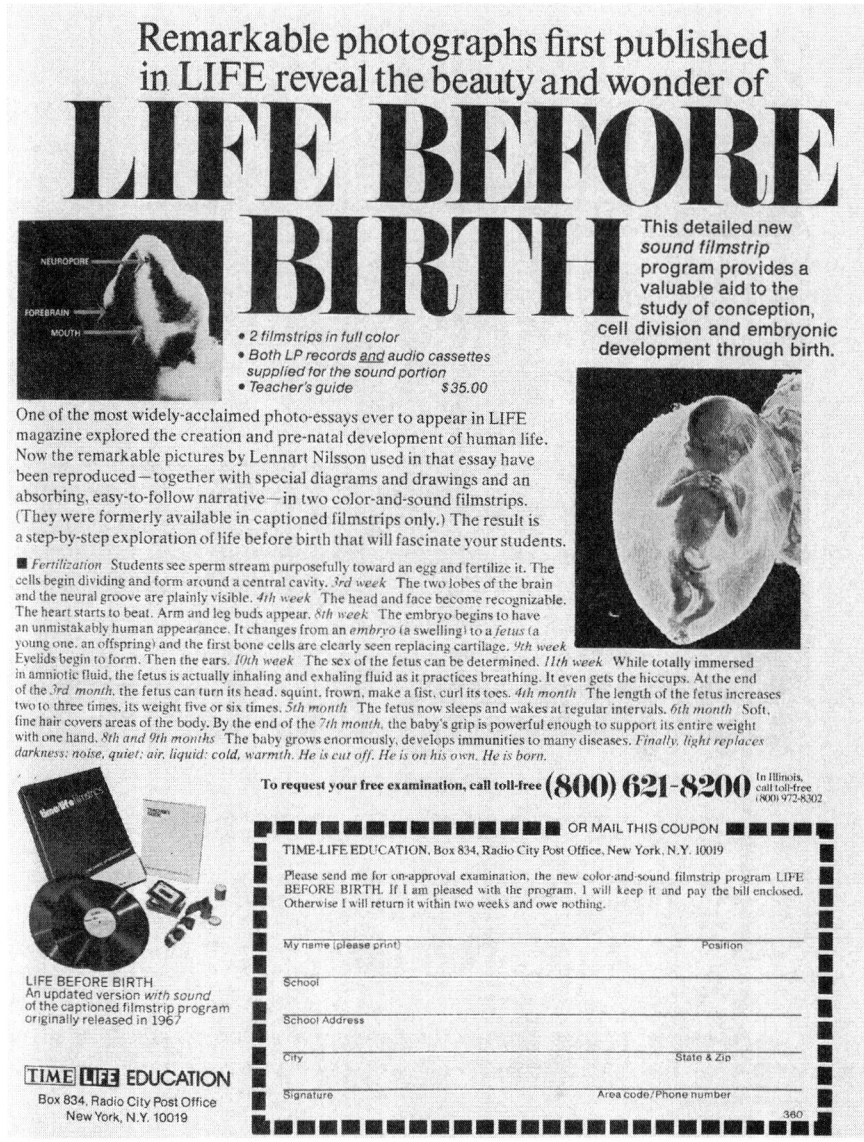

Figure 10.1 Sexual education in the age of audiovisual media. Ad from *The American Biology Teacher* 23 (May 1973). Courtesy of Time-Life Pictures/Getty Images.

At the end of the 1960s these investments on audiovisual media products appeared to be a successful move. Although Nilsson's publications sold well, there were recurrent reports of an international publishing crisis. It was a commonly held belief that videocassettes and other new media would replace books, newspapers, and other printed information. As a consequence, the largest book-publishing companies in different countries started to invest capital in experimenting with and assessing new technologies and new media.[16] In 1973 Esselte Bonnier Audio Visual (EBAV), a company jointly owned by the Bonnier Group and Esselte, started the subsidiary Science AV that produced educational multimedia material. One of its major commissions was the manufacture, sale, and rental of media products based on Nilsson's photographs. Educational packages, filmstrips, slide series, and overhead projector pictures in different versions for different class levels were sold to about fifty countries. Also, films on human conception and development were converted to TED videodiscs, an early predecessor of the DVD format that never achieved much market traction against the recordable videocassettes. Around 1980 this experimentation with new media continued with a model for an electronic encyclopedia stored on a video laserdisc. A search on an early personal computer using the letter *F* (as in "fetal development") led to the presentation of elements of text, image, and sound.[17] Thus, new media were made through old media and directed toward an increasingly differentiated market.

Somewhat paradoxically, as they themselves noted, the group associated with Esselte Bonnier Audio Visual published several books on the topic of new media during the 1970s. McLuhan, who was also invited as a keynote speaker at a conference EBAV organized in Stockholm in 1974, was frequently referred to in these publications. For instance, the director Nils B. Treving introduced the book *Nya media* (New Media, 1970) with the words "Open letter to friends in the global village," and apologized for not using a videocassette, telephone facsimile, or a communication satellite to transmit the information to the recipients of the message.[18] In another book Treving and his coauthors referred to McLuhan's conviction that the globalization of audiovisual cassettes would become a strongly decentralized factor in societal change. Instead of watching the same broadcast program, large parts of the population would be able to choose individual programs on audiovisual cassettes.[19]

As pointed out by Treving and the EBAV-people, there were many possibilities in this envisioned future but also problematic effects. From a business perspective the most worrying issue concerned, of course, copyright. Another aspect touched upon involved the difficulties associated with selling products for an international market. To a large extent these had to be "culturally neutral."[20] Both of these concerns were mirrored in the daily practice of handling the Nilsson material. Rune Pettersson, the director of Science AV, was quite aware that biology teachers, antiabortion activists, and other people took copies of the photographs from *A Child is Born* even though it was illegal to do so. Esselte Bonnier Audio Visual tried to counter this by offering higher-quality images and by controlling their circulation within and across national borders. All images that had been rented out for publication in international journals or magazines were supposed to be returned to the Science AV archive, but unauthorized uses were difficult to prevent. The other concern with which Pettersson was confronted stemmed from the great differences between countries on how the publishers wanted to frame educational programs on human sexuality. As a consequence of long dialogues with foreign publishers who wanted to replace some of the images they considered to clash with domestic national sexual morals, Science AV chose not to sell prepackaged series of slides. Instead they offered to sell them to the publishers separately so that they could supply texts with alternative wording and add some images of their own. All the names connected to the production except Nilsson's were removed. After a while Pettersson realized this material could be used at so many levels—from primary school up to medical studies—simply by focusing on different elements in the picture.[21]

In this way, then, the Bonnier Group and its associated partner Esselte adapted the educational multimedia material based on Nilsson's photographs to the national and international market. This involved niche marketing as well as standardization of the products. Filtering out information made it easier for buyers, and also for unauthorized users, to fill in the details they considered crucial for experiencing the drama of life before birth. Or, to borrow from McLuhan, the hot medium of photography was cooled down in the new electronic environment.

SEXUAL EDUCATION AND THE AV REVOLUTION

The Bonnier Group's launch of the Nilsson material coincided with an extensive expansion and reform of the education system in Sweden. When the new comprehensive and compulsory school was fully introduced in 1962 it created a basic nine-year curriculum for all children from seven to sixteen years old. Keywords that were used to guide teaching on all levels were activity, self-activity, individualization, and concretization. Many educators and pedagogues felt this reform demanded a richer and more differentiated educational technology. Textbooks and verbal tools were not enough; instead, a wide range of audiovisual media was needed. The pedagogical attraction of television and film, in particular, was that these media absorbed the whole attention of the student by engaging both eyes and ears.[22] More generally, it was argued that educational institutions had to adapt to the electronic age in which people created new ways of perceiving and structuring information and knowledge. Again, McLuhan was invoked, this time to argue for a shift in the attitude toward the students: "As the audience becomes a participant in the total electric drama the classroom can become a scene in which the audience performs an enormous amount of work."[23]

Interestingly, these reforms also brought with them a reorganization of sex education in schools, a subject that had been compulsory in Sweden since 1956. In view of strong criticism of the sex instruction offered, a state commission was set up in 1964 and presented its proposal ten years later. One recommendation was that sexual education must be taught using new audiovisual material that had been designed specifically for the needs of the different levels.[24] Earlier the biological aspects of the subject had been taught mainly verbally by the teacher and with the aid of object lessons, blackboard sketches, and anatomical drawings. Eleven- to thirteen-year-old children were not allowed to copy any of the pictures since it was feared they would be used "in an unsuitable manner."[25] The 1956 handbook on sex instruction, still in use in the 1960s, was strongly prescriptive and declared that lessons should aim to foster young people who "understand what society demands of them as citizens."[26] The members of the state commission and other experts in the field who advocated more progressive sexual education were enthusiastic about Nilsson's photographs. These made it possible to present the topic of conception and fetal development in "a fresh and relaxed way" and thereby stimulate the interest not least of the young people. Thus, the Nilsson products were thought to fit well into the program of the "active school" since they encouraged the children to talk freely and participate in discussions on different aspects of sexuality.[27] However, this reformed sexual education still aimed to bring up young people to appreciate society's morals; but they were to be citizens of a new kind who shared an ability to reflect upon controversial values such as ethical attitudes toward abortion and views on birth control methods.[28]

The Bonnier Group played an active part in promoting Nilsson's photographic work as first-rate sexual education material designed for the progressive Swedish society. To secure business interests in times that were "a-changin'," it was important to wash out the stamp of antiabortion propaganda still associated with Nilsson's embryonic and fetal images. In the autumn of 1965, concurrent with the publication of *A Child is Born*, one of the magazines owned by the Bonnier Group printed a special supplement with Nilsson's color photographs that was distributed to Swedish school children. Over a period of a few weeks, the photographer traveled around schools in Stockholm and documented how the folder with his images was used in sexual education lessons. He also took pictures that showed how the political goal of achieving greater gender equality was put into pedagogical practice: boys nursing, knitting, and baking; and girls manufacturing handicrafts. In addition, an accompanying photographer portrayed Nilsson seated at a desk together with some of the younger children while studying the images of fetal development. Several of these photographs were then published in the aforementioned Bonnier Group magazine as well as a book oriented at the American audience, *Sex and Society in Sweden*.[29] Clearly, this project was just as much about demonstrating the vitality of the embryos and fetuses in Nilsson's photographs as documenting sexual education in school.

132   Solveig Jülich

Figure 10.2   "To have a child ... A lesson for life." Photographer Lennart Nilsson with school children looking at his famous images of embryos and fetuses. Cover of *Idun Veckojournalen*, 1 October 1965. Photo by Pål-Nils Nilsson. Courtesy of NordicPhotos.

From this time onward, sexual educators began to collaborate with Nilsson on several mixed-media projects. Maj-Briht Bergström-Walan, a member of the state commission on sex education, wrote the script for the film *The Child* that combined Nilsson's fetal photographs with drawings and live shooting to portray the experience of pregnancy from the moment of conception to childbirth and the homecoming from the hospital with the baby. The film was used in schools as well as in maternal and childcare education. On the basis of this material, four sets of slides were produced that had been adapted for different levels from the lower grades to medical school. All these media productions were promoted as scientific, accurate views of embryonic and fetal development. They constructed a narrative in which heterosexuality was taken for granted, that focused largely on the biological differences between the sex organs. Fetal development was presented in a linear manner with images showing different stages of growth from conception to birth. Together, these representational strategies worked to give the impression that the audience was indeed watching the beginning of life for an individual. Although there was no talk about personal rights, as had begun among antiabortion activists in the United States, referring to the embryo as "the little child" created associations to a human being that existed from the moment of fertilization.[30]

With reference to Lauren Berlant it can be claimed, then, that the relationship between sex, citizenship, and commercial media was no less intimate in Sweden than in the United States. As she has pointed out, the early 1970s marked an important phase in the emergence of fetal photography as a defining feature of American citizenship. Of particular interest here is her discussion on how the uses of Nilsson's photographs in the visual tactics of the early antiabortion movement contributed to promote the notion of fetal personhood and rights.[31] Sexual education in Sweden was also part of a national pedagogy project although with a very different agenda.

SOCIAL MOVEMENTS AND VISUAL ACTIVISM

Nilsson's photographs of conception and embryonic development in the April 1965 issue of *Life* magazine have often been described as creating a worldwide sensation; eight million copies of the issue were sold in three days.[32] The responses were mixed, however, and the editors of *Life* received letters from their readers that conveyed everything from feelings of awe and admiration to disgust and repulsion. Some wished to express their appreciation to the editors for providing a visual means for proper sex instruction for the young, whereas others condemned the pictures for violating personal privacy.[33] These different concerns were soon echoed in the social movements of the late 1960s and early '70s.

Historians and other scholars have often described the 1960s as an era of progressive social movements that was followed by the more conservative subsequent decades. However, as Richard L. Hughes has argued, it is important to account also for the similarities between progressive and conservative activists during and after the 1960s. In order to illustrate the complexity of American social activism, he has demonstrated how key grassroots antiabortion activists appropriated the rhetoric and tactics of the antiwar movement and the African-American civil rights movement. Interestingly, a powerful visual link between Vietnam War protests and antiabortion movements can be found in the use of images of children and motherhood to affect public opinion. As suggested by Hughes, Nilsson's pictures of embryos and fetuses provided such a link.[34] In addition, I would like to further emphasize the creative appropriation and remediation of these photographs by social movements of the early 1970s.

For instance, Nilsson's photographs came to play a small but visible part of the program performance of the second Atlanta International Pop Festival in 1970. Like the Woodstock Festival of the previous year, it was promoted as "three days of peace, love and music." According to some estimates there were as many as 500,000 attendees at the Atlanta festival, but 200,000 was probably a closer guess.[35] When the Allman Brothers Band appeared on the stage during the Fourth of July weekend the (unknown) presenter introduced them with a story inspired by Nilsson's photographs of the fertilization of the human egg in *Life* magazine. He told the audience that when he was a boy attending school he had been taught that the beginning of life was a "big race"; the sperm race to the egg and the first one to get there aggressively penetrates it and enters. But now the pictures by the Swedish photographer had disclosed that "what really happens is the sperm surround the egg, the female ovum, and they twirl it with their tails in a rate of eight times per minute in this pheromonal dance—and this actually happens, you know eight times per eight is the sign of infinity, right." He ended excitedly, raising his voice, by saying "that is what we all come from, it is this dance, so life is not a race, it is not competing with anyone, it is playing together, like Allman play together." Then the band started the session and, one must imagine, people began to move their bodies in a mass dance.[36] In many ways, then, this creative appropriation of Nilsson's images as symbols of peace, love, and music at "the Woodstock of the South" can be seen as an illustration of the progressive efforts of the time.[37] In August 1970 McLuhan, in reference to (often televised) media events like these, stated that important changes had taken place in society, and as an effect, "[t]he audience has now become an actor."[38]

During the same period, antiabortion activists started to bring Nilsson's photographs to their lectures, exhibits, and gatherings. The pro-life movement emerged as a reaction to a growing struggle for abortion rights in the years before the *Roe v. Wade* Supreme Court decision in 1973 that legalized abortion in the United States. Although in opposition to many of the ideals that fueled the social activism of the '60s, the antiabortion activists used similar kinds of media strategies and images.[39] The architects behind the

Fetal Photography in the Age of Cool Media 135

Figure 10.3 "This is my client." Lawyer Stephen Foley was one of the members of early antiabortion groups that started to bring Nilsson's images to lectures, meetings, and debates. Photo by Art Rickerby, first published in *Life*, 17 April 1970. Courtesy of Time-Life Pictures/Getty Images.

visual tactics in the early pro-life movement were a Catholic couple from Cincinnati, the physician Jack Willke and his wife, Barbara Willke, who had professional experience from training nurses. Before turning to the subject of abortion they had traveled around the country for many years giving public talks about sexual education for children. Apart from lecturing and giving television and radio talks, they also produced audiovisual presentations and wrote several books that became the canonical literature of the National Right to Life Committee.[40]

In 1973 the Willkes published *How to Teach the Pro-Life Story*, a handbook that covered everything from organizing a local group and teaching guides to a wide variety of media and suggestions for their use. The authors stressed the importance of pictures since they believed this to be the most effective way to convince people that what grows inside the womb is human life. The pictures they used, however, had to have scientific credibility and look "lifelike." For this reason, Nilsson's photographs were much recommended by the Willkes, although the couple seemed to be aware that they showed aborted embryos and fetuses. These and other images of developmental embryos were so "powerful" in themselves that they could be used in nearly any way and still be successful. But the Willkes strongly suggested that lecturers should use the pedagogical technique of starting with the known—pictures of premature babies—and then backing chronologically to earlier and more unknown stages of embryonic development.[41]

At their lectures Barbara Willke held up the cover of the issue of *Life* magazine with the Nilsson photograph of the eighteen-week-old fetus and challenged the audience with the question "Is this being human?" Then the Willkes showed images of embryos at sixteen, fourteen, twelve, and eleven weeks and in each case repeated, "Is this one human?" When confronted with the images of fetuses at eleven and ten weeks, people usually began to question if what they saw was really human life; for this reason, the lecturers detailed the perfection of the bodily functions and organs at these stages. The last photographs were of embryos at eight and six weeks, and the Willkes told the audience that although these no longer looked human, this would not be the case if the people in the lecture hall were to amplify their eyes with a microscope and become aware of the cellular life that makes us human. No images prior to the six-week developmental stage were shown since, according to the authors, this could make the viewers change their minds. When the lesson in fetal development was complete, the Willkes showed a nine-minute film of an actual vacuum abortion. The tactics suggested by the Willkes' performance was thus first to educate the people in the audience and then to shock them. Visual media were deemed so crucial because these were thought to engage and affect the audience's bodies and minds.[42]

As stressed in the Willkes' book, media strategies were central to the action program of the pro-life movement. The best teaching approach was to adapt to various situations and types of audiences. For this reason a wide range of old and new media should be assimilated and combined in various ways. The most effective use of media would involve "a number of primetime documentaries to saturate the nation from the TV screen."[43] Also, it could be quite effective to bring very large blown-up photographs, such as the *Life* magazine cover, to the television studio and to hold it up as the camera zoomed in on it while being interviewed about involvement in pro-life activities. In a classroom or lecture hall, slides and filmstrips offered the most engaging and moving presentation. The educational filmstrip program with Nilsson's material sold by the Time-Life Education company was cited as an already classic example. Public exhibits could be used to affect a large number of people that never came to lectures or attended church. For instance, exhibiting pictures of fetal development could attract the attention of people who came to state or county fairs and walked past the booth. Readers of the Willkes' book were urged to buy or rent an exhibition from the Cincinnati Right to Life Committee that presented fetal development according to the pedagogical idea of succeeding from the known to the unknown—Nilsson's images appeared once again.[44]

In this manner the Willkes went through all sort of media, including brochures, billboards, poster, bumpers stickers, envelope stickers and decals, tapes, calendars, T-shirts, and even jewelry. Each medium, or rather mix of media, was said to be suited for a special situation and audience. They also greatly encouraged the creativity of local pro-life groups: exhibits could be made, banners produced, cassettes duplicated, posters reproduced. Organizing a pro-life rally was described as especially productive since it mobilized many people and was in itself a kind of multimedia event that could potentially attract the attention of the whole nation.[45] Antiabortion activists like the Willkes were, then, both consumers and producers of Nilsson-material.

Earlier feminist and historical research has focused on the role of Nilsson's fetal photography in the growing pro-life movement. Highlighting the playful use of the *Life* magazine images at progressive events such as the Atlanta International Pop Festival can add to an understanding of the complexity of social activism. It has also been a contention of this chapter that a closer look at the mixed-media strategies employed by activists can further the historical analysis of the making of the public fetus.

REMIXING THE PUBLIC FETUS

Today, Nilsson's photographs of embryos and fetuses can be found everywhere in our mediatized culture. This is not simply an effect of the successful business strategies of the Bonnier Group and their associated partners but also of the unauthorized circulation and use of these images. Digital technologies have indeed provided a means for people to actively reshape the content of Nilsson's photographs as they adopt it for their personal use

138 *Solveig Jülich*

or modify it for the needs of grassroots organizations and online communities. For instance, at photo-sharing websites like Flickr, fans of the Swedish photographer borrow his famous pictures to create slideshows on the beginnings of life. YouTube members upload videos that combine Nilsson's pictures, often unacknowledged, with their own images to tell their pregnancy and childbirth stories. Individuals and organizations use his fetal imagery on internet forums, blogs, and other websites to mobilize support for arguments about reproductive rights, sexual education, and abortion. These tendencies and phenomena seem in many ways to be characteristic of the emergence of a new participatory culture.[46]

But, as this chapter has demonstrated, the creative circulation and appropriation of Nilsson's photographs is hardly something unique for the contemporary mediascape. On the contrary, the making of the public fetus was always a matter of remixing new and old media content. Also, when viewing Nilsson's images over a longer period of time, it seems less certain that the convergence of media companies and grassroots communities is a feature of internet culture. From the very start, the Bonnier Group supported and capitalized on the photographic project Nilsson pursued in collaboration with physicians and scientists opposed to abortion at the women's clinics in Stockholm. The effect was that the distribution of Nilsson's photographs in a range of media became a small but burgeoning industry in Sweden and elsewhere. These images of dead embryos and fetuses, staged to look humanlike and alive, were combined and integrated with the new media of the time: television, the videocassette player, the overhead projector, the slide projector, and the tape recorder. Marketed as audiovisual aids to stimulate active and sensory learning, the Nilsson products were targeted at educators and teachers of sexual education during a period of great reforms in the Swedish public school system. However, in the early 1970s grassroots movements in the United States made productive new use of Nilsson's mixed-media images. At "the Woodstock of the South" as well as at media events organized by antiabortion activists, the remediated photographs of conception and embryonic development were employed to affect people, to make them move and act.

Contrary to McLuhan's conviction, this essay suggests that the media involved in the creation and circulation of Nilsson's images had no intrinsic qualities that determined the temperature of participation. Photography was no less cool than television, at least if judged by the large groups of people who used the pictures to visualize different kinds of stories of embryonic life. But neither can it be said that these mixed-media images were more radical, alternative, or democratic than others. The Nilsson slides and filmstrips that the Bonnier Group produced could be used in progressive sexual education in Sweden as well as in the increasingly conservative antiabortion movement in the United States. This points to a somehow more complicated picture of "resistance" to hegemonic mass culture than has often been described by media and cultural studies scholars.[47]

At the same time, however, it can be argued that McLuhan was right in insisting on the materiality of media. Although this may at first appear trivial, it did make a difference that the Willkes manufactured a slideshow that included the *Life* magazine cover and was distributed nationwide. In comparison to reprints, these slides were cheap, small, and easy to circulate. Thus, the technological properties of audiovisual media could facilitate and inspire certain uses. From yet another aspect, the media involved were crucially material. With the help of slide and overhead projectors Nilsson's (already) enlarged photographs of embryos could be magnified to even greater proportions than in magazines and books. When the images were remediated in sex educational films and televisions programs, both eyes and ears were engaged and stimulated. In these and several other ways audiences were bodily and affectively induced to experience the drama of life before birth. But still more important, the symbolic physicality of the images must be taken into account when reflecting over participatory practices and material media. It was hardly a coincidence that sexual educators as well as antiabortion activists were attracted to Nilsson's work. The pictures of embryos and fetuses had been designed to look humanlike and living, a feature emphasized by the accompanying texts. This character of the images made it easier to teach, involve, and activate young citizens in learning about sex and society. As has also been noted in this chapter, it was the babylike look of the pictures of human development that made them fit so well for the Willkes' lectures. Although Nilsson's images of embryos and fetuses were themselves silent, they were increasingly asked to speak. Depending on the social context this talk included everything from progressive politics to cultural conservatism. In the age of cool media, then, school children, hippies, and antiabortion activists as well as mediated fetuses were recruited as participants and publics.

This article is a result of a research project entitled "Scientific Research, Photojournalism or Special Effects? Lennart Nilsson's Visual Hybrid Practices," funded by the Swedish Research Council.

NOTES

1. W. Chun, "Introduction," p. 1.
2. M. McLuhan, *Understanding Media*, esp. Chap. 2.
3. S. Goldstein, "One Man's Media Is Another Man's Poison," *The Village Voice*, 1 January 1970, p. 3.
4. L. Nilsson and A. Rosenfeld, "Drama of Life before Birth," *Life*, 30 April 1965; L. Nilsson, A. Ingelman-Sundberg, and C. Wirsén, *A Child is Born: The Drama of Life before Birth in Unprecedented Photographs; A Practical Guide for the Expectant Mother* (New York: Delacorte Press, 1967). Subsequent American editions were published in 1977, 1990, 2003, and 2009. A presentation of the photographer's career is given in L. Nilsson, *Lennart Nilsson: Images of His Life*, ed. J. Forsell (Stockholm: Bonnier, 2002).

5. R. Petchesky, "Fetal Images."
6. See, e.g., K. Newman, *Fetal Positions*; and the essays by M. Michaels, "Fetal Galaxies," and C. Stabile, "The Traffic in Fetuses."
7. L. Morgan, *Icons of Life*.
8. S. Jülich, "Visions of Life and Death: A Cultural History of Lennart Nilsson's Hybrid Images" (working title for book manuscript, in progress).
9. J. Bolter and R. Grusin, *Remediation*; L. Lessig, *Remix*.
10. For example, see A. Sreberny-Mohammadi and A. Mohammadi, *Small Media, Big Revolution*; J. Downing, *Radical Media*; M. Waltz, *Alternative and Activist Media*; H. Jenkins, *Convergence Culture*. Although Jenkins (*Convergence Culture*, p. 133) is anxious to distance himself from any form of technological determinism, his use of the term "participatory media" could be interpreted as if he nevertheless believes that some media are more participatory than others.
11. This early history of the contexts for the production of Nilsson's embryonic and fetal photographs is described in detail in Jülich, "Visions of Life and Death" (see note 8). All translations are by the author, unless stated otherwise.
12. For the full references to "Drama of Life before Birth" and *A Child is Born*, see note 4. Several researchers have pointed out that Nilsson's fetal photographs, which are used to symbolize life, are of dead specimens. See for instance S. Matthews and L. Wexler, *Pregnant Pictures*, esp. Chap. 6. This aspect is also discussed and related to a wider social history of embryo collecting in the United States in L. Morgan, *Icons of Life*, p. 206. In "Visions of Life and Death" I situate Nilsson's fetal image-making in the context of medicine and media relations in postwar Sweden, based among other things on personal interviews with his scientific collaborators as well as the Bonnier Group editors.
13. H. Jenkins, *Convergence Culture*, Chap. 3.
14. L. Nilsson, "Ett barn blir till," *Idun Veckojournalen*, 1 October 1965; L. Nilsson, "Det är du!" *Se*, 6 May 1965. The film *Så börjar livet*, written by C. Wirsén and B. Bernholm, was produced by L. Wallén, SoL-film, and first broadcast on Swedish television in 1965.
15. "Life before Birth," ad for Time-Life Education, *The American Biology Teacher* 35 (1973), p. 241.
16. A. Steiner, *I litteraturens mittfåra*. This description of the "publishing crisis" is also based on an interview with Rune Pettersson by S. Jülich, 13 January 2009. Pettersson was a zoologist who became an editor at the professional publishing division of the Bonnier Group in 1968 and from 1973 was the director of Science AV, a subsidiary of Esselte Bonnier Audio Visual (EBAV).
17. R. Pettersson, interview, 13 January 2009.
18. "Video och nya media 1974," ad from EBAV, *Utbildningstidningen* 5 (1974), p. 27; N. Treving and B.-A. Vedin, *Nya media* (Halmstad: Ingenjörsförlaget, 1970), p. 6.
19. G. Bergvall, R. Pettersson, N. Treving, and S.-E. Westerlund, *Nya AV-media* (Stockholm: Bonnier, 1971), p. 58.
20. G. Bergvall et al., *Nya AV-media*, pp. 58–64.
21. R. Pettersson, interview, 13 January 2009.
22. E. Wallin, "Mot en pedagogisk teknologi," *Undervisningsteknologi* 1 (1966), pp. 9–11; S. Lidman, *Bildning i bildåldern* (Lund, Sweden: Corona, 1966), p. 57.
23. M. McLuhan and Q. Fiore, *The Medium is the Massage*, p. 101. This phrase was quoted in "Mediernas värld," *Undervisningsteknologi* 3 (1968), p. 13.

24. Utredningen rörande sexual- och samlevnadsfrågor i undervisnings- och upplysningsarbetet, *Sexual- och samlevnadsundervisning* (Stockholm: LiberFörlag/Allmänna förlaget, 1974). See "Summary of the Proposals of the Commission," pp. 802–14.
25. *Handbook on Sex Instruction in Swedish Schools* (Stockholm: National Board of Education in Sweden, 1968), p. 35.
26. Ibid., p. 11.
27. B. Linnér, *Sex and Society in Sweden* (New York: Pantheon Books, 1967), Chap. 10, esp. pp. 93–4, 109–12.
28. "Summary of the Proposals of the Commission," esp. pp. 803–4.
29. B. Linnér, *Sex and Society in Sweden*.
30. L. Nilsson, C. Wirsén, and M.-B. Bergström-Walan, *Barnet* 1–2, a film produced and directed by H. Cronsioe, Svensk Tonfilm, 1967; and *Barnet: En bildserie för skolans sexualundervisning*, 4 vols., Svensk Tonfilm, 1969–70, slides and audio cassettes.
31. L. Berlant, *The Queen of America Goes to Washington City*, esp. Chap. 3.
32. M. Holborn, "Lennart Nilsson and Photography," p. 285.
33. G. Hunt, "Editor's Note," *Life*, 21 May 1965, p. 3; "Letters to the Editors," *Life*, 21 May 1965, p. 27.
34. See the two articles by R. Hughes: "Burning Birth Certificates and Atomic Tupperware Parties"; and " 'The Civil Rights Movement of the 1990s?'."
35. See the memorabilia websites of Alex Cooley, online, available HTTP: <http://www.alexcooley.com/fest-atlpop2.html>; and Carter Tomassi, online, available HTTP: <http://www.messyoptics.com/bird/APF_00.html> (both accessed 5 March 2010).
36. The Allman Brothers Band, "Introduction," *Live at the Atlanta International Pop Festival: July 3 & 5, 1970* (Sony Music Entertainment, 2003). Many thanks to research colleague Johan Jarlbrink who tipped me off about this soundtrack. I would also like to express my gratitude to festival participant Carter Tomassi and his friends for jogging their memories and trying to find out who was the presenter of the festival. However, their search was fruitless and it remains a mystery who this fan of Nilsson's photographs was.
37. The expression "the Woodstock of the South" is used, among others, by S. Schinder and A. Schwartz, *Icons of Rock: An Encyclopedia of the Legends Who Changed Music Forever*, vol. 1 (Westport, CT: Greenwood, 2008), p. 250.
38. M. McLuhan and T. Wolfe, "TV News as a New Mythic Form (1970)," in M. McLuhan, *Understanding Me: Lectures and Interviews*, p. 164.
39. R. Hughes, "Burning Birth Certificates and Atomic Tupperware Parties."
40. C. Gorney, *Articles of Faith*, pp. 99–106. Also see Stabile, "The Traffic in Fetuses," p. 145.
41. J. Willke and B. Willke, *How to Teach the Pro-Life Story* (Cincinatti, OH: Hiltz & Hayes, 1973), esp. Chap. 1.
42. Ibid. Also see C. Gorney, *Articles of Faith*, pp. 101, 104–5.
43. J. Willke and B. Willke, *How to Teach the Pro-Life Story*, quotation on p. 36.
44. Ibid., esp. Chaps. 4–6.
45. Ibid., esp. Chaps. 7–18, 22.
46. This is, of course, an argument in line with H. Jenkins, *Convergence Culture*.
47. A similar argument is made in H. Hendershot, *Shaking the World for Jesus*, p. 14.

11 *Expedition Robinson*, Reality TV, and the History of the Social Experiment

Per Wisselgren

In Peter Weir's award-winning film *The Truman Show* (1998), we are told the story of Truman Burbank, a seemingly ordinary and happy guy who is leading a strictly routinized and not-too-dramatic life in a small, well-ordered American town. The only thing that is really unusual about Truman is that he is unaware that every step he takes and every move he makes is being surveilled and broadcast live twenty-four hours a day, seven days a week, to millions of viewers around the globe; and that the whole town is a constructed stage peopled by professional actors, including his wife, his mother, and his best friend. In the prelude to the film, the fictional character Christof, a former producer of documentaries and himself the creator of the successful reality TV format, explains the success of his "extraordinary experiment":

> We've become bored with watching actors give us phony emotions. We're tired of pyrotechnics and special effects. While the world he inhabits is in some respects counterfeit, there's nothing fake about Truman himself. No scripts, no cue cards. It isn't always Shakespeare but it's genuine. It's a life.[1]

In one of the following opening sequences Marlon, the actor who plays Truman's best friend, confirms "it's all true, it's all real"—and adds: "it's merely controlled."[2]

Although *The Truman Show* in itself is a fictional and by now more than ten-years-old historical document, one of the facts that makes it useful in this context is that the film coincided in time with the early breakthrough of the reality TV genre. Few people at that time were probably able to foresee the enormous expansion of the genre that was to follow and the extent to which the basic formula of reality TV, as prescribed by Christof, with its mixture of ordinary people, unscripted situations, and serialized documentation of actual events, was to be put into systematic practice—especially after the advent of groundbreaking formats such as *Big Brother* (1999) and *Survivor* (2000) and the worldwide plethora of local adaptations and similar formats that have followed in their aftermath.

In the context of the recent developments of the global media industry, however, *The Truman Show* can also be seen as a meta-comment on the deep impact of television on today's late modern culture in general and the significance of the reality TV genre in particular. Like the rapidly expanding research on reality TV, *The Truman Show* explicitly reflects on the current tendencies toward a blurring of genres between fact and fiction, documentary and drama, information and entertainment, and also on more general issues regarding the changing relationships between the private and the public, surveillance and visuality, authenticity and performativity, as well as what some theorists have identified as our related preoccupation with "everyday social experiments."[3]

Another recurrent theme within this rich body of research concerns the dynamic relationship between television and its audiences and the ways in which this relationship has changed in recent years, sometimes described in terms of a "participatory turn."[4] Henry Jenkins, for example, has discussed *Survivor* and *American Idol* as examples of how new converging media tend to encourage new and more democratic forms of participation, while other, more critical voices, such as Mark Andrejevic and John Corner, have problematized the often made equation of media participation with political citizenship.[5] A general tendency among these studies, which often have their disciplinary base in contemporary media studies, is that most of them regard reality TV as emblematic of our late-modern digital era. But is this phenomenon, as well as the themes and issues it has generated, actually as unique and entirely new as it is often claimed?

In this chapter, I will discuss reality TV as a participatory medium with a special focus on its social experimental character and put it in a considerably broader historical context. Empirically, the chapter focuses on the Swedish reality TV show *Expedition Robinson* during the period in which it was broadcast by the domestic public service broadcasting company Sveriges Television (SVT) from 1997 to 2004.[6] The choice of focus is motivated by the fact that the Swedish version of the format, originally created by Charlie Parsons and the UK-based television production company Planet 24, was the very first one to be broadcast, that is, even before it was licensed by Mark Burnett and produced for the American CBS as *Survivor* in 2000.[7] It has been said that *Survivor* started the reality television trend and that its audience is one of the largest in broadcast television, which may be true for the American context.[8] But the format also became extremely popular in Sweden and attracted an even larger proportion of viewers in relation to its population. During the seven seasons it was broadcast by SVT, it never dropped out of the domestic top-ten list of the most viewed programs for each year. The peak was reached in 2000 when no fewer than 4 million Swedes—out of a population of 8.8 million—viewed the final episode of that season![9] Since its inception, the format has been adapted not only in the U.S. but also in more than forty other countries.[10] Although it is possible to argue that it was not the very first reality TV show, not even in the Swedish context, *Expedition Robinson* was definitely the program that brought the genre over to the major domestic networks, made it prime-time entertainment, and through its sheer popularity pioneered the reality television trend in Sweden—and in some respects, internationally.[11]

The main argument developed in this context is that one of the attractions of *Expedition Robinson* lay precisely in its character of a social experiment and that this idea, in combination with the realistic and participatory aspects, encouraged a specific way of reading the program that made the viewers identify with the participants and their social interplay within the group. Another aspect of the argument is that the experimental idea was especially important in the way it established a common basic tripartite consensual understanding between the producers, the participants, and the audience. The third and final part of the argument is that the social experimental character of the program makes it plausible to analyze it within a wider historical context of media-based social experiments, which in the end both points to the need for a more historically nuanced view of reality TV as an entirely new media phenomenon and problematizes some of the power-related aspects inherent in *Expedition Robinson* and other reality TV formats.

EXPEDITION ROBINSON: THE FORMAT AND ITS GENRE

Although "reality TV" is today a firmly established term and *Expedition Robinson* most often classified as a typical representative of the genre, it is important to emphasize that both the phenomenon and the concept have undergone significant changes since they first appeared in the 1990s. Today the term "reality TV" is used for formats as different as *Big Brother, American Idol, Who Wants to Be a Millionaire, Cops,* and *The Apprentice*—just to mention a few of the most well-known and widespread ones. Accordingly, the definitions of the genre tend to differ substantially depending on which of the formats are envisaged, who is consulted, and the local context of the interpretation.[12] At the same time, the very classification of genres plays a decisive role in how viewers make sense of the formats and their contents.[13] For the reality TV or docusoap genre as such, the conscious hybridization of genres is key to understanding its function in the interplay between producers, viewers and participants. When the first episodes of *Expedition Robinson* were launched, for example, this mix of established genres was a crucial part of its attraction and its innovative profile. The format was quite literally marketed as a hybrid of the documentary, with a focus on the everyday lives of ordinary people in reality, and the serialized format of the soap opera that focused on the dramatization of everyday events with their microsocial intrigues and conflicts. Basically, however, it is possible to argue that the genre had its origin, historically as well as conceptually, in the documentary tradition.[14]

History of the Social Experiment   145

Hence, before Charlie Parsons formulated the original idea behind *Expedition Robinson* in the mid-1990s—to bring together a number of "ordinary" people with different social backgrounds on an isolated island—he had produced another program as series editor of Network 7 for British Channel 4. The idea was similar: a stockbroker, a soap opera star, a tennis player, and an ex-prisoner were placed together on an island outside Sri Lanka and interviewed by the camera team once a day about what had happened in the last twenty-four hours.[15] That program was not a great success, however. Like MTV's format *The Real World* (1992), which was based on a similar concept and gathered a group of young strangers in a house for several months as cameras recorded their interpersonal relationships, the social experimental idea was there from the very beginning.[16] The only problem was that the outcome of each episode depended very heavily on the specific group of individuals and their initiatives or, in the worst case, lack thereof. Parsons' solution was to add a dramatized element with a certain set of formalized rules.[17]

The result was the *Expedition Robinson* format, based on the mixture of documentary and dramatized elements. The original idea was still there, to assemble a number of ordinary people on a seemingly isolated island. Their "ordinariness" was important. Hence, when the Swedish production team drafted people to the program they explicitly sought "ordinary" people from different parts of Sweden and of different ages, genders, and social backgrounds.[18] The idea was to mirror Sweden in microcosm: "All groups in Sweden should be represented in the program."[19] In contrast, the setting was extraordinary, the "exotic" tropical island Tengah in Malaysia. By following the participants in their everyday lives in this extreme situation and seeing how they handled it physically and socially, the program had, as the producer of the Danish adaptation of the format explicitly described it, the character "of a public and social realistic laboratory, in which the viewers follow the experiment, staged in a hopefully entertaining way."[20] The dramatized addition, which ensured plot progression, consisted of a specific set of game rules according to which the group was divided into two rival subgroups, "Team North" and "Team South," that competed against each other in order to win prizes and, most important, decided which team had to go to the "island council" and vote one of its members out of the game. When only a limited number of participants remained, the two teams merged and its individual members competed until there was only one sole "survivor" left, that is, the "Robinson."[21]

FROM MORAL PANIC TO PUBLIC SUCCESS

When the first episode of *Expedition Robinson* was aired on the major Swedish channel TV1 at 8 p.m. on Saturday 13 September 1997, that is, best prime time, the hybridized form was explicitly emphasized, as was the basic social experimental idea. "Castaway in Paradise. Sixteen Swedes have to survive on a desert island in Malaysia," the announcements in the television tableaux declared. The introductory sequences stressed repeatedly that the participants were "ordinary Swedes," that they did not know each other beforehand, and that their task was to survive, as the program leader dramatically explained the unusual situation, "without contact with the outer world, without refrigerators, without supermarkets, without telephones, without showers."[22]

One million viewers watched the first episode. Statistically it was a success, but still it caused a public scandal.[23] The very first person to be voted out of the program at the first "island council" committed suicide only four weeks after his return to Sweden. The tragic incident occurred after the show's final shooting but more than a month before the first episode was aired. Although there were no signs that any specific experience from the program had caused the suicide, the public debate soon ran hot. Strong expressions were frequently used to describe the character of the program, like "prostration TV," "elimination TV," and "bullying TV." A psychologist drew explicit parallels to social experiments and commented, "Had it been a scientific experiment, then the program would never have passed the ethical review."[24] The massive criticism forced SVT's current director-general Sam Nilsson to take the exceptional step of making a speech to the nation in the major domestic news program, *Rapport*, where he declared that SVT had decided to temporarily stop the program for two weeks. In the meantime, the planned two episodes were reedited and "sensitive" sequences censored.[25]

The intensive media coverage, which started even before the first episode was aired, was double-edged. In spite of the initial predominantly critical tone, the wide publicity triggered the curiosity of many who still had not seen the program. The attention from the surrounding media remained strong throughout the whole period. The domestic evening newspapers in particular kept following the program's development. During its seven seasons and ninety episodes it was headlined no fewer than 180 times by the two major evening papers, *Aftonbladet* and *Expressen*, and more than 10,000 articles about it were published, in addition to the coverage on radio and other television programs.[26] There was a clear pattern of intermedial symbiosis: The newspapers increased their sales of single copies, which made people even more interested in the program. Especially in the beginning, everyone seemed to be talking about it. If for no other reason, one almost had to watch the episodes for social reasons, as one of the viewers commented in retrospect:

> [I]t's like when *Robinson* started if you didn't know what *Robinson* was you might as well have said "what do you mean, *Riksdagen*, what's that?" You'd get totally alienated, you can't communicate with people, they like "what, haven't you watched *Robinson*"?[27]

Despite the initial massive criticism, it was not long before there was a marked shift of opinion. When the second episode was aired on 4 October 1997, the atmosphere had already become quite different. After that, the number of viewers kept rising each episode. The finale of the first season, which aired in December 1997, attracted no less than 2,345,000 viewers.[28] It may seem that the timeout was needed to enable people to calm down and that the measures taken by SVT—among other things, the program director responsible left her post—had positive effects. However, even more important than these measures, the actual reediting or the director-general's speech to the nation, I would like to argue, was one single debate article.

READING REALITY, ENROLLING THE PUBLIC

The article in question was published on 1 October 1997 in *Dagens Nyheter*, the largest domestic morning newspaper, on its op-ed, which is commonly regarded as one the most influential spaces for opinion making and agenda setting in the Swedish context. Most important in this context, however, is that the article was coauthored by the sixteen participants of the show. The timing was also crucial, that is, after the shooting had finished, after the first episode had been aired, and after SVT's timeout had been announced. During this period of silence, the participants decided to step forward and testify to their experiences from the "other side" of the screen:

> We think it is a pity that the media has given such a strange image of us, of the program, and of its idea. The idea of the format is new and exciting. There is no script, and what is happening, is happening in reality . . . We were well informed about the rules of the social game in which we were supposed to participate. The island council shows the result of how social roles are formed when 16 unknown individuals unknown to each other spend time together on an isolated island . . . [W]e are convinced that people will be able to form their own opinions when they see the program.[29]

Hence, the participants actually emphasized three things in their article: first, they affirmed the program's realistic character, that one of the format's new ingredients consisted of the unscripted events. Second, they underlined the character of a social experiment by explaining that the idea was to see how social roles were formed during the process. Third and most important, by bearing witness to their own experiences, they precluded any criticism that ascribed the role of victim to the participants. What they did in the article, in that sense, was to defend the basic idea of the format as such, and also give the audience new and clarified reading instructions on how the program should be viewed and interpreted.

Their testimony was important. Who would know better what it was all about than the participants themselves? One way of understanding the sharp shift of public opinion after the article was published is that the audience took the participants seriously and watched the program, not as a form of television bullying whereby evil producers had exploited uninformed consent to hoax the participants into a scripted plot, but on the contrary, as a social experiment whereby the participants, completely ordinary citizens like you and me, had voluntarily applied to participate out of curiosity to see how they would handle the situation, both physically and socially, together with other ordinary but completely unknown people. And all this was indeed something that required a new mode of watching and understanding, a different way of reading the program.

Provided with these new reading instructions, the viewing audience could be enrolled as a more active public in the shared understanding that hitherto, according to the participants, had united them and the television production team. Speaking in terms of "media literacy," one might say that the participants provided the viewers with the necessary conceptual tools for understanding, analyzing, and evaluating the meaning of the new format.[30] Anna Edin has argued for the importance of including not only the viewing audience as producers of meaning but also the participants' role in this process, by speaking about a "tripartite shared responsibility."[31] I agree with Edin but would like to take the approach one step further and emphasize the importance of a basic tripartite consensual understanding of the format, in the sense that lack of such a shared understanding often results in disagreement about what the different participants conceive as the proper meaning. The point to be made in this context is that the newspaper article with its reading instructions made this less-conflicted understanding of the new blurred genre possible. In that sense, a new kind of "reality literacy" was established.

Basically, this way of reading the program lay pretty much in line with Charlie Parsons's original idea about a kind of social experiment. The participants already understood this. One of the participants in the first season of the program, for example, explained that she "believed it to be an experiment of some kind"; another participant emphasized that he did not know what to expect or what kind of program it would be.[32] Now the viewers were invited to watch it accordingly, which they seemed to do:

> [I]t is such a thrilling idea, like with *Robinson*. Take a bunch of people who do not know each other and cast them away on an isolated island to see what happens then, kind of. One can imagine how oneself would be and behave, with the group dynamics and so . . . in a way these programs become a mirror of what society is like.[33]

A crucial component in this reading is the role of identification and the way it combined the realistic and the participatory aspects: It was all about ordinary people and our social relations, like in everyday life, but in a constructed setting, like a social experiment. Watching *Expedition Robinson* was in that sense like observing, reflecting on, and learning about oneself. And conversely, it was not so much about regarding objectified people that one could not identify or cope with.

This steadily growing popularity not only resulted in a rising number of viewers, but also in an increase of applicants. The first season had attracted 6,000 applicants. By the second season, the number had already doubled to 12,000; and by the fourth, applications had risen to 14,000.[34] Altogether, during the seven seasons, 92,000 applied to become one of the 108 lucky participants. This actual traffic of people that literally turned viewers into participants in combination with the identificatory reading, the role of reality TV viewers as producers, and the sheer magnitude of its popularity, I would like to argue, make it plausible to describe *Expedition Robinson* and its format as a "participatory medium" in Henry Jenkins's sense, that is, a format "made to be discussed, dissected, debated, predicted, and critiqued" and made to increase the viewer's engagement. And as in the case of *Survivor* and *American Idol*, "at every step along the way, the viewers are invited to imagine that it could be me or someone I know."[35]

THE SOCIAL EXPERIMENTAL CHARACTER OF REALITY TV

When the American adaptation of the format, *Survivor*, was launched in 2000, Mark Burnett and the host Jeff Probst from the very beginning repeatedly described and promoted the new program in terms of a "social" or "human experiment"—as did the journalists and the participants.[36] However, the social experimental idea is typical not only of the *Expedition Robinson* and *Survivor* format, but also for a number of other reality shows.[37] Even more evident is the social experimental character of the *Big Brother* format, created by John De Mol and his television production company Endemol, first broadcast in the Netherlands in 1999, in the UK the year after, and subsequently in almost seventy more countries.[38] In the United Kingdom, *Big Brother* was explicitly marketed as "a social documentary offering the audience a chance to get 'pore close' to the experimental subjects."[39] But the participants in the U.S. version of the format have also described the show as "an experiment in human behavior and strategic planning."[40] Furthermore, it is revealing that the viewers in a study by Janet Megan Jones explained the attraction of *Big Brother* in ways that are very similar to the Swedish audience's reading of *Expedition Robinson*:

> I feel that watching and commenting on *Big Brother* tells us a lot about ourselves: how we judge people, what our values are in relationships. How we interact with others and how we would handle relationship dilemmas if put in a similar position.[41]

> I would love to see how I actually am as a person. I have opinions about myself but have never seen the real me. It (being in the house) brings out the real personality of the person that's there.[42]

Besides Jones's study, a number of other researchers who have focused on *Big Brother* have developed similar analyses.[43] John Corner, for example, characterizes the format as a "popular 'experiment' in modern human interaction" amongst "a whole range of documentary-style projects . . . that have made strong and successful connections with the idea of the 'game' (one often also cast as an 'experiment' with location spaces—interior or exterior—as 'laboratory')."[44]

Another reality TV format that fits into Corner's description is the British production *The Nightmares Next Door* (Channel 4, 2005) about a constructed community of caravans set up in a remote and isolated valley in Dorset, where four groups of "troublesome" neighbors live together for four weeks and share restricted supplies of food, water, and electricity under the supervision of a professional psychologist. When the format was shown in Sweden (in four episodes, under the title *Grannjävlar*, SVT, 2006) it was typically announced with the line "Odd neighbors in a social experiment."[45] The same basic social experimental idea was at play in MTV's *The Real World*; coproducer John Murray explained the importance of the casting process: "We try to cast really interesting people who, when they come together, something interesting is going to happen . . . It's like a chemical experiment—you wait and see what kind of compounds are going to be created."[46] And, once again, the participants were initiated, here represented by one of the participants in MTV's spinoff show *Road Rules*: "I knew going into it it's kind of a human experiment, kind of to see how people react under certain situations."[47]

The clearest expression of the social experimental idea was probably the BBC production *The Experiment*, broadcast in 2002, whose main idea quite simply was to show a real social psychological experiment, supervised by two prominent British social psychologists. The setup was that fifteen participants, selected from a group of more than 300 people who had responded to an advert placed in several British newspapers, were brought to a totally enclosed television-studio north of London in Elstree, especially rigged for the purpose with a "vast army of cameras." The participants, until then unaware of the idea of the television show/the experiment, were then divided into two groups and informed that ten of them were given the role of prisoners and the other five the role of warders and the task of running the prison.[48]

In all of the contemporary cases referred to, reality TV as well as its social experimental character can certainly be interpreted as typical of our self-reflexive late-modern age, wherein our "performed selves" are seen as our "true selves" (to borrow from John Corner) and wherein our individual lives often are formulated as open projects, encouraging us to devote ourselves to what Giddens calls "social everyday experiments."[49]

TOWARD A HISTORY OF MEDIA-BASED SOCIAL EXPERIMENTS

At the same time, however, the reality TV formats can also be seen as inscribed in a broader historical context, as I will argue. Such a broadened understanding at once problematizes the presupposition of the reality phenomenon and its related issues as something entirely new and typical of our late modernity. One of the most significant things about *The Experiment* is that the experiment as such was not new, but a replication of a classical social psychological experiment originally set up by the Stanford psychologist Philip Zimbardo in 1971. There is a broad literature about that experiment, which I will not explore in this context. The point here is that the basic idea of *The Experiment* was to encourage the viewers—in the typical reality TV manner—to identify themselves with the participants: not *as if*, but exactly because it actually was an experiment. In the original social psychological experiment, Zimbardo had to end the experiment earlier than planned because it went out of control, and it turned out that the BBC was forced to act in the same way as well.[50]

There is, however, one additional point to be made with reference to the history of the social experiment: that this history is often closely intertwined with its contemporary media contexts. As Anna McCarthy has argued, for example, it is no coincidence that Zimbardo collaborated with Allen Funt, the creator of the comedic hidden-camera program *Candid Camera* (1959–67), which has sometimes been seen as an early progenitor of reality TV in its use of ordinary people and purported lack of manuscripts in real-life situations in order to make us observe ourselves. But Stanley Milgram was also inspired by Funt's work and made use of his films as teaching tools. The point in this context, following McCarthy, is that these early forms of participatory television formats "served as a place where popular culture and social science overlapped . . . and modes of interaction were put on display."[51] Paul Hillier makes a similar argument but emphasizes even further the interaction and reciprocal exchange of legitimacy between the two spheres, where one additional point is that *Candid Camera* in its cold-war contemporaneity turned social surveillance into an entertaining practice and hence naturalized the contemporary social experiments.[52] My addition to these arguments is that several reality TV formats of today have continued to fill this transactional and partly legitimizing function.[53] Hence it is no coincidence that the doctor commissioned by SVT to ensure the well-being of the participants in *Expedition Robinson* spontaneously drew a parallel from the shootings of the program to the psychological experiments set up in the postwar decades—although he could not imagine SVT permitting anything like that to be repeated. In that, he was probably both right and wrong: right in that there are indeed strong resemblances between the postwar social science experiments and today's reality TV, but wrong that a public service broadcasting company would never allow such a thing—since the BBC has already done so.[54]

Consequently, there is more than one reason to widen the temporal horizons when studying and trying to understand reality TV as a participatory media. Whereas McCarthy focuses on the heritage from *Candid Camera*, Bridget Griffen-Foley draws a slightly different sequence of influences in highlighting earlier forms of audience participation from the partly reader-produced periodicals and magazines of the late nineteenth century, through talkback radio with listeners dialing in, to the emerging reality TV formats of the 1990s.[55] Another important strand of research on reality TV has focused on the heritage from the documentary tradition.[56] To these attempts to broaden historical contextualizations, I would like to contribute the interconnectedness of the history of social science and the history of media in general, and the relationship between the history of social experiments and the historical origins of reality TV in particular. In his study of the historical interplay between media technology and social psychological experiments, Nicolas Pethes pinpoints several of the most striking cases in this intermediary sphere.[57] But there are certainly more to be found. As Matthias Gross and Wolfgang Krohn have suggested, the "self-experimental society" is not typical of our late-modern age, but rather a conceptual understanding that can be dated back at least to the late nineteenth century and the programmatic ideas of the Chicago School to investigate the city as a social laboratory in which the social scientist partook as an observing participant.[58] In that sense, the social experimental character of reality TV is not that unique for our time.

Having said that, another question arises: How far back in time can one go and how far can the perspective be widened without losing too much focus? I would actually like to suggest, at least tentatively, that the perspective could be prolonged and widened at least one step further to include the social *thought* experiment and the rise of the modern novel as a new media in the eighteenth century. When the original program leader of *Expedition Robinson*, Harald Treutiger, was about to characterize and explain the basic idea of the new program, he drew parallels to three novels, namely, William Golding's *Lord of the Flies* (1954), Agatha Christie's *And Then There Were None* (1939), and last but not least, Daniel Defoe's *Robinson Crusoe* (1719)—all of them typically literary narratives with their plots staged on islands. There is an important reductionist quality that unites experiments and islands: their isolated character, which gives both of them important theoretical and narrative functions in making it possible to eliminate external disturbances and create a microcosm through which it is possible to reflect upon and study ourselves as human beings.[59] In that sense, the name of the original Swedish adaptation of the format was congenial. This argument implies, of course, that the concept of participatory media must not be narrowly restricted to the so-called "new media" of our time but remain broad enough to include the novel as well, which since its emergence has in similar ways encouraged social reflection and active participation by its readers.[60]

REALITY TV, PARTICIPATORY MEDIA, AND THE ASYMMETRIES OF POWER

So what is actually new and what is old with reality TV? And what value is added when bringing the social experiment into the picture?

When reality television is discussed, which is quite often nowadays, it is most commonly referred to and characterized as a typical signifier of our late-modern society with its increased reflexivity, the role of media, technological control and surveillance, our obsession with identity-creation and performativity, commercialization and branding, etc. But it has also been suggested that as an active element in the tendencies toward the convergence of media technologies, reality TV has encouraged new forms of participation, which it is hoped will ultimately have a positive effect on our political culture. In that sense reality TV, which welcomes ordinary people onto the screen without distinguishing between celebrities and everyday men and women, may be seen as a tool for democracy.

In this chapter I have chosen to connect this discussion to the social experimental idea as it was expressed in *Expedition Robinson* and a few other reality TV formats. I have argued that two other basic components of this idea are its realistic and participatory aspects, in the sense that they encourage a reading that makes the viewing audience actively identify with the participants and reflect upon themselves as social beings. I have also, in relation to the concept of media literacy, argued for the importance of a basic consensual understanding in the tripartite relationship between producers, participants, and viewers. Both of these arguments can be said to speak in favor of the idea of the democratic potential of participatory media.

The social experimental idea does, however, at the same time relate the reality TV phenomenon with other media-based and scientific experiments. The widened historical perspective suggests that reality TV as a participatory media is not as entirely new as many tend to think. Instead, reality TV can be said to highlight one of the basic ideas in the history of experimental knowledge production, namely, that controlled investigations usually require isolated spaces, like laboratories or islands, to eliminate external disturbances. Another important aspect, however, is that the isolation must not be total. Scientific knowledge requires synoptic arrangements, that is, possibilities for public review to legitimize the knowledge as credible.[61] Nick Couldry makes an important argument about the experimental character of reality TV when he reminds us how the French psychologist Jean-Martin Charcot invited audiences in the 1870s to witness his demonstrations of hysterical women.[62] Whereas Couldry mentions this as an historical exception, however, my point is the opposite: that the public (and the policing of it), as Shapin and Schaffer have shown, has always played a decisive role as witness and guarantor in assuring the credibility of the knowledge produced in the history of the experiments, where the laboratory has historically been seen as a public rather than as a private space.[63] In other words, there have been not only producers and participants but also publics—and hence ethical and power-related aspects to be aware of—in the history of the social experiment as well as in today's reality TV.⁶⁴

This parallel to the history of the social experiment, however, problematizes the idea about a consensual understanding in its democratic political sense. Although Milgram and Zimbardo no doubt had democratic intentions with their social experiments—in their endeavors to explore human nature and its tendencies toward obedience and evil—they can nonetheless be criticized from the point of view of their unintended ethical consequences for the participants.⁶⁵ To speak about participation on equal terms in that respect is to underestimate the power-related aspects of knowledge production. Although reality TV as a participatory medium sometimes invites the audience to affect the outcome of the programs and even makes it possible to switch roles and become a participant, and although reality shows—like the literary novel—rhetorically invite the audience to play the part of the social analyst to observe the behavior of the participants, this may testify to important qualities of participatory media that encourage our engagement in partaking in it.⁶⁶ But that is, after all, something completely different from sharing the power of the heavily capitalized global media industry. Hence, there are as many reasons for skepticism about the commonly made equation of media participation with political democratization as for problematization of the increasing disconnectedness between consuming publics and political citizenship.⁶⁷

Seen as a meta-comment on our own time, *The Truman Show* highlights not only the social experimental character of reality TV but also its power-related and ethical aspects. At the precise moment Truman Burbank realizes that Seahaven, the island on which he lives, is a stage, the asymmetrical relationships between producers, participants, and the audience becomes apparent. And actually, as Andrew Niccol, the screenplay writer, has commented, it is not self-evident who "the real captive [is]—is it Truman, or is it the viewers watching Truman?"⁶⁸ It is easier to conclude that it certainly is not Christof.

This essay has been funded by the Swedish Research Council as part of the project "The History of the Social Reportage and its Relation to the Social Sciences in Sweden, 1840–2000."

NOTES

1. P. Weir, *The Truman Show* (Paramount Pictures, 1998). The characterization of the reality TV show as an "extraordinary experiment" is Peter Weir's, used in the background material to the film. See P. Weir, "Introduction," in A. Niccol, *The Truman Show: The Shooting Script* (New York: Newmarket, 1998), p. xvii.
2. P. Weir, *The Truman Show*.

3. Cf. R. Bishop, "Good Afternoon, Good Evening, and Good Night"; S. Zizek, "Welcome to the Desert of the Real," pp. 385–89; R. Kilborn, *Staging the Real*, pp. 157–61; N. Pethes, *Spektakuläre Experimente*, pp. 117–40. Regarding "social everyday experiments," see A. Giddens, "Living in a Post-Traditional Society," pp. 59–60.
4. G. Enli, *The Participatory Turn in Broadcast Television*.
5. H. Jenkins, *Convergence Culture*, p. 25; M. Andrejevic, *Reality TV*, p. 11; J. Corner, "Performing the Real," pp. 265–66.
6. All episodes of the program during the period 1997–2004 are accessible via the Department of Audiovisual Material (formerly SLBA) of the National Library of Sweden (KB).
7. The television production company Planet 24 was co-owned by Charlie Parsons, Bob Geldof, and Waheed Alli. When the company was bought by Carlton Communications in 1999, the three co-owners retained the rights to the format and transferred them to a new company, Castaway Television Productions. Regarding the background of the American *Survivor*, see M. Burnett and M. Dugard, *Survivor: The Ultimate Game: The Official Companion Handbook to the CBS Television Show* (New York: TV Books, 2000), pp. 9–15.
8. H. Jenkins, *Convergence Culture*, p. 25.
9. According to *TV-tittandet 2000: Årsrapport* (Stockholm: Mediamätning i Skandinavien [MMS], 2000), p. 6, 3,915,000 viewers watched the final episode on 30 December 2000.
10. See the entry "Survivor (TV Series)" at the Wikipedia website, online, available HTTP: <http://en.wikipedia.org/wiki/Survivor_(TV_series)> (accessed 23 November 2009).
11. Regarding the impact of *Expedition Robinson* on Swedish television programming more generally, see S. Hadenius and L. Weibull, *Massmedier*, p. 430; K. Asp, ed., *Svenskt TV-utbud 2003*, p. 87. For comments about *Expedition Robinson* as a pioneer of reality TV more generally, see the interview with Charlie Parsons in the television program *Carin 21:30*, SVT2, 12 February 2004 (accessible via SLBA: TVB–20040221): "Reality started on SVT with Robinson." Cf. Gary Carter's comment in F. Rydén, *Det sista örådet*, SVT1, 15 February 2004 (SLBA: TVB–20040236): "Sweden pioneered reality TV."
12. For an overview of different definitions of the concept and the tendency to use it as an umbrella term or catchall phrase, see A. Hill, *Reality TV*, pp. 44–50.
13. A. Hill, L. Weibull, and Å. Nilsson, *Audiences and Factual and Reality Television in Sweden*, pp. 10, 34.
14. Cf. J. Corner, "Performing the Real"; A. Hill, *Reality TV*, pp. 17–20; S. Murray, " 'I Think We Need a New Name For It'," pp. 40–56.
15. See N. Svensson, *Robinsonboken: Sanningen om Expedition Robinson* (Stockholm: Bazar, 2003), p. 16; J. Såthe, *TV-fabriken: Ett reportage om en ny industri* (Stockholm: Ekerlid, 2003), pp. 100–1; J. Leijonhufvud, "Strix gör såpa-expert till mentor," *Svenska Dagbladet*, 1 March 2004; T. Conlan, "Parsons Follows His Nose to Support Talent," *The Observer*, 15 April 2007.
16. See M. Andrejevic, *Reality TV*, p. 104. Cf. P. Hillier, "Entertaining Reality."
17. J. Leijonhufvud, "Strix."
18. J. Såthe, *TV-fabriken*, p. 104.
19. Citation of Mattias Olsson, producer at Strix Television, in F. Rydén, *Det sista örådet* (see note 11). Cf. M. Burnett and M. Dugard, *Survivor*, p. 14:

"The island is a microcosm of real life." All translations are by the author, unless stated otherwise.
20. Citation from A. Jerslev, "Autenticitetsstrategier i Robinson Ekspeditionen 2000," p. 28.
21. For characterizations of the program and the rules for the first season, see *Expedition Robinson*, SVT1, 13 September 1997 (SLBA: TVB97–1232); for the second season, see *Inför Expedition: Robinson*, SVT2, 5 September 1998 (SLBA: TVB98–2288); for the fourth season, see Y. Andersson and D. Lundberg, *Dokusåpor*, pp. 17–18.
22. *Expedition Robinson*, SVT1, 13 September 1997 (SLBA: TVB97–1232).
23. P. Andersson and J. Lineruth, "*Expedition Robinson*: En massmedial knockout!," unpublished paper (Luleå, Sweden: Luleå tekniska universitet, 2000), appendix I. For overviews of the debate, see A. Edin, *Verklig underhållning*, p. 15; N. Svensson, *Robinsonboken* (see note 15), p. 35.
24. Citation from N. Svensson, *Robinsonboken*, p. 15. According to a survey made by the domestic evening paper *Expressen*, more than two-thirds of the viewers, or 70 per cent, were critical.
25. Two scenes were reedited, one wherein a hen was decapitated and another showing the votings at the island council. See N. Svensson, *Robinsonboken*, p. 35; and F. Rydén, *Det sista örådet* (see note 11).
26. N. Svensson, *Robinsonboken*, p. 212; F. Rydén, *Det sista örådet*; P. Andersson and J. Lineruth, "*Expedition Robinson*."
27. Citation from A. Hill, L. Weibull, and A. Nilsson, *Audience and Factual and Reality Television*, p. 38.
28. P. Andersson and J. Lineruth, "*Expedition Robinson*," app. I. Cf. N. Svensson, *Robinsonboken*, p. 36.
29. E. Bälldal et al., "'Robinson spännande och lärorikt': Vi visste spelreglerna, skriver deltagarna i '*Expedition Robinson*,'" *Dagens Nyheter*, 1 October 1997.
30. Cf. S. Livingstone, "Media Literacy and the Challenge of New Information and Communication Technologies," p. 3.
31. A. Edin, *Verklig underhållning*, p. 88.
32. Citation of Åsa Vilbäck and reference to Martin Melin, in F. Rydén, *Det sista örådet* (see note 11).
33. Citation from A. Edin, *Verklig underhållning*, pp. 57–58.
34. The number of applicants to the first season is mentioned by the program leader Harald Treutiger in the first episode, *Expedition Robinson*, SVT1, 13 September 1997 (SLBA: TVB97–1232). Regarding the second and fourth seasons, see *Inför Expedition: Robinson*, SVT2, 5 September 1998 (SLBA: TVB98–2288), and Andersson, *Dokusåpor*, p. 17.
35. H. Jenkins, *Convergence Culture*, pp. 25, 71.
36. J. Poniewozik, "A Star is Borneo," *Time*, 28 October 1999; P. Hillier, "Entertaining Reality," pp. 2, 7; M. Burnett and M. Dugard, *Survivor*, "Prologue," p. 14.
37. See, e.g., A. Fetveit, "Det kannibalistiske øje"; H. Søndergaard et al., "Indledning," p. 3.
38. The conceptual resemblance between *Big Brother* and *Expedition Robinson/Survivor* is not least illustrated by the fact that Parsons accused Endemol of plagiarism. See C. Milmo, "Big Breakfast's Mr Big Wants Big Brother Back," *The Independent*, 24 August 2000.
39. J. Jones, "Show Your Real Face," pp. 401 and 419, note 3.
40. M. Andrejevic, *Reality TV*, p. 119.
41. Citation from J. Jones, "Show Your Real Face," p. 408.
42. Ibid., p. 409. I have normalized Jones's italics in this citation.

43. See, e.g., R. Kilborn, *Staging the Real*; L. van Zoonen, "Desire and Resistance"; N. Couldry, "Teaching Us to Fake It," p. 57–74; S. Seifarth, "Den iscensatta maskeraden," p. 122.
44. J. Corner, "Performing the Real," pp. 257, 261.
45. Citation of "Udda grannar i socialt experiment" from SVT's website, online, available HTTP: <http://svt.se/svt/jsp/Crosslink.jsp?d=44596> (accessed 3 February 2006). The lecturer in psychology was George Erdos, Newcastle University. The four groups of neighbors were described as "noisy students," "a family with tear-away kids," "dog lovers," and "a lone busybody."
46. Citation from M. Andrejevic, *Reality TV*, p. 104. Cf. P. Hillier, "Entertaining Reality."
47. M. Andrejevic, *Reality TV*, p. 104–5.
48. Citation from "Shocking Experiment Recreated for TV," BBC News website, 14 May 2002, online, available HTTP: <http://news.bbc.co.uk/2/hi/entertainment/1986889.stm> (accessed 15 April 2010). The two social psychologists were Alex Haslam (University of Exeter) and Stephen Reicher (University of St. Andrews). See also the official website of the so-called BBC Prison Study, online, available HTTP: <http://www.bbcprisonstudy.org/index.php> (accessed 15 April 2010). Cf. N. Couldry, "Teaching Us to Fake It," p. 64; and N. Pethes, *Spektakuläre Experimente*, pp. 110–16.
49. J. Corner, "Performing the Real," p. 261; A. Giddens, "Post-Traditional Society," pp. 59–60; and idem, *The Transformation of Intimacy*, p. 8.
50. See especially N. Pethes, *Spektakuläre Experimente*, pp. 83–116, 142–50, for a closely related perspective. Cf. S. Brenton and R. Cohen, *Shooting People*, pp. 81–163; N. Couldry, "Teaching Us to Fake It," p. 64.
51. A. McCarthy, " 'Stanley Milgram, Allen Funt, and Me'," pp. 26, 28.
52. P. Hillier, "Entertaining Reality," pp. 13, 18. Cf. B. Clisshold, "*Candid Camera* and the Origins of Reality TV," pp. 33–53.
53. Cf. D. Jermyn, "This Is About Real People!"; E. Carlsson, *Medierad övervakning*, pp. 18–21.
54. F. Rydén, *Det sista örådet*.
55. B. Griffen-Foley, "From *Tit-Bits* to *Big Brother*."
56. See note 14.
57. N. Pethes, *Spektakuläre Experimente*.
58. M. Gross and W. Krohn, "Society as Experiment." See also Seifarth, "Den iscensatta maskeraden," p. 122.
59. Cf. J. Gillis, *Islands of the Mind*, p. 25.
60. I. Watt, *The Rise of the Novel*. See also A. Öhman, *Äventyrets tid*, p. 10.
61. T. Mathiesen, "The Viewer Society."
62. N. Couldry, "Teaching Us to Fake It," p. 66.
63. S. Shapin and S. Schaffer, *Leviathan and the Air-Pump*, pp. 55–60.
64. See T. Dehue, "Social Experiments, History of," pp. 509–16.
65. L. Slater, *Opening Skinner's Box*, pp. 32–63.
66. P. Hillier, "Entertaining Reality," p. 17. For a striking example of the role of the novel in the context of "the birth of the observer" in the history of the social sciences, see C. Fox, "Introduction," pp. 1–30.
67. M. Andrejevic, *Reality TV*, p. 11; J. Corner, "Performing the Real," pp. 265–66; B. Griffen-Foley, "From *Tit-Bits* to *Big Brother*," p. 545.
68. Quoted from R. Bishop, "Good Afternoon, Good Evening, and Good Night," p. 7.

12 History on the Web
Museums, Digital Media, and Participation

Bodil Axelsson

Late-modern mediatized societies offer many arenas for interpreting and staging the past. The past is not simply given but is made meaningful to the present by means of communication and mediation. One of the most powerful institutions for mediating the past is the museum. Since their inception, museums have comprised a set of heterogeneous and dynamic institutions involved in the framing of the relationship between objects, media, and people.[1] In this context, digital media and the internet can be perceived as forces for renewal.[2] In common with popular culture of history in general, hopes are high that a disintegration of the hierarchies of knowledge presumed to have restricted public engagement with the past will occur.[3] However, Ross Parry points out that there are two accounts, which are not mutually exclusive, of how museums have related to digital media. More and more museums embrace them, but among other things, it is the presumed capacity of new media to overthrow institutional stability and controlled authorship that has slowed down their expansion within the world of museums.[4]

The present chapter examines how one particular museum, the Swedish Museum of National Antiquities, deals with new media by investigating the ways in which the politics of participation are conveyed through two websites created by the museum. I begin with the proposition that it is neither the museum nor the media per se that sets the conditions for participation, but the socio-technical arrangements they form. According to Andrew Barry, socio-technical arrangements combine devices, practices, and people in specific settings.[5] Due to this yoking of the technological to the social, socio-technical arrangements might produce, or be drawn into, political struggles. According to Barry, there is a difference between politics and the political. "Politics" refers to processes striving to encode and control social and cultural interaction. For example, there is a politics of the democratic process, which among many other things includes the protocols of public debate. By the "political," on the other hand, Barry refers to all those spaces open to debate and dissent.[6] In this essay, the notion of politics refers to the ways in which power relations between people, and between people and technology, are produced at the two websites under scrutiny.

INTRODUCING THE MUSEUM AND ITS WEBSITES

The two websites to be discussed and contrasted are the homepage of the Swedish Museum of National Antiquities and the online discussion forum Historical Worlds. The museum is situated in Stockholm, and is committed to collecting, maintaining, and displaying a national heritage of archaeological artifacts. It also possesses and displays collections of medieval ecclesiastical art and gold handicrafts. Like many other national museums, it promotes the abstract ideas of nationhood and national identity by providing a space in which the culture and history of the nation is defined in material form—by objects on display.[7] As indicated by Flora Kaplan, two competing ideals seem to be manifest in national museums. On the one hand, they are intended to contribute to the ongoing process of democratization via the downward dissemination of information to their respective citizens. On the other hand, museums should be spaces in which competing worldviews are expressed and debated.[8]

Along with the directives of government cultural policy, the Swedish Museum of National Antiquities emphasizes democratic development, public access, and increased public participation. As a state-funded institution, its director is appointed by the government and its mission is to classify and curate Sweden's cultural heritage and provide perspectives on human existence in order to strengthen society's democratic development. In this context, knowledge of the past is seen as a prerequisite to civic involvement. The museum therefore aims at fulfilling a public service role and to present independent, reliable, and critically scrutinized information in order for people to understand the ways in which cultural heritage is used to promote various interests.[9] In order to increase easy public access, the Swedish Museum of National Antiquities has extensively invested in the digitization of its collection. It has published several reports on information technology and carried out several projects aimed at advancing access and encouraging public communication.[10]

In 2007, the museum launched a new website. According to the head of the museum's media department at that time, the main goal of the new website was to attract visitors and provide supplementary material before and after visiting the museum. To a lesser extent, the website was intended to function as a substitute for museum visits for those unable to do so physically. The online forum Historical Worlds was created in 2001 for live role-players, aiming to appeal to a much narrower target audience. However, rather than providing a medium for social interaction between live role-players and museum staff, the de facto social interaction between participants established the forum as a peer-to-peer medium for practitioners of living history and reenactment. The online forum is still linked to the main museum website but is now set up on a different domain. When restructuring the main museum website, the forum was deemed the residue of a superannuated, project-based approach to the internet that had been funded with temporary finances. The museum's main site contained disparate information and links to external websites including Historical Worlds. The restructuring of the museum's website was aimed at working out a more integrated approach to the use of the internet. Its overall aim was to improve the structure of information and graphic design to make the museum's presence on the internet more visually striking and accessible to the general public.[11]

In the following I embark on an analysis of the socio-technical arrangement generated by the process of restructuring the main website. Thereafter, the chapter discusses the types of participation and interactivity the museum's socio-technical arrangement encourage. I then proceed to introduce the practice of living history and reenactment and the way in which a politics of participation takes shape through digital technology. The chapter concludes with a discussion of how participation can turn into a political issue within an institution.

In preparing this discussion, I scrutinized public documents and conducted two interviews, one with the administrator of the forum and one with key staff at the media department. The fact that the main museum website is constantly being refurbished and contains about 7,000 pages, and that at the time of this study the forum contained some 40,000 postings, obviously made it unfeasible to attempt to capture the essence of the websites in their entirety. Therefore I approached the sites ethnographically. I scrolled, clicked, read, and viewed my way around the two websites to narrow my focus and understand the way its visitors were positioned in terms of participation and interactivity.[12]

GENERATING A SOCIO-TECHNICAL ARRANGEMENT

The website launched in 2007 was the culmination of a process drawn out over several years and led by the media department and hired consultants, parts of which have been explained and defended in a final report published online. In the following paragraphs I will unravel how the report describes the ways in which technical devices, practices, and people were united in a socio-technical arrangement.

The interface of the website was designed for navigation within a set of pre-provided information. The page was given a plain white background and divided into three columns, each of which featured an abundance of color photographs and links. The items on the website were designed to be handled by a content management system that allowed web editors to efficiently rearrange a vast range of texts, photos, and video features to add news value to the site.[13] Furthermore, even though exclusive images were produced on a regular basis, the website was technically integrated with the museum's digital database in order to avoid double storing images.[14] However, the then head of the media department stated that to him, the digitized objects were "raw data." He therefore strongly advocated that these digital depictions be embedded in narratives and interpretations produced by the museum's staff.[15] The low public-information value the media department ascribed to the digitized collection at the time of the restructuring of the website was underscored by the fact that the entrance to the database was placed at the bottom left-hand side of the museum's entry page.[16]

Segments of the general public were drawn in to the process of restructuring the website in their capacity as internet users. The process was initiated by asking relevant target audiences to fill in usability questionnaires. These included teachers, students, regular museum visitors, tourists, senior citizens, and immigrants.[17] The special interest in teachers and their pupils suggests that the museum placed great value on the website's educative function. The interest in senior citizens might be explained by the fact that they comprise a rapidly expanding segment of the population presumed to have a lot of spare time and, to some extent, money on their hands. Pinpointing immigrants may also be interpreted as an educative effort. It may perhaps also be explained by the fact that minority representation in cultural production and consumption has been a recurrent theme in Swedish cultural policy for the last fifteen years. Museums, as well as other cultural institutions, struggle with the issue of how to adjust cultural heritage policy and practice to reflect the diversity that recent globalization and migration has brought to Sweden.

The choice of targeted audience categories underlines the museum's role as a civic institution of popular education. The new website featured specific entries for teachers and pupils as well as for families and newly arrived immigrants in need of "easy to read" Swedish. However, it behooves us to accentuate the way in which different audience groups were collapsed into a single, generalized one based on the broad-based perception of a common denominator. The usability tests indicated that the aforementioned groups were those whose new media literacy and level of education would set the standard for the site's future accessibility to a general public.

Museum staff was assigned the task of producing content. For its part, the staff wanted the website to reflect the narratives of the exhibitions, public lectures, and museum publications. Early in the process of restructuring the website, the staff was interviewed and summoned to workshops. In the workshops, the development of the website was integrated into discussions on the overall aim and vision of the museum. A new working model was conceived for producing website content. The task of composing text was delegated to experts such as antiquarians and exhibition curators who would work under the supervision of an editorial board that consisted of representatives from different departments at the museum.[18]

The result was that the navigational paths of the website, and the narratives presented there, were very much modeled after the way the objects were presented in the museum's galleries. The museum, as well as its website, echoes at least two well-established articulations of the temporal and spatial order of the Swedish nation. First, the entries under the heading "history" are ordered according to a chronology that divides human prehistory into distinct periods such as the Stone Age, the Bronze Age, and the Iron Age, followed by the Middle Ages. These periods are not specifically Swedish, of course, having long been established in both international scholarly and popular discourse, but they are still very much part of the popular imagination of the nation's evolution. Second, the website narratives placed both objects and people within a national geography of regions, parishes, and communities. Although the texts emphasize that the Swedish nation did not exist in prehistoric times, the collection and scope of the museum are constantly referred to as "Swedish." As pointed out by one of the archaeologists at the museum, this exclusive focus on a national material heritage might exclude those with a different geographical background who live within the current nation.[19]

THE VOICE OF THE MUSEUM

The report summarizing the creation of the museum's website states that texts ought to be written in accordance with linguistic and dramaturgical guidelines set out in a manual compiled by hired specialists in the field of language cultivation. The texts should also fit into predesigned formats produced to be compatible with the overall design and structure of the website. Few of the published texts were actually signed by members of the staff, often with the caveat that they were highly personal and creative interpretations.[20] Otherwise, the majority of texts address its readers as the manual prescribes.

The editorial process, the manual, and the formats propagate the politics of publishing. This particular socio-technical arrangement might be seen as a means to create an "unassailable voice" on behalf of the museum. According to Peter Walsh, the unassailable voice has the "flattened, vaguely evasive tone of a text created by a committee." It appears, for example, on interpretative exhibit labels in displays and is often the result of compromise. The unassailable voice is impersonal and disembodied. Walsh argues that the internet threatens the continued existence of the unassailable voice since the web is disorganized and nonhierarchal. He continues: "The tone of institutional authority that has been the essential medium of museums for decades will not easily cross the barriers of modems and HTML where all authority yields to a kind of electronic leveling."[21] However, Walsh's 1997 depiction of the internet as disorganized and nonhierarchal seems no longer relevant. More and more organizations carve out their own niche on the internet and design it to suit their own needs. In fact, the head of the media department of the Swedish Museum of National Antiquities stated that the technology for publishing and the technological solutions for internet publication had matured to the extent that the museum finally was able to implement both a unified and structured system for administration of website content and a system of publication that could be used by people with no previous experience of HTML coding.[22] And, as pointed out by several scholars of new media, users are themselves establishing their own politics of participation.[23]

INVITATION TO PARTICIPATE

Whereas "participation" is a concept referring to social arrangements for engagement in common matters and affinity with communities of various scale and interest, "interactivity" can be defined as the technical device for getting there. Interactivity allows for reciprocal communication as well as hypertextual navigation, i.e., the exercise of choice within databases.[24] The concepts of participation and interactivity are often intertwined in highly normative and persuasive discourses according to which the technological solutions for interactivity will translate into more active forms of participation, even in the field of traditional governmental politics.[25] There is, according to Andrew Barry, an interactive model that stresses the need of working with rather than directing the political imagination of ordinary citizens.[26] This model draws upon the ideals of deliberative democracy and encourages dialogue and reciprocity between politicians and citizens rather than top-down communication.[27]

Both interactivity and participation have a positive ring to them. In the field of museology, scholars and practitioners alike have praised initiatives that invite ethnic minority communities or specific age groups to participate in the production of exhibitions, hence allowing communities to represent themselves in institutional spaces.[28] Not surprisingly, new media formats emerge as technologies that open up for active participation and co-creation of museum narratives.[29] According to this line of reasoning, careful implementation of new media applications might transfer agency from the museums to individuals and communities outside the institutions and enhance the opportunities for the museum's visitors to co-create meaning together with the institutions.[30] This entails the development of socio-technological frameworks that encourage two-way communication between institutions and communities.[31]

The website launched by the Swedish Museum of National Antiquities in 2007 did not invite communities to represent themselves. Neither was the general visitor invited to publicly express an opinion. Instead, users were invited to navigate between narratives and images produced by the staff. In particular, a set of web-television features represented ways for citizens to engage with cultural heritage by prescribing and stipulating relationships between the museum and citizens or visitors.

Several web-television features offer "object lessons." Archaeologists lecture on objects and conservators discuss their procedures. The visitor is thus addressed as the recipient of expert knowledge. This form of address is supported and underlined by two other invitations to participate. The first is produced by narratives of discovery. In a movie made in 1945, farmers who by chance discover archeological objects in their fields and immediately call for the archaeologists are portrayed as exemplary citizens. Such scenes teach their viewers to turn any unearthed archaeological object in to the authorities.[32] Yet another form of exemplary citizenship is produced in the final scenes of the 1945 movie as well as in a film produced by a freelancer only a few years ago. In both, citizens are depicted as reverent spectators in relation to objects on display at the museum. Moreover, the latter film highlights the way in which cultural heritage is mediated by digital technology. In the final scene, museum visitors are shown admiring a digital representation of one of the most highly valued gold objects in the museum's collection.[33]

Another position for participation is suggested by a web-video feature produced in 2007. The short feature is a teaser for the reopening of the museum's permanent exhibit on prehistoric times, the design of which employs a "transit-hall metaphor," intended for what Australian museum scholar Andrea Witcomb calls "spatial interactivity." Visitors are encouraged to circulate and crisscross the space in order to make their own connections between the objects on display.[34] For this particular exhibit, visitors are made to choose between several entrance points and reflect upon lifestyle choices. In the video feature, the encouragement of individual choice and personal responsibility is underscored by authoritative voices, such as that of the designer of the exhibit who states that "we make demands on the visitor, we actually demand involvement."[35]

This video marks a break with the museum's past invitations. It seems to want to increase the level of visitor activity. It jibes with the ways in which interactivity works in science museums, according to Andrew Barry. Interactive devices encourage museum visitors to become something more than mere spectators; they invite people to become informed, engaged, and skilled in governing and improving their learning potential.

Barry equates interactivity with participation, creativity, and positive injunctions like "discover" or "you may." However, he also argues that interactivity has become a political, even ideological force associated with "advanced liberal forms of government." It addresses citizens in their capacity to govern themselves according to a preconceived logic.[36] Furthermore, when visitors are only allowed to choose from a set of options provided by the staff, which is the case on the website of the Swedish Museum of National Antiquities as well as in its exhibit on prehistoric times, the choices becomes limited and predictable. The result is what Barry, borrowing a term from Slavoj Zizek, calls "interpassivity." He contrast this with "creative passivity," a term Georgina Born coined to characterize instances in which individuals are not visibly active but rather invited to imagine, dream, or invent experiences.[37] Barry means that even though spectatorship appears to be passive since there is no immediately visible or audible feedback, it still might serve to ignite the imagination. Furthermore, Barry points out the ways in which the idea of interactivity per se governs social relationships in contemporary society, providing the impetus for both individuals and institutions to embrace technological solutions.

When restructuring its website, the media department chose to follow the museum's democratic imperative by creating access and providing people with information—information selected and produced by the staff.[38] A complementary approach was proposed by some of the archaeologists in the research department. They advocated "public archaeology," that laymen be included in the production of archaeological projects and interpretations.[39] In the end, however, this suggestion failed to have an impact on the restructuring of the museum's website. The representations of prescribed positions for participation inherent in the website's video features and the socio-technical arrangement with which the website was imbued invited people to be merely "interpassive" and "creative passive." They were encouraged to co-create meaning, if not content. Since people are not passive recipients of media messages but active readers and coproducers of meaning, they are bound to interpret the objects, narratives, and images on the website in a variety of ways. But when restructuring the website, the museum steered clear from technical solutions that would allow visitors to publish their reflections or post links to direct other visitors to alternative sources—with one exception, Historical Worlds.

LIVING HISTORY AND REENACTMENT ON THE WEB

The devotees of living history and reenactment games who populate online discussion forum Historical Worlds share with the host museum the goal of portraying the past as accurately as possible. The reconstruction of material culture, especially attire from the Viking era and the Middle Ages, is its main focus. But there are differences, too. For example, while the museum is first and foremost committed to displaying unique objects and findings found within the current national borders (some brought to Sweden as items of trade or trophies of war), living history and reenactment buffs produce the material objects they use to display the past themselves. They sew their own clothes and craft their own props. They don historical garb and stroll among period settings at markets and fairs. In an English-speaking context, reenactment refers to the staging of specific historical events such as famous battles.[40] Living history and reenactment are genres for the reconstruction of times past in which participants display and relive the past by immersion in dynamic webs of sensuous meaning. In the forum, habitués discuss how to stay warm in the winter and cool in the summer in their period outfits. Bodily experiences are thus relevant to the way both reenactors and practitioners of living history experience proximity to times past and gain historical knowledge.[41]

The online forum's setup is not nearly as meticulously documented as that of the new main museum website. According to the few archived documents, it was created to offer points of contact between the museum and noninstitutional applied-history practiced by enthusiastic young people. It was made possible by a grant from a foundation dedicated to advancing innovative cultural projects.[42] Along with the forum, the website includes glossaries, virtual exhibitions, and costume patterns. The grant made it possible for the museum to hire an administrator for the forum, according to whom neither the website in its totality nor the online forum succeeded in creating a dialogue between museum staff and the young lay experts. He suggests the reason for this lies in the fact that the staff's entries were far too theoretical and that it simply did not know how to give straight, pragmatic answers to the young people's questions. Furthermore, due to its open access, the live role-players to whom the site originally intended to appeal were amiably outmaneuvered by the more sophisticated living history and reenactment enthusiasts.[43]

In many ways, the fate of the forum is a case in point of the emerging digital culture characterized by Mark Deuze with three key terms: participation, remediation, and bricolage.[44] Like the independent online journalistic practices he discusses, members of the forum offer a collection of hyperlinks to documents, archival content, and images. All members can pose questions, answer each other's questions, or post links. The software and interface enable them to participate in meaning-making processes aimed at producing material culture. In contrast to the museum's main website, the sources presented in the forum are not confined to domestic archaeological finds; they are imported through hyperlinks from a vast, mostly European archive of digitized pictures, patterns, and manuscripts. Hence, to a certain extent, contemporary Swedish reenactors and living historians reach out to an imagined historical Europe.[45]

Interaction between members of the forum is very much the remediation and extension of real-world social networks. In relation to living history and public reenactment events, the online forum is a supplementary media that details the effort and craft put into reconstruction. Discussions of period garb revolve around procedures such as selecting the right model for the chosen time period and geographical area, combining colors and materials, how to dye cloth, design, and cutting and stitching. Standards of historical accuracy are constantly balanced with the member's contemporary knowledge of practical procedures and aesthetic considerations.

NEGOTIATING BRICOLEURS

To some extent, the discussions at the forum mimic the way historians of practical activities as varied as warfare and weaving draw on the testimony of images and engage in source criticism.[46] However, there is almost no general discussion about the social distribution of power during the periods in which the members take interest. Class and gender are indeed important issues discussed frequently, but the emphasis is more on what pictures reveal about the visual signs of class and gender in specific contexts than on what the depicted material culture implies about political attitudes or social and cultural inequality.

Although the focus on materiality is sometimes up to debate, most discussion about the rules of the game concern the standards of historical accuracy to which the members of the forum should adhere. In one of these meta-discussions, a moderator suggests that clothes and props should be modeled on original archaeological objects, a contemporary manuscript, or a contemporary visual depiction. In addition, the source of the paraphernalia should originate in a period within fifty years of the time the bearer claims to depict. Other members partly agree with him, but some state that standards of historical accuracy should be allowed some leeway.[47] Time after time, forum members repeat that the rules are contextual, that they depend on the event and the more or less informal guidelines worked out by each group. Thus standards of historical accuracy emerge as negotiations between social context and individual choice. Living history encourages individual skills, and some of the forum members have university degrees in heritage-related topics and professions. One of the moderators, for example, boasts a degree in archaeology and acts as an expert in several fields. Aside from keeping track of topics and enforcing forum rules, she offers advice on dressmaking design and participates in discussions on historical accuracy. Her expert position is characterized by humility and context sensitivity, and in some respects she sets the tone for how to interact in the forum.

According to Deuze, online digital cultures assign "active bricoleur-identities" to people, who are able to publish and provide others with links at the same time as the they find their own way through the material presented and rework it according to their own needs.[48] But it is also made obvious by examining posts to this particular forum that online discussions seem determined to reduce interpretative choices. This reduction of options is exercised by mimicking historians' source criticism and testing evidence and theory through the practical experience of producing attire and other attributes. Daniel Chandler, upon whom Deuze draws, accentuates the ways in which the choices bricoleurs make are influenced by common conventions about material and procedures generated by groups of members.[49] The sociotechnical arrangement of the online forum generates common conventions of historical accuracy among practitioners of living history and reenactment, although these conventions may vary from context to context.

THE FORUM AS A SOCIO-TECHNICAL ARRANGEMENT

The Historical Worlds forum offers open access and anyone who registers may post. However, the way the software is set up allows for the participants to be ranked. Here, as in many other forums, participatory statuses are produced. Each new post features a record of the number of contributions this particular member has posted. Ranking is also produced by each submission being accompanied by individual profiles such as "member," "veteran," or "moderator." Status is also subtly accrued by participants "casually" mentioning their profession. This hierarchy among members is also maintained by the way in which new contributors often enter the discussion by posing questions and making propositions in a meek manner, excusing themselves by stating that they are only beginners. Moreover, status is bestowed by the way individual posts are taken up and included in discussions.

The software provides forum members with a tree structure comprised of main topics and threads (i.e., sub-topics). Since the forum is asynchronous, hours, days, and even years can pass between posts to particular threads. Since most questions receive one or more answers, the threads often consist of a variety of entangled themes. In order to keep the threads reasonably coherent topicwise, a group of moderators has been commissioned by the forum administrator to lock threads and to move posts from one thread to another when appropriate. Both the moderators and the administrator perform housekeeping functions insofar as they retain the right to turn away members who do not adhere to the forum's netiquette or its stated topics. Since they do not vet messages prior to publication, the forum is post-moderated.

Thus moderators and administrators have rights and obligations ordinary forum members lack. As an additional example of this special status, several years ago they refurbished the structure of the forum, as it had grow almost organically and could no longer handle all the new threads and subjects. The administrator undertook a process of restructuring, and threads were culled and sorted with general posts on textiles and dressmaking at the top and less popular subjects like carpentry, leatherwork, and metalwork relegated to a place further down the entry page.[50]

Generating different participatory statuses and arrangements for administering and housekeeping reinforce the members' negotiations of standards of historical accuracy. In the end, it shows that this particular use of a medium produces a politics of participation that contributes to the formalization of reenactment and living history. According to folklorist Regina Bendix, reenacting battles and dressing up in period or regional clothing runs parallel to establishing several other avenues for staging and materializing socially constructed accounts of the past in the late nineteenth and early twentieth century.[51] The museum would be one such "parallel venue." Bendix suggests that "experience-centered hobbies" took a different path from heritage productions located in more politically and economically controlled areas, but that they now might be headed toward greater degrees of social control.[52] The interaction evident between members of Historical Worlds supports this observation.

CONCLUSION

The socio-technical arrangements of the two websites discussed in this chapter differ insofar as concerns the kind of participation they encourage and the way they deploy technological interactivity. The present discussion highlights the way socio-technical arrangements, and the politics of participation they produce, are intimately bound up in the context from which they emerge. Software that provides for discussion among people who share the same interests seems to be congenial to experienced-centered hobbies like living history and reenactment, whereas an interface set up for hypertextual navigation within a set of pre-provided information might be more appropriate for an institution intent on educating the general public. I will end this chapter by referring to an instance in which the normative and value-laden ideals of interactivity and participation have become a political issue at the Swedish Museum of National Antiquities.

In contrast to the "interpassivity" or "creative passivity" proffered on its main site, the museum's online discussion forum Historical Worlds invites people to actively engage with the past. Whoever enters participates in the production of interpretations and accounts of the material culture of an imagined historical Europe. Visitors are also invited to critically engage with the divergent contextual standards of historical accuracy presented and debated at the forum. However, the circumspect tone that seems to be encouraged by the forum's politics of participation downplays tensions and dissonances between members. The fact that members mainly accept the offer of technological interactivity in order to create a sense of community seems to cow them into avoiding confrontation both with fellow members and with their host. Forum members do not prioritize information provided by the museum, but neither do they reject it outright. Instead, they participate in a parallel, mainly aesthetic, practical, and sensuous engagement with the past. They do not confine themselves to spectatorship but produce "object lessons" of their own out of experiences and a fluid archive of digitized resources.

Neither the socio-technical arrangement of the museum nor the intertwining of the social and the technical in the online forum are open to the political, i.e., the airing of contentious contemporary issues. However, the internet policy of the media department became a political issue for the administrator of the forum. Although at times among the museum's most popular web pages, the media department maintained a reluctant stance toward the forum. The forum administrator, on the other hand, disagreed with what he considered to be a public address based on the one-too-many mass-media paradigm associated with television and newspapers. He himself advocated a combination of one-way communication, in which the museum staff provides expertise, and two-way communication between the museum and the public.[53]

What emerges as most significant in light of this is that the museum harbored conflicting attitudes toward new media and participation. The forum administrator and the then head of the media department advocated divergent politics of participation and therefore promoted different socio-technical arrangements. While the media department insisted on the museum's final authority, the forum administrator had greater confidence in noninstitutional and experience-centered involvement with the past. In addition, some archaeologists at the museum discussed the possibility of including laypersons in the production of archaeological knowledge. At the time of the restructuring of the museum's main website, the matter of just what digital media and the internet could offer in terms of participation in this particular context had yet to be settled.

NOTES

1. A. Witcomb, *Re-Imagining the Museum*, p. 127.
2. F. Cameron and S. Kenderdine, eds., *Theorizing Digital Cultural Heritage*; R. Parry, *Recoding the Museum*.
3. J. de Groot, *Consuming History*, pp. 90–101.
4. R. Parry, *Recoding the Museum*.
5. A. Barry, *Political Machines*, p. 11.
6. Ibid, p. 207. Barry here draws on Georgio Agamben.
7. L. Jordanova, *History in Practice*; introduction to F. Kaplan, ed., *Museums and the Making of Ourselves*, pp. 1–15.
8. F. Kaplan, *Museums and the Making of Ourselves*, pp. 2–3.
9. *Statens historiska museer*, "Policy för Statens historiska museer," online, available HTTP: <http://www.shmm.se/Documents/SHMM_policy_20030813.pdf> (accessed 30 April 2008).
10. *Statens historiska museer*, "Museum.se: Handlingsplan för hur museers resurser på internet kan samordnas för att öka tillgängligheten för användarna," 2006, online, available HTTP: <http://www.shmm.se/Documents/museum_se.pdf> (accessed 23 November 2007).
11. Interview with the head of the media department B. Johansson and the main web editor A. Ståhlberg, Stockholm, October 17, 2007.
12. *Historiska museet*' main website, online, available HTTP: <http://www.historiska.se>; *Historiska världar*, online, available HTTP: <http://histvarld.historiska.se/histvarld/forum/> (both accessed 14 January 2010). All translations are by the author, unless stated otherwise.
13. Interview with B. Johansson and A. Ståhlberg; J. Berthling and A. Engquist, "Slutrapport från webbprojektet på historiska museet," 2007, online, *Historiska museet*, available HTTP: <http://www.shmm.se/Documents/webbprojektet_rapport.pdf> (accessed 8 December 2007).
14. J. Berthling and A. Engquist, "Slutrapport," p. 8.
15. Interview with B. Johansson and A. Ståhlberg.
16. Two years later, in 2009, a system for individual annotation was added to the database's search function.
17. J. Berthling and A. Engquist, "Slutrapport," p. 4.
18. Ibid., pp. 4–5, 7, 9–10.
19. F. Svanberg, "Museum Narration and the Collection Machine." pp. 175–82. Online. Available HTTP: <http://www.ep.liu.se/ecp/030/> (accessed 25 May 2008).

20. J. Berthling and A. Engquist, "Slutrapport," p. 7.
21. P. Walsh, "The Web and the Unassailable Voice," p. 81.
22. Interview with B. Johansson and A. Ståhlberg.
23. Cf. H. Jenkins, *Convergence Culture*; R. Rosenzweig, "Can History Be Open Source?".
24. M. Lister et al., *New Media*, pp. 20–22.
25. For critical discussions on this matter, see for instance A. Barry, *Political Machines*, p. 14; Lister et al., *New Media*, pp. 40–44; S. Livingstone, "Critical Debates in Internet Studies," pp. 9–28.
26. A. Barry, *Political Machines*, p. 148.
27. M. Lister et al., *New Media*, pp. 20, 43–44.
28. J. Graham and S. Yasin, "Reframing Participation in the Museum."
29. See for instance R. Parry, *Recoding the Museum*, pp. 109–16.
30. S. Hazan, "A Crisis of Authority," pp. 133–47.
31. A. Russo and J. Watkins, "Digital Cultural Communication," pp. 148–64.
32. *Hur vår historia rädddas* (1945), online, *Historiska museet*, available HTTP: <http://video.historiska.se/index.aspx?id=221> (accessed 12 December 2007). The film was produced by the National Heritage Board, then in the same national governmental agency as the Museum of National Antiquities, and with the then head of the agency in a prominent role. *Glänsande gudaoffer del 1*, online, *Historiska museet*, available HTTP: <http://video.historiska.se/index.aspx?id=159> (accessed 12 December 2007). These films were produced in 1986 and 1987 by Skaraborgs länsmuseum, a regional museum in the south of Sweden.
33. J. Forssell, dir., *I historiens djup*, online, *Historiska museet*, available HTTP: <http://video.historiska.se/index.aspx?id=171> (accessed 3 May 2008).
34. A. Witcomb, *Re-Imagining the Museum*, pp. 141–47.
35. *Invigningen av forntider* (2007), online, *Historiska museet*, available HTTP: <http://video.historiska.se/index.aspx?id=234> (accessed 11 November 2007).
36. A. Barry, *Political Machines*, pp. 127–35.
37. Ibid., pp. 140–41.
38 Interview with B. Johansson and A. Ståhlberg.
39 F. Svanberg and K. Wahlgren, *Publik arkeologi*.
40. "Re-enactment, Reänacktmänt eller vad?" *Historiska världar*, postings dated 7 April 2003–11 May 2003, online, available HTTP: <http://histvarld.historiska.se/histvarld/forum/topic.asp?TOPIC_ID=172> (accessed 20 December 2007); C. Åsberg and B. Axelsson, "Digital Performances of Gendered Pasts," pp. 153–54.
41. R. Bendix, "CP, TK, TCE & Co."; de Groot, *Consuming History*, pp. 105–9.
42. K. Berg, "Ansökan från Statens historiska museum till Stiftelsen framtidens kultur," 21 February 2000, Statens historiska museum, Dnr 642-774-2000; H. Summanen, "Redovisning av Historiska världar," email to author, 26 June 2006.
43. Interview with forum administrator H. Summanen, Stockholm, 28 September 2007.
44. M. Deuze, "Participation, Remediation, Bricolage."
45. C. Åsberg and B. Axelson, "Digital Performances of Gendered Pasts," p. 174.
46. P. Burke, *Eyewitnessing*, pp. 81–84.
47. Cf. Arild Krake, "Definition av historiskt återskapande," posted 15 February 2004, online, *Historiska världar*, available HTTP: <http://histvarld.historiska.se/histvarld/forum/topic.asp?TOPIC_ID=1049>; see also the thread "Att återskapa historia: Hur långt ska man gå," posted 23 February 2004–1 January 2006, online, *Historiska världar*, available HTTP: <http://histvarld.historiska.se/histvarld/forum/topic.asp?TOPIC_ID=1073> (accessed 20 December 2007).

48. M. Deuze, "Participation, Remediation, Bricolage," p. 70.
49. Ibid., pp. 70–71. D. Chandler, "Personal Homepages and the Construction of Identities on the Web."
50. Interview with H. Summanen.
51. R. Bendix, "CP, TK, TCE & Co.," p. 53; see also M. Sandberg, *Living Pictures, Missing Persons*, p. 149. These parallels have also attracted the Swedish artist Martin Karlsson; see the artist's website, esp. "Old Stockholm," 2006, online, available HTTP: <http:/www.martinkarlsson.net/martin081030/oldstockholm.html> (accessed 9 January 2010).
52. R. Bendix, "CP, TK, TCE & Co.," p. 54.
53. Interview with H. Summanen.

Bibliography

Abercrombie, N., and B. Longhurst. *Audiences: A Sociological Theory of Performance and Imagination*. London: Sage, 1998.
Andersson, E. *Väckelse och andra kristna folkrörelser i Kongo*. Uppsala, Sweden: Svenska institutet för missionsforskning, 1997.
Andersson, Y., and D. Lundberg. *Dokusåpor: En "verklighet" för sig?* Stockholm: Granskningsnämnden för radio och TV, 2001.
Andrejevic, M. *Reality TV: The Work of Being Watched*. Lanham, MD: Rowman and Littlefield, 2004.
Asp, K., ed. *Svenskt TV-utbud 2003: En undersökning på uppdrag av Granskningsnämnden för radio och TV*. Haninge: Granskningsnämnden för radio och TV, 2004.
Axelsson, S. *Culture Confrontation in the Lower Congo: From the Old Congo Kingdom to the Congo Independent State with Social Reference to the Swedish Missionaries in the 1880s and 1890s*. Stockholm: Gummesson, 1970.
Bailey, P. *Popular Culture and Performance in the Victorian City*. Cambridge: Cambridge University Press, 1998.
Barry, A. *Political Machines: Governing a Technological Society*. New York: Athlone, 2001.
Beegan, G. *The Mass Image: A Social History of Photomechanical Reproduction in Victorian London*. New York: Palgrave Macmillan, 2008.
Bellanta, M. "Voting for Pleasure, Or a View from a Victorian Theatre Gallery." *M/C Journal* 11, 2008. Online. Available HTTP: <http://journal.media-culture.org.au/index.php/mcjournal/article/view/22> (accessed 8 April 2010).
Bendix, R. "CP, TK, TCE & Co.: The End of Freewheeling Culturalization?" In *INTER: A European Cultural Studies Conference in Sweden 11–13 June 2007*, ed. J. Fornäs and M. Fredriksson, 2007. Online. Available HTTP: <http://www.ep.liu.se/ecp/025/> (accessed 12 May 2008).
Benkler, Y. *The Wealth of Networks: How Social Production Transforms Markets and Freedoms*. New Haven, CT: Yale University Press, 2006.
Bennet, J., et al. *1900: The New Age, A Guide to the Exhibition*. Cambridge: Whipple Museum of the History of Science, 1994.
Bennett, T. *The Birth of the Museum: History, Theory, Politics*. London: Routledge, 1995.
Bennett, T. *Pasts Beyond Memory: Evolution, Museums, Colonialism*. London: Routledge, 2004.
Berlant, L. *The Queen of America Goes to Washington City: Essays on Sex and Citizenship*. Durham, NC: Duke University Press, 1997.
Berlin, G., and A. Simon, eds. *Music Archiving in the World*. Berlin: VWB, 2002.
Berman, M. *All That is Solid Melts into Air: The Experience of Modernity*. New York: Simon & Schuster, 1982.

Bishop, R. "Good Afternoon, Good Evening, and Good Night: The Truman Show as Media Criticism." *Journal of Communication Inquiry* 24 (2000): 6–18.
Björkin, M. "Industrial Greta: Some Thoughts on an Industrial Film." In *Nordic Explorations: Film before 1930*, ed. J. Fullerton and J. Olsson. London: John Libbey, 1999.
Björkin, M. "Platser i rörelse: Industrifilm och mediehistoria." In *Kultur, plats, identitet: Det lokalas betydelse i en globaliserad värld*, ed. J. Johannisson and H. Englund. Stockholm: SISTER, 2003.
Bolter, J., and R. Grusin. *Remediation: Understanding New Media*. Cambridge, MA: MIT Press, 1999.
Boström, M. "The Phonogram Archive of the Stockholm Ethnographic Museum (1909–1930): Another Chapter in the History of Ethnographic Cylinder Recordings." *Fontes Artes Musicae* 50 (2003): 22–35.
Boström, M. "Den falske kungen i den sanna återgivningen: Fonograf som utställningsattraktion kring 1900." In *1897: Mediehistorier kring Stockholmsutställningen*, ed. A. Ekström, S. Jülich, and P. Snickars. Stockholm: Statens ljud- och bildarkiv, 2006.
Bowker, G. *Memory Practices in the Sciences*. Cambridge, MA: MIT Press, 2005.
Brady, E. *A Spiral Way: How the Phonograph Changed Ethnography*. Jackson: University of Mississippi Press, 1999.
Brenton, S., and R. Cohen. *Shooting People: Adventures in Reality TV*. London: Verso, 2003.
Breslau, D. "The American Spencerians: Theorizing a New Science." In *Sociology in America: A History*, ed. C. Calhoun. Chicago: The University of Chicago Press, 2007.
Brown, J. *Health and Medicine on Display: International Expositions in the United States, 1876–1904*. Cambridge, MA: MIT Press, 2009.
Burchell, G., C. Gordon, and P. Miller, eds. *The Foucault Effect: Studies in Governmentality*. Chicago: University of Chicago Press, 1991.
Burgess, J., and J. Green. "The Entrepreneurial Vlogger: Participatory Culture Beyond the Professional-Amateur Divide." In *The YouTube Reader*, ed. P. Snickars and P. Vonderau. Stockholm: National Library of Sweden, 2009.
Burke, P. *Eyewitnessing: The Uses of Images as Historical Evidence*. London: Reaktion Books, 2001.
Burton, A. *Archive Stories: Facts, Fictions, and the Writing of History*. Durham, NC: Duke University Press, 2005.
Burton, N., and H. Fraser. "Mirror Visions and Dissolving Views: Vernon Lee and the Museological Experiments of Patrick Geddes." *Nineteenth-Century Contexts* 28 (2006): 145–60.
Butsch, R. *The Making of American Audiences: From Stage to Television, 1750–1990*. Cambridge: Cambridge University Press, 2000.
Butsch, R., ed. *Media and Public Spheres*. Basingstoke, UK: Palgrave Macmillan, 2007.
Butsch, R. *The Citizen Audience: Crowds, Publics, and Individuals*. New York: Routledge, 2008.
Cameron, F., and S. Kenderdine, eds. *Theorizing Digital Cultural Heritage: A Critical Introduction*. Cambridge, MA: MIT Press, 2007.
Carlsson, E. *Medierad övervakning: En studie av övervakningens betydelser i svensk dagspress*. Umeå, Sweden: Department of Culture and Media Studies, 2009.
Chandler, D. "Personal Homepages and the Construction of Identities on the Web." Online. 1998. Available HTTP: <http://www.aber.ac.uk/media/Documents/short/webident.html> (accessed 1 May 2008).
Chansky, D. *Composing Ourselves: The Little Theatre Movement and the American Audience*. Carbondale: Southern Illinois University Press, 2004.

Chapman, J., M. Glancy, and S. Harper, eds. *The New Film History: Sources, Methods, Approaches*. Basingstoke, UK: Palgrave Macmillan, 2007.
Christensson, J. *Lyckoriket: Studier i svensk upplysning*. Stockholm: Atlantis, 1996.
Chun, W. "Introduction: Did Somebody Say New Media?" In *New Media, Old Media: A History and Theory Reader*, ed. W. Chun and T. Keenan. New York: Routledge, 2006.
Classen, C., and D. Howes. "The Museum as Sensescape." In *Sensible Objects: Colonialism, Museums and Material Culture*, ed. E. Edwards, C. Gosden, and R. Phillips. Oxford: Berg, 2006.
Clisshold, B. "*Candid Camera* and the Origins of Reality TV: Contextualising a Historical Precedent." In *Understanding Reality Television*, ed. S. Holmes and D. Jermyn. London: Routledge, 2005.
Coombes, A. *Reinventing Africa: Museums, Material Culture and Popular Imagination in Late Victorian and Edwardian England*. New Haven, CT: Yale University Press, 1994.
Comment, B. *The Panorama*. London: Reaktion Books, 1999.
Condon, Y. "St. Louis 1904: Louisiana Purchase International Exposition." In *Historical Dictionary of World's Fairs and Expositions, 1851–1988*, ed. J. Findling and K. Pelle. New York: Greenwood Press, 1990.
Corner, J. "Performing the Real: Documentary Diversions." *Television & New Media* 3 (2002): 255–69.
Couldry, N. "Teaching Us to Fake It: The Ritualized Norms of Television's, 'Reality' Games." In *Reality TV: Remaking Television Culture*, ed. S. Murray and L. Oullette. New York: New York University Press, 2004.
Critcher, C. *Moral Panics and the Media*. Buckingham, UK: Open University Press, 2003.
Curran, J., and J. Seaton. *Power without Responsibility: The Press and Broadcasting in Britain*. London: Routledge, 1997.
DaMatta, R. "Carnival in Multiple Planes." In *Rite, Drama, Festival, Spectacle: Rehearsals toward a Theory of Cultural Performance*, ed. J. MacAloon. Philadelphia: ISHI Publications, 1984.
Darnton, R. "An Early Information Society: News and the Media in Eighteenth-Century Paris." *American Historical Review* 105 (2000): 1–35.
Debord, G. *The Society of the Spectacle*. Translated by D. Nicholson-Smith. New York: Zone Books, 1994. Originally published as *La société du spectacle* (Paris: Buchet-Chastel, 1967).
de Groot, J. *Consuming History: Historians and Heritage in Contemporary Popular Culture*. New York: Routledge, 2009.
Dehue, T. "Social Experiments, History of." In *Encyclopedia of Social Measurement*. Vol. 3, ed. K. Kempf-Leonard. Oxford: Elsevier, 2005.
Deuze, M. "Participation, Remediation, Bricolage: Considering Principal Components of Digital Culture." *The Information Society* 22 (2006): 63–75.
Dooley, P. *Taking Their Political Place: Journalists and the Making of an Occupation*. Westport, CT: Greenwood, 1997.
Downing, J. *Radical Media: Rebellious Communication and Social Movements*. Thousand Oaks, CA: Sage, 2001.
Drotner, K. "Dangerous Media? Panic Discourses and Dilemmas of Modernity." *Paedagogica Historica* 35 (1999): 593–619.
DuPuis, E. *Nature's Perfect Food: How Milk Became America's Drink*. New York: New York University Press, 2002.
Edgren, H. *Publicitet för medborgsmannavett: Det nationellt svenska i Stockholmstidningar 1810–1831*. Uppsala, Sweden: Uppsala University Press, 2005.
Edin, A. *Verklig underhållning: Dokusåpor, publik, kritik*. Stockholm: Institutet för mediestudier, 2005.

Edwards, E., C. Gosden, and R. Phillips, eds. *Sensible Objects: Colonialism, Museums and Material Culture*. Oxford: Berg, 2006.
Ekström, A. *Den utställda världen: Stockholmsutställningen 1897 och 1800-talets världsutställningar*. Stockholm: Nordiska museets förlag, 1994.
Ekström, A. "Det vertikala arkivet: Om översiktmedier och historiska svindelkänslor." In *1897: Mediehistorier kring Stockholmsutställningen*, ed. A. Ekström, S. Jülich, and P. Snickars. Stockholm: Statens ljud- och bildarkiv, 2006.
Ekström, A. "'Showing at One View': Ferdinand Boberg's 'Statistical Machinery' and the Visionary Pedagogy of Early Twentieth-Century Statistical Display." *Early Popular Visual Culture* 6 (2008): 35–50.
Ekström, A., S. Jülich, and P. Snickars. "I mediearkivet." In *1897: Mediehistorier kring Stockholmsutställningen*, ed. A. Ekström, S. Jülich, and P. Snickars Stockholm: Statens ljud- och bildarkiv, 2006.
Eliade, M. *The Sacred and the Profane: The Nature of Religion*. New York: Harcourt Brace Jovanovich, 1959.
Enli, G. *The Participatory Turn in Broadcast Television: Institutional, Editorial and Textual Challenges and Strategies*. Oslo: Unipub AS, 2007.
Fabian, J. *Time and the Other: How Anthropology Makes Its Object*. New York: Columbia University Press, 1983.
Fabian, J. *Out of Our Minds: Reason and Madness in the Exploration of Central Africa*. Berkeley: University of California Press, 2000.
Feldman, J. "Contact Points: Museums and the Lost Body Problem." In *Sensible Objects: Colonialism, Museums and Material Culture*, ed. E. Edwards, C. Gosden, and R. Phillips. Oxford: Berg, 2006.
Fetveit, A. "Det kannibalistiske øje: Verklighedsshow, eksperimentfjernsyn og den nye kreativitet i fjernsynsunderholdningen." *Mediekultur* 34 (2002): 14–27.
Forsslund, T. *Frisk och stark med skolradion: Pedagogik och retorik i hälsoprogram 1930–1959*. Stockholm: HLS Förlag, 2002.
Foucault, M. "The Ethic of Care for the Self As a Practice of Freedom." In *The Final Foucault*, ed. J. Bernauer and D. Rasmussen. Cambridge, MA: MIT Press, 1988.
Foucault, M. "Questions of Method." In *The Foucault Effect: Studies in Governmentality, with Two Lectures and an Interview with Michel Foucault*, ed. G. Burcell, C. Gordon, and P. Miller. Chicago: University of Chicago Press, 1991.
Fox, C. "Introduction: How to Prepare a Noble Savage: The Spectacle of Human Science." In *Inventing Human Science: Eighteenth-Century Domains*, ed. C. Fox, R. Porter, and R. Wokler. Berkeley: University of California Press, 1995.
Frisby, D. *Cityscapes of Modernity: Critical Explorations*. Cambridge: Polity, 2001.
Garberding, P. *Musik och politik i skuggan av nazismen: Kurt Atterberg och de svensk-tyska musikrelationerna*. Lund, Sweden: Sekel, 2007.
Gelatt, R. *The Fabulous Phonograph, 1877–1977*. London: Cassell, 1977.
Giddens, A. *The Transformation of Intimacy: Sexuality, Love and Eroticism in Modern Societies*. Cambridge: Polity Press, 1992.
Giddens, A. "Living in a Post-Traditional Society." In *Reflexive Modernization: Politics, Tradition and Aesthetics in the Modern Social Order*, ed. U. Beck, S. Lash, and A. Giddens. Oxford: Polity, 1994.
Gillis, J. *Islands of the Mind: How the Human Imagination Created the Atlantic World*. New York: Palgrave Macmillan, 2004.
Gitelman, L. *Scripts, Grooves, and Writing Machines: Representing Technology in the Edison Era*. Stanford, CA: Stanford University Press, 1999.
Gitelman, L. *Always Already New: Media, History, and the Data of Culture*. Cambridge, MA: MIT Press, 2006.

Gitelman, L., and G. Pingree, eds. *New Media, 1740–1915*. Cambridge, MA: MIT Press, 2003.
Gorney, C. *Articles of Faith: A Frontline History of the Abortion Wars*. New York: Simon & Schuster, 1998.
Graham, J., and S. Yasin. "Reframing Participation in the Museum: A Syncopated Discussion." In *Museums after Modernism: Strategies of Engagement*, ed. G. Pollock and J. Zemans. Malden, MA: Blackwell, 2007.
Griffen-Foley, B. "From *Tit-Bits* to *Big Brother*: A Century of Audience Participation in the Media." *Media, Culture & Society* 26 (2004): 533–48.
Griffiths, A. "Media Technology and Museum Display: A Century of Accommodation and Conflict." In *Rethinking Media Change: The Aesthetics of Transition*, ed. D. Thorburn and H. Jenkins. Cambridge, MA: MIT Press, 2003.
Gross, M., and W. Krohn. "Society as Experiment: Sociological Foundations for a Self-Experimental Society." *History of the Human Sciences* 18 (2005): 63–86.
Gunning, T. "An Aesthetic of Astonishment: Early Film and the (In)credulous Spectator." *Art & Text* 34 (1989): 31–45.
Gunning, T. "The Cinema of Attractions: Early Film, Its Spectator and the Avant-Garde." In *Early Cinema: Space-Frame-Narrative*, ed. T. Elsaesser. London: British Film Institute, 1990.
Gunning, T. "The World as Object Lesson: Cinema Audiences, Visual Culture and the St. Louis World's Fair, 1904." *Film History* 6 (1994): 422–44.
Gustafsson Reinius, L. "Förfärliga och begärliga föremål: Om modernitetens materiella manifestationer på två utställningar." In *1897: Mediehistorier kring Stockholmsutställningen*, ed. A. Ekström, S. Jülich, and P. Snickars. Stockholm: Statens ljud- och bildarkiv, 2006.
Gustafsson Reinius, L. "Exhibiting the Congo in Stockholm." In *Encountering Foreign Worlds: Experiences at Home and Abroad; Proceedings from the 26th Nordic Congress of Historians, Reykjavik 8–12 August 2007*, ed. C. F. Ax, et al. Reykjavik: University of Iceland Press, 2007.
Gustafsson Reinius, L. "Innanför branddörren: Om etnografiska samlingar som sammansatta medier och materialitet." In *Mediernas kulturhistoria*, ed. S. Jülich, P. Lundell, and P. Snickars. Stockholm: Statens ljud- och bildarkiv, 2008.
Gustafsson Reinius, L. "Exhibiting the Congo in Stockholm." In *National Museums*, ed. S. Knell, A. Amundsen-Bugge, and P. Aronsson. London: Routledge, forthcoming.
Habel, Y. *Modern Media, Modern Audiences: Mass Media and Social Engineering in the 1930s Swedish Welfare State*. Stockholm: Aura förlag, 2002.
Habermas, J. *Strukturwandel der Öffentlichkeit*. Neuwied, Germany: Herman Luchterhand, 1962.
Habermas, J. *The Structural Transformation of the Public Sphere: An Inquiry into a Category of Bourgeois Society*. Translated by T. Burger and F. Lawrence. Cambridge: Polity Press, 1989. Originally published as *Strukturwandel der Öffentlichkeit*.
Hadenius, S., and L. Weibull. *Massmedier: En bok om press, radio och TV*. Stockholm: Bonnier, 2005.
Hagberg, J.-E. *Tekniken i kvinnornas händer: Hushållsarbete och hushållsteknik under tjugo- och trettiotalen*. Malmö, Sweden: Liber, 1986.
Hampton, M. *Visions of the Press in Britain, 1850–1950*. Urbana: University of Illinois Press, 2004.
Hansen, M. *Babel and Babylon: Spectatorship in American Silent Film*. Cambridge, MA: Harvard University Press, 1991.
Hartley, J. *Popular Reality: Journalism, Modernity, Popular Culture*. London: Arnold, 1996.

Hazan, S. "A Crisis of Authority: New Lamps for Old." In *Theorizing Digital Cultural Heritage: A Critical Introduction*, ed. F. Cameron and S. Kenderdine. Cambridge, MA: MIT Press, 2007.
Hemmungs Wirtén, E. *No Trespassing: Authorship, Intellectual Property Rights, and the Boundaries of Globalization*. Toronto: University of Toronto Press, 2004.
Henare, A., M. Holbraad, and S. Wastell, eds. *Thinking Through Things: Theorising Artefacts Ethnographically*. New York: Routledge, 2007.
Hendershot, H. *Shaking the World for Jesus: Media and Conservative Evangelical Culture*. Chicago: University of Chicago Press, 2004.
Hill, A. *Reality TV: Audiences and Popular Factual Television*. London: Routledge, 2005.
Hill, A., L. Weibull, and Å. Nilsson. *Audiences and Factual and Reality Television in Sweden*. Jönköping, Sweden: Jönköping International Business School, 2005.
Hillier, P. "Entertaining Reality: Media as Social Experiments." Unpublished paper presented at the annual meeting of the Association for Education in Journalism and Mass Communication, The Renaissance, Washington DC, 8 August 2007. Online. Available HTTP: <http://www.allacademic.com/meta/p200384_index.html> (accessed 24 October 2010).
Hirdman, Y. *Magfrågan: Mat som mål och medel 1870–1920*. Stockholm: Rabén och Sjögren, 1983.
Hobsbawm, E. *The Age of Revolution: Europe 1789–1848*. London: Weidenfeld & Nicholson, 1962.
Holborn, M. "Lennart Nilsson and Photography." In L. Nilsson, *Life*. London: Random House, 2006.
Holt, J., and A. Perren, eds. *Media Industries: History, Theory, and Method*. Oxford: Wiley-Blackwell, 2009.
Horkheimer, M., and T. Adorno. *Dialectic of Enlightenment: Philosophical Fragments* (1944). Translated by E. Jephcott. Stanford, CA: Stanford University Press, 2002.
Hughes, R. "Burning Birth Certificates and Atomic Tupperware Parties: Creating the Antiabortion Movement in the Shadow of the Vietnam War." *The Historian* 68 (2006): 541–58.
Hughes, R. "'The Civil Rights Movement of the 1990s?' The Anti-Abortion Movement and the Struggle for Racial Justice." *The Oral History Review* 33 (2006): 1–24.
Jackson, G. "Cultivating Spiritual Sight: Jacob Riis's Virtual-Tour Narrative and the Visual Modernization of Protestant Homiletics." *Representations*, no. 83, 2003: 126–66.
Jarlbrink, J. *Det våras för journalisten: Symboler och handlingsmönster för den svenska pressens medarbetare från 1870-tal till 1930-tal*. Stockholm: Kungliga biblioteket, 2009.
Jenkins, H. "Quentin Tarantino's *Star Wars*? Digital Cinema, Media Convergence, and Participatory Culture." In *Rethinking Media Change: The Aesthetics of Transition*, ed. D. Thorburn and H. Jenkins. Cambridge, MA: MIT Press, 2003.
Jenkins, H. *Convergence Culture: Where Old and New Media Collide*. New York: New York University Press, 2006.
Jenkins, H. "What Happened Before YouTube?" In *YouTube: Online Video and the Politics of Participatory Culture*, ed. J. Burgess and J. Green. Cambridge: Polity Press, 2009.
Jermyn, D. "This Is About Real People! Video Technologies, Actuality and Affect in the Television Crime Appeal." In *Understanding Reality Television*, ed. S. Holmes and D. Jermyn. London: Routledge, 2005.

Jerslev, A. "Autenticitetsstrategier i Robinson Ekspeditionen 2000." *Mediekultur* 34 (2002): 28–37.
Johannesson, E. "Med det nya på väg (1858–1880)." In *Den svenska pressens historia II: Åren då allting hände (1830–1897)*, ed. K. Gustafsson and P. Rydén. Stockholm: Ekerlid, 2001.
Jones, A. *Powers of the Press: Newspapers, Power and the Public in Nineteenth-Century England*. Aldershot, UK: Scholar, 1996.
Jones, J. "Show Your Real Face: A Fan Study of the UK Big Brother Transmissions (2000, 2001, 2002); Investigating the Boundaries Between Notions of Consumers and Producers of Factual Television." *New Media & Society* 5 (2003): 400–21.
Jönsson, H. *Mjölk: En kulturanalys av mejeridiskens nya ekonomi*. Stockholm: Symposion, 2005.
Jordanova, L. *History in Practice*. 2nd ed. London: Hodder Arnold, 2006.
Jülich, S. "Media as Modern Magic: Early X-Ray Imaging and Cinematography in Sweden." *Early Popular Visual Culture* 6 (2008): 19–33.
Kaplan, F., ed. *Museums and the Making of Ourselves: The Role of Objects in National Identity*. London: Leicester University Press, 1996.
Keen, A. *The Cult of the Amateur: How Today's Internet is Killing Our Culture*. New York: Doubleday, 2007.
Kern, S. *The Culture of Time and Space 1880–1918*. Cambridge, MA: Harvard University Press, 1983.
Kessler, F., and N. Verhoeff, eds. *Networks of Entertainment: Early Film Distribution 1895–1915*. Eastleigh, UK: John Libbey, 2007.
Kilborn, R. *Staging the Real: Factual TV Programming in the Age of Big Brother*. Manchester: Manchester University Press, 2003.
Kirshenblatt-Gimblett, B. "Objects of Ethnography." In B. Kirshenblatt-Gimblett, *Destination Culture: Tourism, Museums, and Heritage*. Berkeley: University of California Press, 1998.
Kitchen, P. *A Most Unsettling Person: An Introduction to the Ideas and Life of Patrick Geddes*. London: Gollancz, 1975.
Knudsen, J. *Justus Möser and the German Enlightenment*. Cambridge: Cambridge University Press, 1986.
Koselleck, R. "Einleitung." In *Geschichtliche Grundbegriffe: Historisches Lexikon zur politisch-sozialen Sprache in Deutschland*. Vol. 1, ed. O. Brunner, W. Conze, and R. Koselleck. Stuttgart: Klett-Cotta, 1972.
Latour, B. *Pandora's Hope: Essays on the Reality of Science Studies*. Cambridge, MA: Harvard University Press, 1999.
Lee, J. "Pastöriseringens försenade triumf." *Lychnos: Årsbok för idé- och lärdomshistoria*, 2005: 175–97.
Lemke, T. "Foucault, Governmentality, and Critique." Paper presented at the conference "Rethinking Marxism," University of Amherst, September 21–24, 2000.
Lessig, L. *Remix: Making Art and Commerce Thrive in the Hybrid Economy*. New York: Penguin, 2008.
Liddle, D. "Who Invented the 'Leading Article'? Reconstructing the History and Prehistory of a Victorian Newspaper Genre." *Media History* 5 (1999): 5–18.
Lindgren, A.-L. *"Att ha barn med är en god sak": Barn, medier och medborgarskap under 1930-talet*. Linköping, Sweden: Linköping University, 1999.
Lippmann, W. *Public Opinion*, London: Allen & Unwin, 1922.
Lister, M., et al. *New Media: A Critical Introduction*. London: Routledge, 2003.
Livingstone, S. "The Changing Nature of Audiences: From Mass Audiences to the Interactive Media User." In *A Companion to Media Studies*, ed. A. Valdivia. Malden, MA: Blackwell, 2003.

Livingstone, S. "Media Literacy and the Challenge of New Information and Communication Technologies." *Communication Review* 7 (2004): 3–14.
Livingstone, S. "Critical Debates in Internet Studies: Reflections on an Emerging Field." In *Mass Media and Society*. 4th ed. Ed. J. Curran and M. Gurevitch. London: Hodder Arnold, 2005.
Livingstone, S. "On the Relation Between Audiences and Publics." In *Audiences and Publics: When Cultural Engagement Matters for the Public Sphere*, ed. S. Livingstone, Bristol: IntellectBooks, 2005.
Lundell, P. *Pressen i provinsen: Från medborgerliga samtal till modern opinionsbildning 1750–1850*. Lund, Sweden: Nordic Academic Press, 2002.
Lundell, P. "Det goda samhällets tjänare iscensatt: Kring en pressutställning 1945." In *Frigörare? Moderna svenska samhällsdrömmar*, ed. M. Kylhammar and M. Godhe. Stockholm: Carlsson, 2005.
Lundell, P. "Pressen är budskapet: Journalistkongressen och den svenska pressens legitimitetssträvanden." In *1897: Mediehistorier kring Stockholmsutställningen*, ed. A. Ekström, S. Jülich, and P. Snickars. Stockholm: Statens ljud- och bildarkiv, 2006.
Lundell, P. "The Medium Is the Message: The Media History of the Press." *Media History* 14 (2008): 1–16.
Lundgren, F. "Social samling: Att ställa ut samhället omkring 1900." In *1897: Mediehistorier kring Stockholmsutställningen*, ed. A. Ekström, S. Jülich, and P. Snickars. Stockholm: Statens ljud- och bildarkiv, 2006.
Lynch, L. "The G Word: Guantanamo, the 'Gulag' Backlash, and the Language of Human Rights." *Politics and Culture* 2007:1. Online. Available HTTP: <http://aspen.conncoll.edu/politicsandculture/page.cfm?key=546> (accessed 1 January 2007).
McCarthy, A. "'Stanley Milgram, Allen Funt, and Me': Postwar Social Science and the 'First Wave' of Reality TV." In *Reality TV: Remaking Television Culture*, ed. S. Murray and L. Oullette. New York: New York University Press, 2004.
McConnell, K. "The Hand-Made Tale: Cassette-Tapes, Authorship, and the Privatization of the Pacific Northwest Independent Music Scene." In *The Resisting Muse: Popular Music and Social Protest*, ed. I. Peddie. Aldershot, UK: Ashgate, 2006.
McGann, J. *The Textual Condition*. Princeton, NJ: Princeton University Press, 1991.
McLuhan, M. *Understanding Media: The Extensions of Man*. New York: McGraw-Hill, 1964.
McLuhan, M., and Q. Fiore. *The Medium Is the Massage: An Inventory of Effects*. New York: Bantam Books, 1967.
McLuhan, M., and T. Wolfe. "TV News As a New Mythic Form (1970)." In M. McLuhan, *Understanding Me: Lectures and Interviews*. Boston: MIT Press, 2005.
Marvin, C. *When Old Technologies Were New: Thinking About Electric Communication in the Late Nineteenth Century*. New York: Oxford University Press, 1988.
Mathiesen, T. "The Viewer Society: Michel Foucault's 'Panopticon' Revisited." *Theoretical Criminology* 1 (1997): 215–34.
Matthews, S., and L. Wexler. *Pregnant Pictures*. New York: Routledge, 2000.
Mauss, M. *The Gift: The Form and Reason for Exchange in Archaic Societies* (1923–24). Translated to English by W. D. Halls. London: Routledge, 2002.
Meller, H. *Patrick Geddes: Social Evolutionist and City Planner*. London: Routledge, 1990.
Michaels, M. "Fetal Galaxies: Some Questions about What We See." In *Fetal Subjects, Feminist Positions*, ed. L. Morgan and M. Michaels. Philadelphia: University of Pennsylvania Press, 1999.

Miller, D., ed. *Materiality*. Durham, NC: Duke University Press, 2005.
Morgan, L. *Icons of Life: A Cultural History of Human Embryos*. Berkeley: University of California Press, 2009.
Mral, B. "Två tidningsstarter i Örebro." In *Ständigt dessa landsortstidningar*, ed. K. Gustafsson and P. Rydén. Gothenburg, Sweden: Nordicom, 1998.
Murray, S. "'I Think We Need a New Name For It': The Meeting of Documentary and Reality TV." In *Reality TV: Remaking Television Culture*, ed. S. Murray and L. Oullette. New York: New York University Press, 2004.
Myers, H., ed. *Ethnomusicology: An Introduction*. London: Macmillan, 1992.
Negroponte, N. *Being Digital*. New York: Alfred A. Knopf, 1995.
Newman, K. *Fetal Positions: Individualism, Science, Visuality*. Stanford, CA: Stanford University Press, 1996.
O'Boyle, L. "The Image of the Journalist in France, Germany and England, 1815–1848." *Comparative Studies in Society and History* 10 (1967–68): 290–317.
Oettermann, S. *The Panorama: History of a Mass Medium* (1980). Translated by Deborah Lucas Schneider. New York: Zone Books, 1997.
Oushakine, S. "The Terrifying Mimicry of Samizdat." *Public Culture* 13 (2001): 191–214.
Owen, D. *Copies in Seconds: Chester Carlson and the Birth of the Xerox Machine*. New York: Simon & Schuster, 2004.
Parry, R. *Recoding the Museum: Digital Heritage and the Technologies of Change*. London: Routledge, 2007.
Petchesky, R. "Fetal Images: The Power of Visual Culture in the Politics of Reproduction." *Feminist Studies* 13 (1987): 263–92.
Peterson, L., and Å. Pettersson. *Medieboken: Massmedier*. 9th ed. Malmö, Sweden: Liber, 2007.
Pethes, N. *Spektakuläre Experimente: Allianzen zwischen Massenmedien und Sozialpsychologie im 20. Jahrhundert*. Weimar, Germany: VDG, 2004.
Ponte, A. "Building the Stair Spiral of Evolution: The Index Museum of Sir Patrick Geddes." *Assemblage*, no. 10, 1989: 46–64.
Porter, R. *Enlightenment: Britain and the Creation of the Modern World*. London: Allen Lane, 2000.
Rabinovitz, L., and A. Geil. "Introduction." In *Memory Bytes: History, Technology, and Digital Culture*, ed. L. Rabinovitz and A. Geil. Durham, NC: Duke University Press, 2004.
Renwick, C. "The Practice of Spencerian Science: Patrick Geddes's Biosocial Program, 1876–1889." *Isis* 100 (2009): 36–57.
Retallack, J. "From Pariah to Professional? The Journalist in German Society and Politics, from the Late Enlightenment to the Rise of Hitler." *German Studies Review* 16 (1993): 175–223.
Rosengren, C. *Tidevarvets bättre genius: Föreställningar om offentlighet och publicitet i Karl Johanstidens Sverige*. Stockholm: Symposion, 1999.
Rosenzweig, R. "Can History Be Open Source? *Wikipedia* and the Future of the Past." *Journal of American History* 93 (2006): 117–46.
Rudenstine, D. *The Day the Presses Stopped: A History of the Pentagon Papers Case*. Berkeley: University of California Press, 1996.
Runcis, M. *Steriliseringar i folkhemmet*. Stockholm: Ordfront, 1998.
Russo, A., and J. Watkins. "Digital Cultural Communication: Audience and Remediation." In *Theorizing Digital Cultural Heritage: A Critical Introduction*, ed. F. Cameron and S. Kenderdine. Cambridge, MA: MIT Press, 2007.
Sandberg, M. *Living Pictures, Missing Persons: Mannequins, Museums and Modernity*. Princeton, NJ: Princeton University Press, 2003.
Schneider, M. *Geschichte der Mehrstimmigkeit*. 1934. Reprint of 1st ed. Tutzing, Germany: Hans Schneider, 1969.

Schück, H., and K. Warburg. *Illustrerad svensk litteraturhistoria*. Vol. 3, *Frihetstiden*. 1927. Facsimile print of 3rd ed. Stockholm: Gidlund, 1985.
Schwartz, H. *The Culture of the Copy: Striking Likenesses, Unreasonable Facsimiles*. New York: Zone Books, 1996.
Seifarth, S. "Den iscensatta maskeraden: Om framställningar och vanställanden i dokusåpor." In *Det vanställda ordet: Om den svåra konsten att värna sin integritet*, ed. M. Kylhammar and J.-F. Battail. Stockholm: Carlsson, 2006.
Sennett, R. *The Fall of Public Man*. New York: Random House, 1977.
Shapin, S., and S. Schaffer. *Leviathan and the Air-Pump: Hobbes, Boyle, and the Experimental Life*. Princeton, NJ: Princeton University Press, 1985.
Short, J., E. Williams, and B. Christie. *The Social Psychology of Telecommunications*. New York: John Wiley, 1976.
Simon, A., ed. *Das Berliner Phonogramm-Archiv 1900–2000: Sammlungen der traditionellen Musik der Welt*. Berlin: Verlag für Wissenschaft und Bildung, 2000.
Singer, B. *Melodrama and Modernity: Early Sensational Cinema and Its Contexts*. New York: Columbia University Press, 2001.
Skeggs, B. *Class, Self, Culture*. London: Routledge, 2004.
Slater, L. *Opening Skinner's Box: Great Psychological Experiments of the Twentieth Century*. London: Bloomsbury, 2004.
Smith, B. *On the Origin of Objects*. Cambridge, MA: MIT Press, 1998.
Snickars, P. *Svensk film och visuell masskultur 1900*. Stockholm: Aura förlag, 2001.
Sreberny-Mohammadi, A., and A. Mohammadi. *Small Media, Big Revolution: Communication, Culture, and the Iranian Revolution*. Minneapolis: University of Minnesota Press, 1994.
Stabile, C. "The Traffic in Fetuses." In *Fetal Subjects, Feminist Positions*, ed. L. Morgan and M. Michaels. Philadelphia: University of Pennsylvania Press, 1999.
Staiger, J., and S. Hake, eds. *Convergence Media History*. New York: Routledge, 2009.
Stange, M. *Symbols of Ideal Life: Social Documentary Photography in America, 1890–1950*. Cambridge: Cambridge University Press, 1989.
Stavenow-Hidemark, E. *Villabebyggelse i Sverige 1900–1925: Inflytande från utlandet, idéer, förverkligande*. Stockholm: Nordiska museet, 1971.
Steiner, A. *I litteraturens mittfåra: Månadens bok och svensk bokmarknad under 1970-talet*. Gothenburg, Sweden: Makadam, 2006.
Surowiecki, J. *The Wisdom of Crowds: Why the Many Are Smarter than the Few and How Collective Wisdom Shapes Business, Economics, Society and Nations*. London: Little, Brown, 2004.
Svanberg, F. "Museum Narration and the Collection Machine: Or How Collections Make Collectors." In *Comparing: National Museums, Territories, Nation-Building and Change. NaMu IV, Linköping University, Norrköping, Sweden 18–20 February 2008: Conference Proceedings*, ed. P. Aronsson and A. Nyblom, pp. 175–82. Online. Available HTTP: <http://www.ep.liu.se/ecp/030/> (accessed 25 May 2008).
Svanberg, F., and K. Wahlgren. *Publik arkeologi*. Lund, Sweden: Nordic Academic Press, 2007.
Sylwan, O. *Svenska pressens historia till statshvälfningen 1772*. Lund, Sweden: Gleerup, 1896.
Søndergaard, H., et al. "Indledning." *Mediekultur* 34 (2002): 3–6.
Sörenson, U. *När tiden var ung: Arkitekturen och Stockholmsutställningarna 1851, 1866, 1897, 1909*. Stockholm: Stockholmia Förlag, 1999.
Tapscott, D., and A. Williams. *Wikinomics: How Mass Collaboration Changes Everything*. New York: Portfolio, 2006.

Taussig, M. *Mimesis and Alterity: A Particular History of the Senses*. New York: Routledge, 1993.
Ternhag, G. "'Ett fonogramarkiv för svensk folkmusik': En idé som aldrig förverkligades." *Svensk tidskrift för musikforskning*, 1993: 83–102.
Ternhag, G. *Jojksamlaren Karl Tirén*. Umeå, Sweden: Dialekt- och folkminnesarkivet, 2002.
Thorburn, D., and H. Jenkins, eds. *Rethinking Media Change: The Aesthetics of Transition*. Cambridge, MA: MIT Press, 2003.
Thrift, N. *Non-Representational Theory: Space, Politics, Affect*. London: Routledge, 2008.
Torbacke, J. "Nu grundläggs den moderna utvecklingen (1809–1830)." In *Den svenska pressens historia I: I begynnelsen (tiden före 1830)*, ed. K. Gustafsson and P. Rydén. Stockholm: Ekerlid, 2000.
Turner, V. *The Ritual Process: Structure and Anti-Structure*. Ithaca: Cornell University Press, 1969.
Turner, V. *Dramas, Fields, and Metaphors: Symbolic Action in Human Society*. Ithaca: Cornell University Press, 1974.
Ullman, R. "The Pentagon's History As 'History'," *Foreign Policy*, no. 4, 1971: 150–56.
Uricchio, W. "Historicizing Media in Transition." In *Rethinking Media Change: The Aesthetics of Transition*, ed. D. Thorburn and H. Jenkins. Cambridge, MA: MIT Press, 2003.
Van Dijck, J. "Users Like You: Theorizing Agency in User-Generated Content." *Media, Culture & Society* 31 (2009): 41–58.
von Hornbostel, E. "Phonogramm-Archiv des Pshychologischen Institut der Universität, Berlin C.2, Schloß/Demonstrations-Sammlung." In *Das Berliner Phonogramm-Archiv 1900–2000: Sammlungen der traditionellen Musik der Welt*, ed. A. Simon. Berlin: Verlag für Wissenschaft und Bildung, 2000.
Walsh, P. "The Web and the Unassailable Voice." *Archives and Museum Informatics* 1 (1997): 77–85.
Waltz, M. *Alternative and Activist Media*. Edinburgh: Edinburgh University Press, 2005.
Warner, M. *The Letters of the Republic: Publication and the Public Sphere in Eighteenth-Century America*. Cambridge, MA: Harvard University Press, 1990.
Warner, M. *Publics and Counterpublics*. New York: Zone Books, 2002.
Watt, I. *The Rise of the Novel: Studies of Defoe, Richardson and Fielding*. London: Pimlico, 1957.
Weber, M. "Bureaucratic Authority." In *Sociological Writings*, ed. W. Heydebrand and trans. M. Black with L. Garmer. New York: Continuum, 1994.
Welch, W., and L. Burt. *From Tinfoil to Stereo: The Acoustic Years of the Recording Industry, 1877–1929*. Gainesville: University Press of Florida, 1994.
Wells, T. *Wildman: The Life and Times of Daniel Ellsberg*. New York: Palgrave, 2001.
Werner, Y., ed. *Kristen manlighet: Ideal och verklighet 1830–1940*. Lund, Sweden: Nordic Academic Press, 2008.
Witcomb, A. *Re-Imagining the Museum: Beyond the Mausoleum*. London: Routledge, 2003.
Woodmansee, M. "On the Author Effect: Recovering Collectivity." In *Construction of Authorship: Textual Appropriation in Law and Literature*, ed. M. Woodmansee and P. Jaszi. Durham, NC: Duke University Press, 1994.
Zaret, D. *Origins of Democratic Culture: Printing, Petitions, and the Public Sphere in Early-Modern England*. Princeton, NJ: Princeton University Press, 2000.
Zizek, S. "Welcome to the Desert of the Real." *South Atlantic Quarterly* 101 (2002): 385–9.

Zoonen, L. van. "Desire and Resistance: Big Brother and the Recognition of Everyday Life." *Media, Culture & Society* 23 (2001): 669–77.
Åsberg, C., and B. Axelsson. "Digital Performances of Gendered Pasts." In *Cyberfeminism in Northern Lights: Digital Media and Gender in a Nordic Context*, ed. M. Sveningsson Elm and J. Sundén. Newcastle, UK: Cambridge Scholars, 2007.
Öhman, A. *Äventyrets tid: Den sociala äventyrsromanen i Sverige 1841–1859*. Umeå, Sweden: Umeå University, 1990.
Öhrneman, J. *Perspektiv från Kongo*. Stockholm: Gummesson, 1968.
Östberg, W. *När Afrika kom oss nära: Missionen och den svenska Afrikabilden*. Stockholm: Etnografiska museet, 2002.

Contributors

Bodil Axelsson is an assistant professor at the Department of Culture Studies, Linköping University, Sweden. Her research interests are mainly in the area of heritage studies, and among her publications is a coedited volume (with J. Fornäs), *Cultural Studies in Sweden* (Lund, Sweden: Studentlitteratur, 2007, title in translation).

Mathias Boström is an archivist at the Swedish Centre for Folk Music and Jazz Research, Stockholm, and a PhD student at the Department of Musicology, Uppsala University, Sweden. Research fields include ethnomusicology and media history. He has coedited *The Great Mission: Perspectives on the Swedish Folk Music Commission 1908–2008* (Stockholm: Nordiska museet, 2010, title in translation).

Anders Ekström is an associate professor in the Division of History of Science and Technology, Royal Institute of Technology, Stockholm. His current research is focused on the history of audiences. Recent publications include a collection of essays on historiography and cultural theory, *Representation and Materiality: Introductions to Cultural History* (Nora, Sweden: Nya Doxa, 2009, title in translation), and articles in journals such as *Early Popular Visual Culture* and *Nineteenth-Century Contexts*.

Lisa Gitelman is an associate professor in the Departments of English and of Media, Culture, and Communication at New York University. Her research specializes in the field of media history, and she is the coeditor (with G. B. Pingree) of *New Media, 1740–1915* (Cambridge, MA: MIT Press, 2003) and the author of *Always Already New: Media, History, and the Data of Culture* (Cambridge, MA: MIT Press, 2006).

Lotten Gustafsson Reinius is an associate professor of ethnology and a curator at the Museum of Ethnography in Stockholm. Her research interests include heritage production and issues of materiality, ritual, and play in contemporary society. Some recent publications are "Sensing Through

White Gloves: On Congolese Objects in Swedish Collections," *The Senses and Society* 4 (2009), and a chapter in the forthcoming anthology *The Nation Exhibited*, ed. S. Knell, A. Amundsen-Bugge, and P. Aronsson (London: Routledge).

Ylva Habel is an assistant professor at the Department of Media and Communication Studies at Södertörn University, Stockholm. Research fields include interwar media culture, postcolonial studies, and critical whiteness studies. Among her recent publications is "Beside Myself with Looking: The Provincial, Female Spectator as Out of Place at the Stockholm Exhibition 1897," in *Strange Spaces: Explorations into Mediated Obscurity*, ed. A. Jansson and A. Lagerkvist (Farnham: Ashgate, 2009).

Solveig Jülich is an assistant professor at the Department of Literature and History of Ideas, Stockholm University. She is the author and coeditor of several books and articles on media history, visual culture, and the history of scientific visualization. Currently, she is completing a book entitled "Visions of Life and Death: A Cultural History of Lennart Nilsson's Hybrid Images."

Patrik Lundell is an associate professor at the Department of Communication and Media, Lund University, Sweden. His main research field is the media history of the press, and his latest books are the coedited volumes *Media and Monarchy in Sweden* (Gothenburg, Sweden: Nordicom, 2009) and *The Media System of the Nineteenth-Century* (Stockholm: National Library of Sweden, 2010, title in translation.)

Frans Lundgren is an assistant professor at the Department of History of Science and Ideas, Uppsala University, Sweden. His main research interests are in European cultural history and especially the intersections of the social sciences, politics, and popular education. His current research project is entitled "A History of the Social Museum: Mediating the Public and Political Subjectivities through Scientific Communication, 1880–1950."

Mark B. Sandberg is a professor at the University of California, Berkeley, jointly appointed in the Department of Scandinavian and the Department of Film and Media. His research fields include visual culture, Scandinavian film history, theater history, and museology. He is the author of *Living Pictures, Missing Persons: Mannequins, Museums, and Modernity* (Princeton, NJ: Princeton University Press, 2003).

Per Wisselgren is an assistant professor at the Department of Sociology, Umeå University, Sweden. His research is focused on the history of the social sciences. Among his recent publications are contributions to the anthologies *Academics as Public Intellectuals*, ed. S. Eliaeson and R. Kalleberg (Newcastle: Cambridge Scholars, 2008) and *Intellectuals and Their Publics*, ed. C. Fleck, A. Hess, and E. S. Lyon (Farnham, UK: Ashgate, 2009).

Index

A
Abercrombie, Nicholas, 22
Adorno, Theodor, 3
agency: actant, 52; distribution of, 5, 113; of tangible things, 94; transfer of, 163
Åhrén, Uno, 76
Anderson, Wes, 63
Andrejevic, Mark, 143
Asplund, Gunnar, 76
audience: active audiences, 3, 6, 7, 10, 29, 94; attracting audiences, 53, 161; audience participation, 3, 21, 27–28, 106, 131–133, 152; audience positions, 22, 164; conceptual demarcations, 49-50, 53–54, 144, 153–154; enrollment of, 5, 53–54, 56, 81, 148, 103–105; physically engaged audiences, 4, 22; learning to act as, 4, 22, 26–30; history of audiences, 21–22, 29; making audiences into publics, 83, 103, 125; television audiences, 143
Axelsson, Bodil, 5

B
Bailey, Peter, 26–27
Barry, Andrew, 158, 163–165
Beegan, Gerry, 26
Bendix, Regina, 168
Bennett, Tony, 82
Bergström-Walan, Maj-Briht, 133
Berlant, Lauren, 133
Boberg, Ferdinand, 25–26
Bolinder, Gustaf, 54
Booth, Charles, 41
Born, Georgina, 164
Boström, Mathias, 5, 7
Brady, Erika, 52

Burnett, Mark, 143, 149
Bücher, Karl, 18

C
camera obscura, 24
Chandler, Daniel, 167
Charcot, Jean-Martin, 153
Christie, Agatha, 152
citizenship, 1, 3, 21, 94, 115, 119, 143, 154, 164; civics, 37–39
community, 1, 60, 92-94, 163; fan community, 1, 112; grassroots community, 7, 93, 112–113
consumer. See media: consumer
copyright, 1, 8, 56, 120–121
Corner, John, 143, 150
Couldry, Nick, 153

D
DaMatta, Roberto, 93
Debord, Guy, 3
Defoe, Daniel, 152
De Mol, John, 149
Densmore, Frances, 56, 58
Deuze, Mark, 166, 167
DuPuis, Melanie, 98–99

E
Edin, Anna, 148
education: pedagogy of simultaneity, 105–106; popular, 34–35, 38, 161; visual, 33, 40–41; of 'the eye,' 42–45; sexual education, 130–134, 138
Ekström, Anders, 4, 83
Ellsberg, Daniel, 113–121
exhibitions, 4, 59–60, 81–82; aesthetic of attraction, 23–24, 27; amusement areas, 4, 20, 71–74; as campaign vehicle, 32; as

community-making mechanism, 45–46; contextual groupings, 69; didactics of, 36, 39–42; exhibition journal, 27; fatigue, 20, 33–35; housing exhibitions, 66–78; materiality of displays, 4, 68–69, 83, 85–86, 94; as media, 32–42, 74–75, 82; mobility of exhibitions, 81, 83, 85–88, 92-94; theatricality of displays, 4, 69–70; world's fairs, 20, 33-38, 41

F
Fey, Tina, 120
film, 2, 4, 28, 76–78, 85–87, 103–105, 142
Forsell, John, 54
Forsslund, Karl Erik, 57–58
Foucault, Michel, 5, 7, 99–103, 109
Funt, Allen, 151

G
Galton, Francis, 39
Geddes, Patrick, 5, 33, 35–46
Gelb, Leslie, 116, 118
Giddens, Anthony, 150
Gitelman, Lisa, 7–8, 12, 100, 106
Golding, William, 152
Goode, Brown, 41
Gorbachev, Mikhail, 120
Griffen-Foley, Bridget, 10, 152
Gross, Matthias, 152
Gustafsson Reinius, Lotten, 4
Gustavus III of Sweden, 15

H
Habel, Ylva, 5
Habermas, Jürgen, 3, 14
Hartley, John, 10
Hillier, Paul, 151
Horkheimer, Max, 3
Hughes, Richard, 134

I
interactivity, 2, 5, 160, 163–165, 169
internet, 1–2, 60, 158, 162, 166, 169–170

J
Jenkins, Henry, 2–3, 6, 7, 58–60, 112, 127, 143, 149
Jevons, William Stanley, 34–35, 41
Jones, Janet Megan, 149-150

Jülich, Solveig, 7

K
Kant, Immanuel, 12
Kaplan, Flora, 159
Kennedy, John F., 116
Key, Ellen, 68
Kibangu, Jeremia, 85
Kirshenblatt-Gimblett, Barbara, 82
Krohn, Wolfgang, 152

L
Laman, Karl Edvard, 50–51, 53–54, 55, 56–57, 60
Laman, Selma, 53–54
Laurell, Yngve, 55
Lazare, Lewis, 63
Le Bon, Gustave, 33
Lee, Jenny, 100
Lemke, Thomas, 102
Leopold II of Belgium, 84
Le Play, Frederic, 41
Liddle, Dallas, 11
Lindblom, Gerhard, 56
Lippmann, Walter, 18
Livingstone, Sonia, 3
Longhurst, Brian, 22
Lundell, Johan August, 51–52
Lundell, Patrik, 6
Lundgren, Frans, 5

M
McCarthy, Anna, 151–152
McLuhan, Marshall, 2-3, 93, 120, 125–126, 129–130, 138–139
McNamara, Robert, 114, 116, 119
magazine, 4, 112, 152
Malkoff, Mark, 63–64, 79
Mauss, Marcel, 92
media: attractions, 35–36, 53; bodily engagement in, 139; concept of, 4, 94, 112; consumption of spectacles, 42–43; convergence, 7, 60, 143; distinction between old and new media, 2, 6–8, 49, 54, 93, 112, 125, 129; distinction between hot and cool media, 2, 125, 130; events, 5, 99, 102, 108–109; historiography of, 1, 3, 6, 10–11, 49; intermediality, 26-27, 106, 146; literacy, 1, 43, 46, 148, 153, 161; materiality of media, 2–5, 22, 27, 49, 52, 83, 94, 126, 139, 167. *See also* exhi-

bition: materiality of displays; media culture, 29–30; media contests, 25–26, 29, 105; participatory media, 1–8, 29, 49, 52, 59, 93, 113–114, 126, 143–144, 148, 152–154; physicality of media, 22, 27–28; platform, 45–46; protocols of, 12–13, 18; remediation, 125–126, 166; remixing of media content, 1, 7, 126, 138; small media, 113, 126; social media, 46, 94; strategies, 81, 94, 136–137; transmediality, 4, 26, 29, 127; as virtual travel, 23, 36
Milgram, Stanley, 151, 154
Morgan, Lynn, 126
Murray, John, 150
museum; and digital media, 6, 158–170; ethnographic museum, 51, 53, 60, 82; folk museum, 66–67; national museums, 81, 91, 93, 159; 'social museums' as a genre, 37–40; See also exhibition

N
Nciama, Yona, 90
Negroponte, Nicholas, 11
newspaper. See the press
Niccol, Andrew, 154
Nilsson, Lennart, 7, 125–139
Nilsson, Sam, 146
Nixon, Richard, 113, 120
Nordenskiöld, Erland, 53
Nzau, Sebuloni, 90

O
observation: lost power of, 42–45; training, 41–45
Öhrneman, Josef, 86
online forum, 1, 159, 165–169
open source, 1, 2, 121
Östberg, Wilhelm, 88

P
Palin, Sarah, 120
panorama, 32, 35, 40; moving panorama, 28
Parry, Ross, 158
Parsons, Charlie, 143, 145, 148
Persson, Maria, 57
participation: asymmetries of, 3, 5, 7, 58, 154; concepts of, 7, 78–79, 163–164; consumer participation, 63–65, 70–71, 75, 79, 101; degrees of, 2, 138; non-participation, 11, 14, 17; participant observation, 45, 81, 152; participatory culture, 2, 6, 21, 58–59, 127, 138; participatory immersion, 65–67, 70, 75–77; protocols of, 5, 14, 158–162; performative aspects of, 4, 10, 51, 54–60, 78–79, 93; socio-technical arrangements of, 6, 158–162, 167; strategies of, 5, 53, 93, 109, 125–126, 133
performance, 23–24; participatory performance, 63–66, 79, 107–108, 110; performativity, 22; performative address, 25, 30; performative inhabitation, 64–66, 76–78; performative subjectivities, 29; performative visibility, 22, 27
Petchetsky, Rosalind, 125
Pethes, Nicholas, 152
Petterson, Rune, 129–130
phonograph, 5–7, 29, 49–59
photography, 5, 7, 36, 39, 51–52, 90, 99–100, 106–107, 125–139
Pinet, Theodor, 21
Pingree, Geoffrey, 100, 106
politics, 7, 13–14, 147, 158; anti-abortion activism, 126–127, 129, 133–138; empowerment thesis, 5, 7; of exclusion, 4, 7, 60, 119; free speech, 113, 121; governmentality, 102; of inclusion, 4, 7, 59–60, 93–94, 102–109, 163; responsibilization, 102–103, 105
press, the, 6, 10–13, 115, 146–147; civic press, 11–14, 17; correspondent, 15–16; editorial ideals, 14–16; historiography of, 11, 15–18; letter to the paper, 13–14; political affiliations of, 16–17; politicization of, 14, 16–17; printer as editor, 10–12; professionalization of, 13–14, 16; publicist, 14–15
Probst, Jeff, 149
public: public experiment, 5, 29, 153; public opinion, 5, 15, 46, 153; public service, 143, 151, 159; public space, 22, 29; theory of public sphere, 3–6, 14, 113

publics: as experimental communities, 40, 45–46; psychology of, 37; self-reflexivity of, 35, 45–46; the making of, 103, 125, 45–46

R
radio, 152
realism, 86–87, 93, 144, 147–148, 152; re-enactment, 165–169
representations: engagement with, 32, 40–45
Riis, Jacob, 35–36
Roosevelt, Theodore, 32
Rostow, Walter, 119
Russo, Anthony, 115–116
Ruong, Lars Nilsson, 58
Rydin, Herman, 15

S
Sandberg, Mark, 4, 7
Schaffer, Simon, 153
Scharp, John, 100
Schneider, Marius, 60
science: ethnographic fieldwork, 5, 49–60, 81; expert knowledge, 163, 167; scientific credibility, 56, 59, 151, 153; scientific experiment, 146; social science and popular culture, 151–152; social experiment, 5, 142–154; sociology, techniques of observation, 39–42; visual statistics, 25, 35
sciopticon, 35-36, 85
seeing: modes of, 41–44; immersive, 36
Sennett, Richard, 3
Shapin, Steven, 153
Simmel, Georg, 33
Singer, Ben, 26
Skeggs, Beverley, 107–108
sociability, 4, 24–25; media sociability, 22, 27, 29, 112; performative sociability, 29–30
social movement, 81, 92–94, 121

sound media, 4, 49, 51, 53–59; *See also* phonograph
Spencer, Herbert, 38
Stanley, Henry Morton, 83
stereoscope, 32
Strömstedt, Margareta, 91
Sydow, Carl Wilhelm von, 52

T
Taussig, Michael, 56
television, 2, 143–145, 163; reality TV, 5, 142–154
Tenow, Kaj, 105
Tirén, Karl, 55–60
Treutiger, Harald, 152
Treving, Nils, 129

U
Ullman, Richard, 118
Ulrich, Valborg, 100

V
visualization, 41, 45
von Hornbostel, Erich, 57, 60

W
Walsh, Peter, 162
Warner, Michael, 103–105
wax display, 4, 65–66
Web 2.0, 1, 112, 121–122, 137–138
Weber, Max, 118
Weir, Peter, 142
Westling, Martin, 84
Willke, Barbara, 136–137
Willke, Jack, 136–137
Wisselgren, Per, 5
Witcomb, Andrea, 164

X
xerography, 6–7, 59, 112–122

Z
Zimbardo, Philip, 151, 154
Žižek, Slavoj, 164